# ALTARS

This book is set in the typeface *Athelas* designed by Veronika Burian and Jose Scaglione.

Paperback ISBN: 979-8-8293-596-14

A Publication of *Tall Pine Books*
119 E Center Street, Suite B4A | Warsaw, Indiana 46580
*www.tallpinebooks.com*

| 1 22 22 20 16 02 |

Published in the United States of America

# ALTARS

STRATEGIES FOR YOUR VICTORY IN SPIRITUAL WARFARE

## CHARLIE SHAMP

# CONTENTS

## CHAPTER ONE

# SACRED SPACE, THIN SPACE

Since the fifth century AD, Celtic spirituality has existed in Ireland and Scotland with a tradition called "thin places," sacred places where the veil between heaven and earth, the supernatural and natural, is thin. Upon encountering such mystical place, the Celts would often mark those places with standing stones like Stonehenge.

Though the thin space metaphor does not appear in scripture, there are other expressions of a thin place. So, if you define a thin place as a place where God's presence is known with particular immediacy, then there are stunning thin places like God's mountain, where the walls are weak between the two worlds. Rabbi Lionel Blue, a reformed rabbi and famous journalist, said, "Eternity is all around us. Part of us inhabits it already."

So, within the scriptures, there are references to thin places called holy places or sacred spaces. These biblical indications of sacred space reflect the manifestation of the holiness of God associated with the dwelling place of God's presence and glory, His transcendence and immanence, with places of worship and revelation.

*Coram Deo* means the presence of God or before His face. To live Coram Deo is to breathe one's entire life in the presence of God, under the authority of God, living holy lives for the glory of God. In the book of St. Augustine's confessions, Augustine makes this classic statement: *"You have made us for yourself, O Lord, and our heart is restless until it rests in you."*

*In the mystic circle of the Inklings,* before C.S. Lewis wrote The Chronicles of Narnia, young Jack Lewis spent his days dreaming up stories of other worlds filled with knights, castles, and talking animals. His brother, Warnie, spent his days imagining worlds filled with trains, boats, and technology. One rainy day, they found a wardrobe in a little room next to the attic, and they wondered, what if the wardrobe had no end?[1] And the adventures in their home became the beginning of a story with a portal to another world where they encountered *Coram Deo*, the face of God, in a Lion in a sacred place.

The scriptures often speak of God's presence in human history. The most common Hebrew term for "presence" is *panim*, also translated as "face," one of the most prolific words in the Hebrew Bible. It shows up over 2,100 times, and it is translated as face, but also as *presence, surface, front, before, and countenance,* implying a close and personal encounter with the Lord.[2]

Being in YHWH's presence meant being in the light, the sparkling glow of YHWH enlightening us. The phrase *"in His Presence"* was often translated as *"before Him"* but means *"before His face"* or *"before/in His Presence." And Jehovah in his holy temple: be silent all the earth before his face* (Habakkuk 2:20).[3]

## THE REALM OF REVIVAL

It is said that when Christianity retreats, evil steps in to fill the gap, but in Ezekiel 22:20, God said, *I sought for a man among them who would make a wall, and stand in the gap before Me on behalf of the land, that I should not destroy it.* In times like that, we seek a mighty manifestation of the presence of God and a demonstration of His glory in revival power with awesome holiness and irresistible power.

In the revival realm, there are three keys as the spirit of God moves on the face of the earth: intercession, reconciliation, and restoration. It is manifested by continuous intercession, spiritual hunger, and profound supernatural expressions resulting in reconciliation, restoration, and a renewed passion for the lost. In the revival of 1904, one hundred and fifty thousand people converted to Christ, adding many to churches and chapels in the Welsh revival. Lives were transformed. Lifestyles were changed. Homes and families were healed. Churches were packed and the fire of God filled the altars in those sacred places.

Revival is a spirit, something God wants to release in all the earth, but He's looking for someone who will fill the gap and carry the torch for Christ to advance His kingdom as written in the Book of Acts and reflected in the early church.

Filling the gap with intercession will bring reconciliation and release restoration. After the death, burial, and resurrection of Jesus, He calls His disciples and future generations to be agents of restoration, bringing supernatural breakthroughs in those sacred places throughout the world.

## WORLDWIDE REVIVALS THROUGH THE CENTURIES

In the 18th century, a great awakening happened, starting with the Methodist movement of the Wesleys in England and Whitefield in the colonies. With a great passion for restoring their countries, they moved forward with passionate determination to change their world through conversion, restoration, and making disciples, reflecting the early church. In the Second Great Awakening, a fresh flood of power with the word and miracles such as Charles Finney and the Cane Ridge revival and the beginning camp meetings with supernatural manifestations.

The Réveil, French for "revival" or "awakening," in 1814 was a movement within western Switzerland and southeastern France, mainly stimulated by the Moravians, which spread to America. The Moravians found a home with Count von Zinzendorf, who gave them the vision to take the gospel to the far corners of the globe. Wesley's heart was "strangely warmed" during his time with the Moravians in the Fetter Lane Chapel in England. Once the Moravians landed in America, they emerged with great influence in Pennsylvania and the Carolinas, including the town of Moravian Falls located in the heart of Wilkes County, North Carolina, when the Moravians arrived in 1753.[4]

Ram Mohun Roy was only the first of many radical Hindu reformers to place the figure and teaching of Christ at the center of a movement of spiritual and social renewal.

On 21 September 1857, Jeremiah Lamphier, a businessman, began a series of prayer meetings in New York. By the beginning of 1858, the congregation was crowded, mostly with people in business. Newspapers reported that over 6,000 were attending various prayer meetings in New York, and 6,000 in Pittsburgh. Daily prayer meetings were held in Washington, DC, at five different times to accommodate the crowds. Other cities followed the pattern. By May, 50,000 of New York's 800,000 people were new converts, a sign of the coming Full Gospel Business Men's Fellowship International, which played a major role in the Charismatic Movement.

In our present time, we have watched and experienced the great revivals in Pensacola and Toronto that started a wave of supernatural manifestations with thousands of lives changed by the Holy Spirit.

## SPIRITUAL ATMOSPHERES

The only thing separating heaven and earth is a spiritual atmosphere, a point of divine connection, and a breeding ground for the miraculous. *To make the weight for the winds; and he weighed the waters by measure* (Job 28:25).

Winds and waters, weight and measures—the weight of Spirit winds and the measures of Spirit waters. When the boat's sail is full, and the kite soars upward, and when the windmill is turning, we know that the Holy Spirit is moving. An atmosphere was created in a time of intercession and worship, now living in closer unity of mutuality and interdependence with Christ.

While the one hundred and twenty were in prayer, *suddenly there*

*came from heaven a noise like a violent rushing wind (Ruach, Spirit), and it
filled the whole house where they were sitting* (Acts 2:1, 2).

Water is the foundation of this planet, the life-giving essence in
all organisms, including human bodies. And **without sound, clean
water, we couldn't survive, and not a single thing we see around us
would be possible.** Water creates the overall quality of life we enjoy.

The earth was a formless void, and darkness covered the face of
the deep, while the <u>wind</u> of the Spirt swept over the face (panim) of
the <u>waters</u> (Genesis 1:2). *The waters prevailed and increased greatly on
the earth, and the ark floated on the face (panim) of the waters* (Genesis
7:18).

There are two very parallel images of the spirit and the ark moving on the face of the waters, a creative and saving act of the Spirit. In
the original Hebrew, moving on the face of the waters portrays something like the flapping of bird wings. Included in the flood story is the
first "life" leaving the ark, a bird sent to fly over the face of the waters.
The underlying metaphor and motif are the miracle of recreation,
restoration, and a remnant.

Out of their innermost being come waters, torrents of living water, which was Jesus' prophecy of the coming of the Holy Spirit (John
8:38, 39, NASB), resulting in a recreation, restoration, and remnant
reflected through the generations.

## EDEN: THE MOUNTAIN AND PARADISE OF GOD

In Genesis 2, there appears for the first time a reference to the "Garden of Eden." *And the LORD God planted a garden in Eden, in the east,
and there he put the man whom he had formed* (Genesis 2:8). The noun
*Eden* means delight, finery, or luxury.

*Daughters of Israel, weep over Saul, Who clothed you in scarlet, with
luxury (eden)* (2 Samuel 1:24). *You (God) give them drink from your river of delights (eden). For with you is the fountain of life; in your light, we see
light* (Psalm 36:8, 9).

Revelation 2:7 says that the "one who overcomes, I will grant to
eat from the tree of life," (PARA), which is in the Paradise of God.

The Hebrew word *paradeisos* means a park, a garden, a paradise, and a great enclosure or preserve. According to many church fathers, the Paradise where Adam and Eve fell still exists, neither on earth nor in the heavens, but above and beyond the world. In 2 Corinthians 12:4, Paul was caught up into Paradise and heard inexpressible words, which a man is not permitted to speak.[5]

The Lord God planted a garden eastward in Eden, a sacred space where humans could experience the manifest presence of God. It was a separate plot of ground, fenced off like an enclosed park separated from the rest of Eden and planted with trees and herbs of choicer kinds, more fit for food, and more beautiful in foliage and blossom than elsewhere (Ellicott's Commentary).[6]

It was a walled garden within the cosmos created by God as a sacred place of communion and pleasure in His presence. Whether you feel it or not, or know it or not, God is present in this space, ascendent but always imminently present. There is a difference between omnipresence and manifest presence. God's omnipresence is not alerted by the observer, for He is there whether we know it or not. Even if you do not believe in God, He is still there. In the New Testament, manifest means to cause to be seen, displayed, or made known or revealed. His presence is revealed in multiple ways.

> And He said, "My presence shall go with you, and I will give you rest." Then he said to Him, "If Your presence does not go with us, do not lead us up from here" (Exodus 33:14, 15).

> Where can I go from Your Spirit? Or where can I flee from Your presence? (Psalm 149:7).

*So God created man in His own image; in the image of God, He created him, male and female* (Genesis 1:27). And God told them to be fruitful, multiply, subdue the earth, and have dominion. God planted a garden on the eastern side of Eden, the mountain of God (Genesis 2:8). Then God informed them about the two trees, the tree of life and the tree of good and evil, which were forbidden (v. 10, 16).

They enjoyed paradise, the manifest presence of God, in that holy and sacred place until they disobeyed God and sinned against Him. The original intention was always to fulfill the Edenic covenant of blessing and dominion, forever living in the presence of God. And while fulfilling that purpose, they would cover the earth with the manifest presence of God. That's why God told Joshua, *"Every place that the sole of your foot will tread upon I have given you, as I said to Moses"* (Joshua 1:3). Dominion was never meant just for the secret place, but dominion was given so that the manifest presence would be revealed in every place around the world, whether a village in Africa or on Wall Street. God's ultimate goal was that they would receive a divine impartation to take dominion over the whole earth and make it look like heaven.

## DEATH BY HOLINESS

Dr. Stephen De Young, the pastor of Archangel Gabriel Orthodox Church and a Ph.D. in Biblical Studies from Amridge University, has a powerful perception on the issue of those who act unworthily in a sacred place and pay the consequences. At several points in the scriptures, humans contact the sacred in ways that result in extremely negative consequences. These persons are immediately struck dead by entering a sacred space or inappropriately contacting holy things. However, there are far more examples in the scriptures of sinful and unworthy individuals coming into direct contact with God and being brought to repentance and otherwise purified. But it is how these persons do what they do that brings the consequences they receive, as illustrated in the following stories.[7]

The sin of Adam and Eve was more than a punishment; it was the mercy of God because it is dangerous to remain in sin while living in the sacred place of God's presence. The theologia holiness" because God's manifest presence is so that it cannot come into contact with sin. It is no God's glory, but that those who sin cannot live in ence of the Lord.

> *Then Nadab and Abihu, the sons of Aaron, each took his censer and put fire in it, put incense on it, and offered profane fire before the LORD, which He had not commanded them. So fire went out from the LORD and devoured them, and they died before the LORD (Leviticus 10:1, 2).*

Another Old Testament episode of violating sacred space is Uzzah (2 Samuel 6:5-11). Many hands must have touched the ark that day in the process of lifting it onto the cart with none of them being smitten; it was not the fact of touching, but the spirit in which he handled the ark that made Uzzah guilty. His rash irreverence, entirely ignoring the sanctity of the ark, regarding it as an unholy common thing. He had no consciousness of the Divine Presence in the ark. It wasn't the act; it was the attitude in that sacred place.

> *It is reported that there is sexual immorality among you, and sexual immorality of such a kind as does not exist even among the Gentiles, namely, that someone has his father's wife; deliver such a one to Satan for the destruction of the flesh, that his spirit may be saved in the day of the Lord Jesus (1 Corinthians 5:1, 5).*

The ancient Greek word *porneia* broadly refers to sexual activity outside of marriage. The ethics of Greek culture clashed with the ethics of Jesus, and though sexual immorality was accepted for the common person in Greek culture, it was not to be so among the followers of Jesus.[8]

Paul rejected this kind of incestuous relationship and considered it taboo even among the pagans of their culture, yet those in the Corinthian church seemed to accept this behavior. The punishment appears to remove spiritual protection and social comfort, not an infliction of evil. Placing this man outside that spiritual protection and eliminating the church's social comfort was the destruction of his rebellious flesh, not the body.

Ananias and Sapphira were not judged for their lack of generosi-doomed for trying to deceive God. They presented themselves as something very different than what they were. When asked by Peter if the financial gift represented the entire sum of the sale, both Ananias and his wife separately lied and were each struck dead. The text is clear that the falsehood was the sin, not the percentage of the money they chose to donate. *Then Peter said, "Ananias, how is it that Satan has so filled your heart that you have lied to the Holy Spirit and have kept for yourself some of the money you received for the land? You have not lied just to human beings but to God." When Ananias heard this, he fell and died. And great fear seized all who heard what had happened* (Acts 5:3-5).

You are not your own. For this cause, many are weak and sickly among you—since we are the temple of the Lord. *Do you not know that your bodies are temples of the Holy Spirit, who is in you, whom you have received from God?* (1 Corinthians 6:19). We understand how a crime against the body and blood of Christ ( v. 23) would deny the body of anyone who committed it in His presence and predisposed to sickness and even death.

. It is the judgment that Paul speaks about in 1 Corinthians 11:30: *For he who eats and drinks in an unworthy manner eats and drinks judgment to himself, not discerning the Lord's body. For this reason, many are weak and sick among you, and many sleep.*

Paul addresses how one should approach the eucharist. The eucharist (from the Greek *eucharistia* for "thanksgiving") is central to prayer and worship, a pivotal belief and practice in Greek Orthodoxy.

The Orthodox Church uses such expressions as symbolical, mystical, and spiritual. All reality is a symbol of mystical truth in manifesting God. Thus, by eating and drinking the bread and wine, we are mystically consecrated by the Holy Spirit, and we have genuine communion with God through Christ, who is "the bread of life" (John 6:34, 41).[9]

In the holy sacrament, it is more than the symbols of bread and wine; it is the body and blood of Christ. During holy communion, unless you are committed to walking in purity, holiness, and the Spirit, you must be cautious about celebrating the eucharist less you are judged. In an unworthy manner, accepting it inappropriately and shamefully, is to eat and drink judgment. So Paul reminds them that eating and drinking of the eucharist is to receive the body and blood of Christ, of God Himself, within one's own body. There is no more intimate contact with God. Participating in the holy communion casually or in an unworthy way without repentance leads some in the Corinthian community to becoming ill, and even to the death of some. Some of you are sick, weak, and even dying because you embraced something holy without living a life of holiness.

## TOWER OF BABEL, PROFANE PLACE

Genesis chapters three and six become part of what Heiser calls a theological prelude that frames the rest of the Bible. Since the tragedy in Genesis and then life after the flood, humans have attempted to recover and rebuild Eden in their way. The angels who once served God, many revolted and were cast down to the earth. Now, these are enemies of Yahweh, humans, and corrupted angels. Any attempt at recreating Eden without God's original plan will end in a world of disaster.

After the flood, Nimrod, whose Semitic name means "to rebel,"[10] is only mentioned in Genesis 10:8, 9, but these two verses speak volumes about the character of Nimrod. He would become the ancestor of the Assyrian and Babylonian nations that would dismantle Israel's original glory. Babylon was a sacred but profane place where people sought to "make a name (*shem*) for themselves" by building a tower that reached the heavens, the realm of the gods.

> Now the whole earth had one language and one speech. And they said, "Come, let us build ourselves a city and a tower whose top is in the heavens; let us make a name for ourselves, lest we be scattered abroad over the face of the whole earth" (Genesis 11:1, 3).

The plural announcement of "let us make man in our image" and "let us go down and confuse their language," was a creative act, and a pivotal redirection of history, which is a difference between Babel and

Abraham. Apart from God's presence, you can't build a sacred space. People can create a majestic tower that is spectacular to the natural eye, but apart from God, it's nothing.

Heiser describes a reversal of the nations: "Deuteronomy 32:8-9 describes how Yahweh's dispersal of the nations at Babel resulted in his *disinheriting* these nations as his people, a nation that was Noah's descendants. The Old Testament equivalent of Romans 1:18-25 is a familiar passage wherein God 'gave (humankind) over' to their persistent rebellion. The statement in Deuteronomy 32:9 that 'the Lord's (Yahweh's) portion is his people, Jacob his allotted heritage' tips us off that contrast in affection and ownership is intended. Yahweh, in effect, decided that the people of the world's nations were no longer going to be in a relationship with him. He would begin anew. He would enter into covenant relationship with a new people that did not exist: Israel."[11]

## ABRAM IN THE SHADOW OF ANCIENT BABEL

Amongst the ancient Mesopotamians, each city had its gods and at the center of the cities were large sacred places called temples or ziggurats built to their gods. But during the era of Babel's Tower, a golden thread of promise is revealed.

Beginning with Genesis 11:10, we can trace the genealogy of the descendants of Shem through his great-grandson, Eber, to a man named Abram. Though a pagan from a pagan home and city, Abraham would become a father of many nations. Joshua said to all the people, *"This is what the LORD, the God of Israel says: 'From ancient times your fathers lived beyond the Euphrates River, namely, Terah, the father of Abraham and the father of Nahor, and they served other gods"* (Joshua 24:2).

In chapter seven of Josephus' *Antiquities of the Jews*, he quoted Berosus of Mochus, a third-century BC Chaldean priest, who said Abram was trained in the celestial sciences of astronomy and astrology. Josephus also said that Abram's study of the heavenly bodies convinced him that they obeyed fixed laws of the universe rather than acting independently of each other as true gods would do.[12]  As he continued to study, Abram became convinced that there must be a supreme god of the whole universe who controlled everything.

When the time was right, God chose Abram from Ur of the Chaldeans, located in southern Mesopotamia, present-day Iraq. *Now the Lord had said to Abram: Get out of your country, From your family And from your father's house To a land that I will show you. I will make you a great nation; I will bless you And make your name great; And you shall be a blessing. I will bless those who bless you, And I will curse him who curses you; And in you all the families of the earth shall be blessed* (Genesis 12:1-3).

When God spoke to Moses and instructed him to communicate with the Israelites in Egypt, He told Moses to refer to Him as the God of Abraham, Isaac, and Jacob (Exodus 3:15, 16). Not only did this distinguish Him from the Egyptian gods, it inherently reminded the Israelites of His longstanding promises to covenant with them.

In Psalm 91:1, the poet mentioned the Almighty: *He who dwells in the secret place of the Most High Shall abide under the shadow of the Almighty*. In Genesis 15:18, Melchizedek king of Salem was the priest of God Most High.

The Hebrew *El Elyon* occurs forty-nine times in the Bible, and it is either as God Most High, the Lord Most High, the Most High God, or simply Most High. El Elyon refers to God as supremely exalted above all, whether gods or kings. *For the LORD Most High is awesome; He is a great King over all the earth* (Psalm 47:2).

## MOUNT SINAI AND MOUNT ZION

It's not God's choice, whether He manifests Himself to you, for it's your choice to live in the place of consecration, set apart unto Him, where He can overshadow you with His glory. But Abraham, Isaac, and Jacob encounter God's mountain. Abraham experienced the God of the mountain, as Isaac brought his son to the mountain and experienced God. And there is Jacob's ladder to heaven, where the angels were ascending and descending.

*For you did not come near to the mountain touched and scorched with fire, and blackness, and darkness, and storm* (Hebrews 12:18, LSV). The author's words echo the retelling of Sinai in Deuteronomy 4 and 5. Mount Sinai looks large in the theological landscape of the Old Testament. It is the mountain of God, a sacred place.

Mount Sinai, the untouchable mountain, refers to a restriction, inferring a command forbidding them to "touch" the mountain, implying that it was tangible but untouchable and uncontrollable. Everything connected to the giving of the Law set boundaries around the mountain which they cannot pass and hedged with the darkness and violent storms on God's mountain, which was created to overawe the soul.

The generation coming out of Egypt was dazed and overawed with the theophany, so much so that they begged for Moses to mediate communication to them rather than for God to speak directly (Exodus 20:19). They did not want to be too close to God (Exodus 20:18) because they knew God had commanded anything would die if it touched this mountain (Exodus 19:12). When the people saw the thunder and lightning and heard the trumpet and saw the mountain in smoke, they trembled with fear. And so terrifying was the sight that Moses said, "I am exceedingly afraid and trembling" (Exodus 12:21).

The author's words, *you cannot come*, is now replaced with *you have come*. The contrast of God's presence is much different under grace rather than the impinging force of the Law. *But you have come to Mount Zion and to the city of the living God, the heavenly Jerusalem, to an innumerable company of angels to the general assembly and church of the firstborn who are enrolled in heaven, to God the Judge of all, to the spirits of just men made perfect to Jesus the Mediator of the new covenant, and to the blood of sprinkling that speaks better things than that of Abel* (Hebrews 12:22-24).

We are not kept at a distance from God as the Israelites were at Mount Sinai, for we enter into the unseen presence. At the edge of the mountain of grace is one grand, ample, and interesting display of the infinite love of God. It is all encouragement, and we breathe nothing but mercy.

The main point of the comparison is that under the Jewish dispensation, everything was adapted to awe the mind and restrained by the exhibition of grandeur and power. Still, while much was sublime under the gospel of grace, much more was adapted to hold the affections of love for God. There were revelations of higher truths and more affecting motives to lead to obedience. There was that of which the former was but the type and emblem.[13]

> *See that you do not refuse Him who speaks. For if they did not escape who refused Him who spoke on earth, much more shall we not escape if we turn away from Him who speaks from heaven whose voice then shook the earth; but now He has promised, (Hebrews 12:25-26).*

Under the threat of persecution, the author addressed those tempted to abandon Christ and return to their Jewish faith. So, he paints a picture contrasting the terrors of Mount Sinai, portraying Jewish life under the law, with the glories of Mount Zion, picturing the joy of life under the new covenant. Right living flows out of right spiritual awareness and knowledge, not by the law. If you know and have experienced the riches you possess in Christ, you will not reverse back to the empty, fleeting pleasures of the world.

Do not refuse Him who speaks—Jesus' words were clearer and greater than the works of the law. He does not speak amid lightning, thunder, and dark clouds, but Jesus teaches the way and power of love, forgiveness, grace, mercy, and promises of a better covenant. So, do not refuse Christ as Israel rejected God under the old covenant.

If all Israel were held accountable for obeying God when He warned them on earth from Mount Sinai, how much more will we be answerable now when He speaks from heaven, from Mount Zion? The Greek *chrematizo* means responding to those consulting an oracle, giving a divine command or warning, and teaching from heaven.[14]

This heavenly warning presents the same peril—that apathy toward spiritual matters and complacency with a religious lifestyle falls far short of what God requires and has made full provision. But such complacency cannot go unjudged forever. It constitutes a refusal of God's grace, a turning of one's back on truth and deliverance. And this is where some, if not many, of the recipients of this letter now stand in peril.

> *Yet once more I shake not only the earth, but also heaven."*
> *Now this, "Yet once more," indicates the removal of those*
> *things that are being shaken, as of things that are made,*
> *that the things which cannot be shaken may remain (He-*
> *brews 12:27).*

The prophecy is a reference to Haggai 2:6, 7. It initially referred to the second temple, the glory of which was to be greater than the glory of the first, but the ultimate prophetic word is the final revelation of Christ coming to his people. Its first fulfillment is rightly seen in Christ's first coming as the prophets spoke in Malachi 3:1: *The Lord, whom ye seek, shall suddenly come to his temple the messenger of the covenant whom you desire.*

But the language used points even to a further fulfillment. The ultimate reference is what is seen dimly in so many prophetic visions and the final dissolution of the whole present order of things, to be succeeded by the kingdom of eternal righteousness. *You have prepared the earth from the first, and your hands made heaven* (Psalm 102:25).[15]

The eternity of God looks backward and forward, beginning and end, when the years of God stretched through all the generations of people and the changes which occurred upon the earth. At the very beginning He existed and He would continue to exist to the very close, unchangeably the same.

*Therefore, since we are receiving a kingdom which cannot be shaken, let us have grace, by which we may serve God acceptably with reverence and godly fear* (Hebrews 12:28). Let us have grace which means "let us hold fast the grace or favor which we have received in being admitted to the privileges of that kingdom."[16]

The author's object is to keep them in the reverent fear and service of God. We pertain to a kingdom that is permanent and unchanging. The past has shown that no power of earth or hell can destroy it and that amidst all revolutions, this kingdom still survives, the only empire destined never to fall. Life isn't easy because we are aliens in this world, and when we walk with Christ, we are out of step with the world. But let us continually have grace to serve God and others.

God is a consuming fire (see Hebrews 12:29) which involves understanding the reflection, the name, and the motion. So, the burning bush, consuming fire image in Exodus 3 is a powerful symbol representing God's miraculous energy, sacred light, illumination, and the burning heart of purity, love, and clarity. It also illustrates reverence and fear before the Divine Presence.

God's identity involves worship, acceptable and which God receives adoration, expressions of love with awe and wonder, who worship Him in spirit and truth. "Earth's crammed with heaven, and every common bush afire with God. But only he who sees takes off his shoes" (Elizabeth Barrett Browning).

The motion of God's consuming fire is seen in holiness that burns up anything unholy. God's holiness separates Him from sin without repentance. The godless, Isaiah writes, tremble before Him: "*Who of us can dwell with the consuming fire? Who of us can dwell with everlasting burning*?" (Isaiah 33:14). The prophet Isaiah answers this by saying that only the righteous can withstand the consuming fire because of Christ in them. The consuming fire draws near us, and we to Him, through His mercy and compassion. God is a consuming fire for those under the new covenant through redemption and adoption into the covenant.

## THE SACRED SPACE OF CHRIST IN YOU

While we are in the world, we are separate from the world but called to be a part of the culture to change the culture reflecting God's kingdom. God's intention for us is to be His agents on the earth to bring the trajectory, the overwhelming arcing glory of God, to the planet.

As God's agents, we seek to create a space where heaven becomes earth. God didn't just want us to walk with Him because His ultimate goal was for God to live inside us, which Christ in us is the hope of glory.

In the Old Testament, God could not find a space of ultimate perfection. He looked for someone to journey with Him and be a friend to Him. So, in the Old Testament, God built a box, a space for His presence, which would become a temple, but even that had to be covered with the blood of bulls and goats because it was imperfect, unholy, and flawed.

We live under the emblem of God's favor, not because of our family or lineage but because the God Most High, El Elyon, the Christ who lives inside you. With His favor, you are consecrated and set apart for Him. You are no longer living, for Christ lives inside of you.

The mystery, hidden for generations, is now revealed to us. To them, *God willed to make known what are the riches of the glory of this mystery among the Gentiles: which is Christ in you, the hope of glory* (Colossians 1:27).

Christ in us, the hope of glory, but the hope of glory remains dormant until that hope is made manifest in Christ. *But all have sinned and fallen short of the glory of God, but we are justified freely by His grace through the redemption that is in Christ Jesus* (Romans 3:23, 24). It's show me the money or show me the glory, and Moses chose the glory, while too many choose the money. First, Moses says, *If Your Presence does not go with us, do not bring us up from here* (Exodus 33:15). Then in verse eighteen, he says, *Please, show me Your glory*.

The sacred space in you is where Christ lives within. *I am crucified with Christ; and it is no longer I who live, but it is **Christ who lives in me**; and the life which I now live in the flesh I live in faith, the faith of the Son of God, who loved me and gave himself up for me* (Colossians 2:20, emphasis added).

That's why you have to recognize who you are in Christ. You must realize that you are a container for Christ identifying you as the sacred and holy space where He abides because of a transformation. *Therefore if anyone is in Christ [that is, grafted in, joined to Him by faith in Him as Savior], he is a new creature [reborn and renewed by the Holy Spirit]; the old things [the previous moral and spiritual condition] have passed away. Behold, new things have come [because spiritual awakening brings a new life]* (2 Corinthians 5:17, AMP).

Christ in you—Christ formed in you. *My children, with whom I am again in labor until Christ is formed in you* (Galatians 4:19). Christ comes and shapes us within if we are willing to be clay on the Potter's wheel. Christ presses the shape of His face into the clay of our souls as we become like Christ. Paul's message and the Judaizers' message contradict each other, one of humility and obedience and the other of pride and self-will.

It is why wherever Abraham, Isaac, and Jacob went, they experienced God, setting up altars, making burning sacrifices to the Lord. Looking back, we see it as types and shadows of the ultimate sacrifice of Christ. And we are called to live in that sacred space as we are consumed by the holiness of God, death by holiness.

## PILLARS, NAMES, AND THE NEW JERUSALEM

That John was the instrument of closing the final book of the New Testament is worthy of consideration. John was distinguished as a disciple of Jesus, prophet, apostle to the churches, and known as the beloved disciple whom Jesus loved. For nearly thirty years following the resurrection of his Lord, John's ministry was as suspected in harmony with his character—quiet and unassuming but resolute with purpose and faithful to the cause of Christ.

Those acquainted with the writings of John and Paul agree that there are no two writers in the scripture more different in style than these two apostles, but both were powerful and the most influential in their writings. One wrote short, pithy statements, the other long and compound sentences. One keeps his personal experience hidden, while the other draws from his experiences. One was called at the beginning of Jesus' ministry, and the other after His death. One saw the Lord in His deepest humiliation in the garden, and the other saw Him in highest glory. One was the closest with Him, while the other did not know Christ but saw Him on the Damascus Road, risen and glorified like a bright light. But of the two, John would write the final book of the New Testament.

In Revelation 1, Jesus tells John what he saw, write in a book, then send it to the seven churches of Asia (v. 11). Either by a vision or a dream, John prophetically saw things: the things which are and the things which will take place afterward (v. 19).

In the Targum, an Aramaic paraphrase, Isaiah 22:22 reads, "I will give *the key of the house of the sanctuary*, and the government of the house of David, into his hand."[17] And in that mystical experience with John, Jesus says, *He who has the key of David, who opens and no one will shut, and who shuts and no one opens* (Revelation 3:7). It doesn't appear to be a door of opportunity but the open door of heaven itself. The purpose of this letter was to offer assurance and encouragement to the church of Philadelphia, which was beleaguered by the Jewish synagogue, which is actually a synagogue of Satan, but the Philadelphian church remained faithful to the testimony of Christ and sought to bring the Jews to understand that Christ is the promised Messiah.

And then John finishes his letter to the church at Philadelphia with these compelling prophetic words: *He who overcomes, I will make him a pillar in the temple of My God, and he shall go out no more. I will write on him the name of My God and the name of the city of My God, the New Jerusalem, which comes down out of heaven from My God. And I will write on him My new name* (Revelation 3:12).

I will make him a pillar in the temple of My God—the promised reward of faithfulness that he who was victorious would be honored as if he were a pillar or column in the temple of God. *Do you not know that you are the temple of God and that the Spirit of God dwells in you?* (1 Corinthians 3:16).

Jachin and Boaz are the names of two bronze pillars erected at the entrance to the vestibule of Solomon's temple. The pillar on the south of the entrance was called Jachin, and one on the north was named Boaz. Both 2 Chronicles and 1 Kings say that "he" set up the pillars, and "he" called them Jachin and Boaz. Commentators are divided on whether "he" refers to Hiram or Solomon. Whoever named them, their names are significant. *Jachin* (pronounced *yaw-keen*) means "he will establish," and *Boaz* signifies "in him is strength" (1 Kings 7:21).[18]

Having received Christ, they will be rooted and built up in Him and *established* in the faith and *strengthened* with all power, according to His glorious might. The name on the pillars of the temple of God will be *stérigmos*[19] (established) and *sthenos*[20] (strengthened).

And he shall go no more out—you are built as a sacred place, a holy place of habitation, the temple of God, and the dwelling place of the Most High God. *In whom ye also are builded together for an habitation of God through the Spirit* (Ephesians 2:22). *Do you not know that you are the temple of God and that the Spirit of God dwells in you? For you are the temple of the living God* (1 Corinthians 3:16). *As God has said: "I will dwell in them And walk among them. I will be their God, And they shall be My people"* (2 Corinthians 6:16).

I will write on him—character and relationship. The rewards for having character built on endurance and perseverance are an abiding presence and an intimate relationship with Christ. *He who dwells in the secret place of the Most High Shall abide under the shadow of the Almighty. I will say of the* Lord, *"He is my refuge and my fortress; My God, in Him I will trust"* (Psalm 91:1, 2). *I will set him on high, because he has known My name. He shall call upon Me, and I will answer him; I will be with him in trouble; I will deliver him and honor him* (v. 14, 15). *If we endure, we will also reign with Him* (2 Timothy 2:12).

My new name—the promise of a new identity. *They shall see His face, and His name shall be on their foreheads* (Revelation 22:4). The Hebrew root denotes something high or elevated, a monument implying majesty or excellence. It is an outstanding mark, sign, or reputation. Thus "name" is a word by which a person, place, or thing is distinctively known.[21] Through His names and titles, God has chosen to reveal a great deal about His attributes, offices, authority, prerogatives, and will. Each name designates some distinct virtue or characteristic of God's nature. Thus, God made known the glory of His nature through His name.[22]

> *So all the peoples of the earth will see that you are called by the name of the Lord, and they will be afraid of you (Deuteronomy 28:10). Everyone that is called by My name, And whom I have created for My glory, I have formed him, yea, I have made him (Isaiah 43:7, JPS Tanakh).*

*So that the rest of mankind may seek the Lord, and all the*
*Gentiles who are called by My name (Acts 15:17).*

The city of my God and the New Jerusalem—the mystic mountain and the place of God's presence where we abide. *His foundation*
*is in the holy mountains... Glorious things are spoken of you, O city of God*
(Psalm 87:1, 3). *For the LORD has chosen Zion; He has desired it for His*
*dwelling place* (Psalm 132:13).

The house of God, Mount Zion, and the New Jerusalem is the
church and community of God's people where Yahweh habitats, and
the bearer of the name belongs to God and the heavenly city and society of God.

*In the last days the mountain of the house of the LORD will be estab-*
*lished as the chief of the mountains; it will be raised above the hills, and all*
*nations will stream to it* (Isaiah 2:2). *I will give in my house and within my*
*walls a monument and a name better than sons and daughters; I will give*
*them an everlasting name that shall not be cut off* (Isaiah 56:5). *The name*
*of the city from that day shall be, 'The LORD is there'* (Ezekiel 48:35).
*And I saw the holy city, new Jerusalem, coming down out of heav-*
*en from God, prepared as a bride adorned for her husband* (Revelation
21:2).

The point made by the prophet is that God bestows freely upon
His people the privilege of invoking His support and entering into
His secret place, the house of God's presence, where we abide forever
under His name. And there are many names associated with the New
Jerusalem, the church who are the followers of Jesus founded on His
word and formed into a community of God's holy people.

*Jerusalem will dwell securely, and this is what she will be*
*named: Yahweh Our Righteousness (Jeremiah 33:16, LSV).*

Jehovah Tsidkenu, the name by which He will be called, "The
Lord our righteousness."[23] In Jeremiah, God pronounced judgment
against Israel and gave them the promise of a righteous Branch: Je-

•

sus the Messiah who would bring restoration. It is only through the Son that we are made righteous. *Jesus Christ became sin for us so that we could become the Righteousness of God* (2 Corinthians 5:21). By the power of believing faith, we have become the righteousness of God. *This righteousness from God comes through faith in Jesus Christ to all who believe* (Romans 3:22).

> *And the name of the city from that day shall be, Jehovah is there (Ezekiel 48:35).*

Jehovah Shammah, "the Lord is there."[24] The new name reflects the identification of the place with the Person and Permanent Presence of the Prince of Peace, the Messiah. *For a child will be born to us, a son will be given to us; And the government will rest on His shoulders; And His name will be called Wonderful Counselor, Mighty God, Eternal Father, Prince of Peace* (Isaiah 9:6, emphasis added).

The city of God, the New Jerusalem, and God's holy church will then take on the same characteristics as the LORD who will dwell within her. God's presence in the secret place made unforgettable this name of the holy city *The Lord is There.* There is only Christ, and He is everything.

## CHAPTER TWO

# THE MYSTERY OF INIQUITY

*The mystery which has been hidden from ages and from generations, but now has been revealed to His saints (Colossians 1:26).*

The Greek mysteries were secret religious doctrines and rites made known only to initiated persons, who formed approved groups assembling at certain sacred spots mostly near Athens. These organizations exercised a vast influence over the Greek mind and literature full of allusions to ambiguities. Still, their secrets were well kept, and little is known of their real character.

The language and ideas connected with the mysteries were readily adopted by the Jewish Church of Alexandria, whose endeavor it was to expand Judaism by a symbolical and allegorizing method into a philosophical and universal religious system, and who were compelled to veil their inner doctrine from the eyes of their stricter, unenlightened (or unsophisticated) fellow believers. In Paul's writing to those accustomed, either as Greeks or the Hellenistic Jews, to this phraseology, he referred to the gospel as "a mystery," which is "hidden from the natural understanding" (see I Corinthians 2:6-16). But in the words that follow, he repudiates the notion of any secrecy or exclusiveness in its proclamation (see 2 Corinthians 3:12-4:6).[25] In Paul's language, "Mystery is the junction to revelation."

## THE MYSTERY OF INIQUITY

In every city Paul went, he brought the gospel with power and the word with great success and faced opposition, but lawlessness and deception sought to destroy his work.

Paul and his gifted team found success in preaching and teaching the people in Thessalonica but were ultimately forced out of the city by detractors. Sometime after they left, Paul learned that the Thessalonians remained faithful and shared Jesus' message with others. Paul had not been back to Thessalonica after he was driven out during his second missionary journey and was unable to return because he was "hindered" by Satan from doing so (I Thessalonians 2:18). Paul did not give any details about how Satan hindered him, but it is clear that persecution from Jews had already forced Paul to take many detours in his journey. Concerning opposition to God's people, Satan is always present and will do everything he can to deceive and defeat the saints of God.

Throughout the New Testament, there are many expressions of mystery like the mystery of the kingdom, the mystery of Christ, the mystery of godliness, and the mystery of iniquity.

*For the mystery of iniquity doth already work* (2 Thessalonians 2:7). Mystery of iniquity— *mustérion anomia*—the revelation of iniquity, lawlessness, disobedience, sin, and the negative influence on a person's *soul* and *status* before God.[26]

*And then I will declare to them, "I never knew you; depart from Me, you who practice lawlessness"* (Matthew 7:23). *Even so you also outwardly appear righteous to men, but inside you are full of hypocrisy and lawlessness* (Mathew 23:28).

## EXALTED ANGEL, LAWLESS ANGEL

The apostasy comes first, and the man of lawlessness is revealed, the son of destruction, who opposes and exalts himself above every so-called god or object of worship so that he takes his seat in the temple of God, displaying himself as being God. The one whose coming is in accord with the activity of Satan, with all power and false signs and wonders (2 Thessalonians 2:2, 3, 9, NASB).

*Corruptio optimi pessimal, meaning* the corruption of the best, is the worst tragedy! With great potential, there is tragedy as happened with Satan and the human couple in Eden's Garden and the antichrist. As it was in the beginning, it will be in the end. In the beginning, there was a departure, defection, a great fall by disobedience caused by the angel of lawlessness, a son of destruction. And in the end, Satan will do it again through another human, the antichrist, Satan's hench-man, a pseudo-Christ who will perform miracles, signs, and wonders by the power of Satan and ultimately deceive the world.

The chronicles of brothers—Gabriel, Michael, and Lucifer—roy-al archangels, united in devotion to their Father and all His works. Gabriel, the strength of God, a voice to the prophets, and the archan-gel of Israel. Michael, the angel of the Lord, chief prince of the heav-ens, and head of the host of angels in the end times.

Lucifer, son of the morning who became the prince of darkness, was the anointed guardian cherub with a high-ranking position in the angelic host, who had great power and influence. In Jonathan Edward's collection of notes, thoughts, observations, and insights known as his *Miscellanies*, he writes these words in *Miscellanies* No. 986: Lucifer, prior to his fall, "was the chief of all the angels, of the greatest natural capacity, strength and wisdom, and highest in honor and dignity, the brightest of all those stars."[27]

Though Satan was exalted above all other angels, Edwards quick-ly points out that Christ is exalted higher than Lucifer as the second person of the Godhead. In other words, while Lucifer was only near the throne, Christ, being supremely higher and more excellent in His being, was allowed to sit down forever with God on the throne.[28]

The fall of Satan and his angels were shrouded behind a veil and cloaked in mystery but most likely elevated his anger because of the beloved Son of God.But Satan was overcome with pride and desire to be God. *You were perfect in your ways from the day you were created, Till iniquity was found in you. By the abundance of your trading, You became filled with violence within, And you sinned; Therefore I cast you as a profane thing out of the mountain of God; And I destroyed you, O covering cherub, From the midst of the fiery stones* (Ezekiel 28:15, 16). When Satan fell, he did not fall alone. Scripture tells us that he took one-third of the angels (see Revelation 12:4).

From the heights of expectation to the depths of a petulant child who seems he can't find acceptance, though the father's love was always there, for God is love. Like most troubled children with a Freudian hatred for their fathers, Satan shifts from the anointed cherub to the lawless one. So, Satan becomes the prodigal son who will spoil Father's delight in Eden's garden.

When Satan learned of God's latest creation of humans, he was consumed with resentment and sought to eliminate them. Unrepentant, he vows he won't suffer alone, for humanity will make a powerful enemy through deception and luring them into darkness and torment any way he can.

So, Satan invites Adam and Eve to do what Father told them not to do. Then, the rebellious kids become a generation of lawless kids throughout the ages. Once they realize the consequences of their sin, the only sound they hear in Eden's garden is the sound of silence. Father knows best, but Adam and Eve left their Lover and chose the path to lawless destruction, starting with their family.

## THE SERPENT IN EDEN'S GARDEN

Satan's tool is always deception, wrecking humanity through trickery, fabrications, and illusions of the truth. Effective resistance requires the spirit of discernment and the wisdom of God. In Genesis 3, the author opens the door to the catastrophic events in God's garden inside Eden's gate. There are four characters in the Edenic story: God, Adam, Eve, and the serpent.

The Hebrew *nachash* is a serpent or snake and, in Arabic, a viper.[29] There is great debate over the snake's character, being the prince of fallen angels, Satan, or a real serpent possessed and stimulated by Satan. Whatever the case, the enemy of God and humans appeared in the form of a serpent who was a supernatural force of some sort.

In the New Testament, there are a couple of references to the snake/serpent. *He laid hold of the dragon, that serpent of old, who is the Devil and Satan* (Revelation 20:2). *But I am afraid that, as the serpent deceived Eve by his trickery, your minds will be led astray from sincere and pure devotion to Christ* (2 Corinthians 11:3). The Greek *óphis* also means snake or serpent, but the ancients believed that the serpent was an emblem of cunning and wisdom and was the serpent who deceived Eve and was regarded by the Jews as the devil.[30] How did a smart "creature of the field" come to be identified with the Prince of Darkness? That's an impressive leap in a reptile's résumé.

*Now the serpent was more cunning than any beast of the field which the Lord God had made. And he said to the woman, "Has God indeed said, 'You shall not eat of every tree of the garden?'"* (Genesis 3:1). The author opens chapter three, referring to the Lord God as Yahweh Elohim, the living God, but the serpent calls God by the name Elohim alone, and the woman does the same. Elohim is a more general and indefinite name; the personality of the living God is obscured by the use of Elohim, knowing that it could refer to a god or angel.[31] It was intentional on the part of the enemy, seeking to attain his end by changing the name of the living, personal God into a mere God to exaggerate God's prohibition of the tree of the knowledge of good and evil, in the hope of exciting in the woman's mind partly distrust of God Himself, and partly a doubt as to the truth of His word.

## TRAGEDY IN THE ANCIENT GARDEN

Jacob Boehme, the 16th-century Christian theologian and philosopher, spoke about "the horrible, lamentable, and miserable fall of Adam and Eve."

Detecting this spiritual handicap, Satan was ready to make his move. He had patiently waited until the humans were secluded in a vulnerable place—when Father was not present with them. Following his cautiously calculated plan, Satan in his serpent form proudly pranced into the Garden, preparing to inflict a mortal wound on the soul of God's beloved creature.

Now the serpent (Genesis 3:1)—The Genesis text does not clearly detect the serpent's identity, but the rest of the Bible clarifies that Satan appears as a serpent. In the books of Job and Isaiah, a serpent or a snake-like creature appears that is pierced and wounded, such as Job 26:13, *His Spirit He adorned the heavens; His hand pierced the fleeing serpent*, and Isaiah 51:9, *O arm of the LORD! Awake as in the ancient days, In the generations of old. Are You not the arm that cut Rahab apart, And wounded the serpent?*

Was more cunning (vs. 1)—it was the fraudulent scam of Satan that made him effective against Eve: *as the serpent deceived Eve by his craftiness* (2 Corinthians 11:3). Satan does not lie by what he says; what is left unsaid deceives. The devious snake is astute and understands the human condition—and the weaknesses of the human spirit— quite well. Using his crafty language, he undermines Eve's trust in God's goodness toward her. Some would characterize Eve as the unsuspecting woman, but it seems clear that the woman never fully understood the portent of the two trees in the center of the Garden nor the nature of Father's restrictions. Was there a failure on Adam's part to communicate with Eve?

Has God said, You shall not eat of every tree of the garden? (vs. 1)—Casting a dark cloud over God's word, the serpent questioned Eve by asking, you shall not eat of every tree of the garden? The serpent assaulted the very heart of spirituality, man's trust in Father. Satan insinuated that man could not trust God's word. With his treasonous question, he inserted himself between God and man. He would be the umpire, if you will, between God and man. As a counterfeit mediator, he would grossly misrepresent Father. Throwing a blanket of ambiguity over the Divine word, the father of all lies projected his insidious nature onto the image of Father. A duplicitous but treacherous question started everything.

You will not surely die (v. 4)—Eve bites into Satan's hook as Satan reels her in; she becomes a slave to Satan's lies. It will be the beginning of the end for the couple in Eden's wonderful garden. With the final subtle words, Satan aspires to cautiously slander God's character and intentions toward His creation by lying and saying, *For God knows that in the day you eat of it your eyes will be opened, and you will be like God, knowing good and evil* (v. 5). The final enticement was the most powerful because it was how Satan fell, wanting to be equal with God. Eve tried to become a god by rebelling against God.

The woman saw that the tree was good (v. 6)—pleasant to the eyes, a tree desirable to make one wise, and then took its fruit and ate it. She also gave to her husband with her, and he ate. *For all that is in the world—the lust of the flesh, the lust of the eyes, and the pride of life—is not of the Father but is of the world* (1 John 3:16).

Naked and ashamed—Adam and Eve once lived in the weightlessness of grace and had not yet experienced the heaviness of shame and guilt. God accepted them wholly for who they were, and they could accept each other totally as they were. Almost instantly, the sweetness of the fruit turned bitter in her mouth. As that first bite was still sliding down her throat, the light in her soul was already slowly but steadily being extinguished. Eve doubled over in a spasm of unexpected agony. Spinning out of control, spiraling downward, she was rapidly floating further and further from her spiritual core; the gravitational pull of God's presence was rapidly losing its attracting power. She turned around and looked at the serpent, and the serpent smiled. ....and she also gave to her husband with her, and he ate.

The couple had now lost all control of the situation. They could not grasp reality and moved blindly, it seems, from one sin to another. A chain reaction of deception and denial was set in motion, establishing future behavior patterns of hiding and blaming. In a blinding, horrific realization of what they had done, Adam and Eve recoiled in shame. Falling to the ground, they groaned deep within their spirits at their treasonous deed. A penetrating sensation of shame and guilt were stripping away the clothing of personal worth they had worn in the presence of Father. Father! Oh no! They became paralyzed at the thought of Father. For the very first time, they feared the presence of Father.[32]

"Millenniums in a moment. A million miles in a step. An ocean in a drop. Volumes in a word. A race in a woman. A hell of suffering in an act. The depths of woe in a glance. The first chapter of Romans in Genesis three, six. Sharpest pain in softest touch. God mistrusted-distrusted. Satan embraced. Sin's door open. Eden's gate shut" (S. D. Gordon).[33]

## SIN, TRANSGRESSION, AND INIQUITY

Therefore, just as through one man sin entered the world, and death through sin, and thus death spread to all men, because all sinned (Romans 5:12). At this point in Paul's writing, he reaches a digression of thought in which a comparison is made between Adam and Christ. For, as by one man—Adam, the common father of the human species, is the representative of humanity.

Sin entered into the world—the transgression of Adam and its consequence, a sinful nature, which took place in him, through his first sin, and which he conveyed to all his future generations. For all have sinned and come short of the glory that God intended at the beginning (Romans 3:23). But as in Adam, all died, so in Christ, all will be made alive (1 Corinthians 15:22). So there is a contrast between the reign of death introduced by the sin of Adam and the reign of life introduced by the atonement of Christ.

Without the law, each generation lived and sinned, but when the commandment came, sin revived, and I died (Romans 7:9). And in the next verse, Paul reaches this logical conclusion: So I discovered that the very commandment that was meant to bring life actually brought death.

Sin, transgression, and iniquity—I acknowledged my sin to You, and my iniquity I have not hidden. I said, "I will confess my transgressions to the LORD," And You forgave the iniquity of my sin (Psalm 32:5).

The word most often translated as sin is chattah. Strong's Hebrew Dictionary defines it as an offense which was first used in Genesis 4:7: If you do well, will not your countenance be lifted up? And if you do not do well, sin is crouching at the door; and its desire is for you, but you must master it. Sin is any thought, word, or action that is in disobedience to the will of God.[34]

The Hebrew pesha means rebellion and trespass, including crossing a boundary and missing the mark. Transgressing against God is choosing to do something God has established clear boundaries against, and willfully doing so. It's proceeding without caring.[35]

The modern Greco-Roman languages commonly use abstract terms, like iniquity. But as Hebrew is a concrete language, rarely using abstracts, we must understand the word "iniquity" from its Hebraic concrete meaning. The Hebrew word for "iniquity" is evel or avel (Strong's #5766)[36], which is derived from the verbal root (Strong's 5753).[37] This verbal root is expressed in the book of Lamentations: He has walled up my ways with hewn stone; he has made my paths crooked (Lamentations 3:9, NASB, emphasis added).

Based on the teaching of Jesus and other passages of scripture, iniquity is doing our own will instead of God's will, even if our own will appears to be "doing good." Jesus said, *Not everyone who says to Me, "Lord, Lord," shall enter the kingdom of heaven, but he who does the will of My Father in heaven. Many will say to Me in that day, "Lord, Lord, have we not prophesied in Your name, cast out demons in Your name, and done many wonders in Your name?" And then I will declare to them, "I never knew you; depart from Me, you who practice lawlessness"* (Matthew 7:21–23).

## MAN OF LAWLESSNESS

This is not your typical charismatic book but is a door begging to be opened as the Apostle Paul was the first to give entrance concerning the man of lawlessness. It's not to diminish any charismatic book, for we are the ones who opened the door to the supernatural, but the entrance into the lawless, iniquitous times we live in requires our attention. The only way to create a theological landscape is the hermeneutical way, one verse at a time, so let's break it down.

*Let no one deceive you by any means; for that day will not come unless the falling away comes first, and the man of sin is revealed, the son of per-*

*dition, who opposes and exalts himself above all that is called God or that is worshiped, so that he sits as God in the temple of God, showing himself that he is God* (2 Thessalonians 2:3, 4). As mentioned, deception is the tool of Satan and is the work of false teachers and prophets and deceptive politicians who are influenced by the evil one and all those who reject God. And by any means, devices of deception, lead God's people away from the truths of God and scripture.

Man of Lawlessness, the Son of Perdition—both are references to their character, and there are many lawless sons of perdition, but only one is <u>the man of lawlessness</u>. The phrase, "the Man of Sin," might, perhaps, be only a poetic personification of a movement, or a class of men, or succession of men. *The enemy shall have no advantage over him: nor the son of iniquity (evel) have power to hurt him* (Psalm 89:22, Douay-Rheims Bible). But one would suppose that

Paul looked for the coming of some actual individual who would head an apostasy movement in rebellion against God. But the man of lawless perdition is doomed to destruction, as with Judas and any who opposed Yahweh.

Some scholars and theologians down through history, including Hippolytus, Luther, Wesley, Manton, and the brilliant Schaff, say that first "Son of Perdition" reference is to Antiochus Epiphanes, the man who attacked the second temple in Jerusalem and defiled it by sacrificing a pig on the altar, erecting a statue of Zeus as himself in the temple, raiding the temple treasury, and minting coins saying "Theos Epiphanes" (God manifest).[38]

But in all the research, Andy Johnson, professor of New Testament at Nazarene Theological Seminary, creates the best viewpoint on the man of lawlessness. "The man of lawlessness has traditionally been identified with the figure of 'Antichrist' characterized by the development of a parallel between Christ and Antichrist, where one is the reverse replica of the other. Irenaeus developed this parallelism using a basic interpretive framework of double recapitulation. Certain textual features of 2 Thessalonians 2:3-4, when situated within the larger Pauline body of work, epitomizes human arrogance as embodied in archetypal kings (Ezekiel 28) It reveals that the man of lawlessness represents the pinnacle of what Christ has reversed. On that basis, the man of lawlessness is appropriately referred to as 'Antichrist.'"[39]

As such, he is also anti-human, anti-God, and anti-holiness, and there are many antichrists. *Just as you have heard that the antichrist is coming, so now many antichrists have appeared. This is how we know it is the last hour. They went out from us, but they did not belong to us. For if they had belonged to us, they would have remained with us* (1 John 2:18).

In biblical language, there is the type and the antitype, which stem from the word *tupos* in the Greek New Testament. *Tupos* originally referred to the mark of a blow, like a stamp, and by extension was used to refer to a copy or image, a pattern, or, in many cases, a type. One might say that types have the stamp of the antitype.[40]

Consider the types in the Old Testament as shadows cast by their antitypes in the New Testament as illustrated with Adam, the first man, and how he foreshadows Jesus Christ, the last man (Romans 5:12-19; 1 Cor. 15:42-49). In this case, opposites exceed similarities. And in Hebrews 10:1, *for the Law, since it has only a shadow of the good things to come and not the form of those things itself.*

And so it is that the many antichrists have brands on their character and action reflecting the image of the antichrist, which is Satan. In this case, Antiochus Epiphanes is only a type where Satan is the antitype. As children of the light, we are always cautious of the subtleties of Satan lest you be deceived. There have always been anti-human, anti-God, and anti-holy antichrists in every generation like Stalin, Hitler, and Mao Tse-tung. But we must be careful in our world where some walk among us in politics, business, and even some churches who preach a different gospel, but you will know them by their character and teaching. The church, indwelt and empowered by the Spirit of God, has always been part of what holds society back from the swelling tide of lawless living.

## RESTRAINING TO BE REVEALED

Restraining to be revealed—restraining prohibits the public unveiling of the man of lawlessness.

The Greek *katechó* means to restrain, hinder, and hold back the advent of antichrist.[41] The restraining power is the Holy Spirit working primarily through us. God's presence in us shines as the light of the world and permeates secular culture as the salt of the earth, resisting all that is of the antichrist, combined with the support of angelic forces in the heavens.

The Greek word *apokaluptó* means to uncover, reveal, lay open, unveil, disclose, and manifest what was previously concealed.[42] While in heaven, Lucifer's love was meant to be centered on God, but he and other angels took a U-turn headed towards himself. Somehow Lucifer *mysteriously* started undermining the importance of God and others and began his *secret* agenda of exalting self and destroying the saints who love God. It is our responsibility to maintain the resistance and activate the revelation of antichrist, whether type or antitype, so they may be exposed and destroyed by the breath of God.

In Isaiah 47, Babylon, the antitype of Satan, was proud of the place of honor she gained among the nations and acts as if she is God thinking she is unconquerable (v. 8, 9). In her arrogance, Babylon believes she can do as she likes and that no one can stop her (v. 10, 11). She thinks that her rise to power results from guidance received through her knowledge of magic and astrology. The prophet challenges her to keep trusting magic and astrology and see if that will save her from God's judgment (v. 12-13). What she will find is that the magicians and astrologers themselves will fall under God's judgment. They will be destroyed, as straw is burnt in a fire. No one will be able to save Babylon from the coming judgment (v. 14-15). And so, it will be for anyone who thinks they are bigger, more powerful than God.

## THE WORKING OF SATAN

The working of Satan—a deceiver, a liar, and a murderer; for such was the working of Satan with our first parents. He seduced Eve, not only by subtlety but by lying. He does not live by truth, for he is the father of lies and a murderer from the beginning, and such is the working of the antichrist. He approaches with cunning words to defeat his chosen enemies, such as Adam and Eve in the Garden, Judas at the table, and Jesus in the desert. But forget his disguise, for he instigates crushing blows on the church through deceptions, seductions, and persecutions of the saints.

In the last days, which seems to be every day, difficult times will come, for they are all around us in the obvious and not so obvious places. *For men will be lovers of themselves, lovers of money, boasters, proud, blasphemers, disobedient to parents, unthankful, unholy, unloving, unforgiving, slanderers, without self-control, brutal, despisers of good, traitors, headstrong, haughty, lovers of pleasure rather than lovers of God, having a form of godliness but denying its power. And from such people turn away* (2 Timothy 3:2-4).

In 2 Thessalonians 2:9, 10, Paul explicitly linked the mystery with the church's archnemesis, Satan. The coming of the lawless one is according to the working of Satan, with all power, signs, and lying wonders, and with all unrighteous deception among those who perish because they did not receive the love of the truth, that they might be saved. But this all changed at the cross of Christ, where Satan was defeated.

## THE MYSTERY OF GODLINESS

The great debate between Christ and Satan is the two mysteries, the mystery of iniquity which we covered and now the mystery of godliness. The mystery of godliness involves resistance and revelation.

The resistance—Being rooted and built up in Christ and established in the faith, *do not allow you to take you captive by philosophy and empty deceit, according to human tradition, according to the elemental spirits of the world, and not according to Christ* (Colossians 2:8).

The revelation—*When Christ, who is our life, is revealed, then you also will be revealed with Him in glory* (Colossians 3:4).

> *Great indeed, we confess great is the mystery of godliness:*
> *God was manifested in the flesh, justified in the Spirit, seen*
> *by angels, preached among the Gentiles, believed on in the*
> *world, received up in glory (1 Timothy 3:16).*

The mystery of godliness and the unraveling is an enigma to the uninitiated, something once unknown, which God's divine providence had carefully concealed. It is rather like an enormous jigsaw puzzle defying all attempts to complete it because vital pieces are missing, and there is no accessible and finalized picture from which to work.

However, that which was prophetically concealed in the Old Testament is revealed in all its richness in the New Testament to those who have ears to hear and eyes to see. This mystery is revealed in Paul's writings by the revelation of God's will to His saints.

In Colossians 1:26, *Even the mystery which hath been hid from ages and from generations, but now is made manifest to his saints.*

And in Ephesians 1:9-11, *Having made known unto us the mystery of his will, according to his good pleasure which he hath purposed in himself: that in the dispensation of the fullness of times he might gather together in one all things in Christ, both which are in heaven, and which are on earth; even in him: In whom also we have obtained an inheritance, being predestinated according to the purpose of him who worketh all things after the counsel of his own will.*

And this mystery of godliness, which was hidden since the foundation of the world, reaches its apex with Paul's words in Colossians 1:27, *To them God willed to make known what are the riches of the glory of this mystery among the Gentiles: which is Christ in you, the hope of glory.*

The mystery of godliness is the heart of the Christian faith. The poetic hymn that Paul records in 1 Timothy 3:16 contains a summation of Jesus' ministry. The godliness of the Father's Son is now to be reflected in us, for Christianity is not a system of rules and actions that must be performed to appease a deity but a life to be lived as Christ lived His life. At the heart of the mystery is God taking on human flesh to live among the people He created. As a Son, Jesus remained completely obedient to His Father in heaven and then offered Himself as a perfect sacrifice in our place. God then raised Him from the dead, thereby conquering death for all who trust in Him. Jesus took our place, so sinful humans may be declared righteous before God and be "born again." The new birth is spiritual and results in a change of heart that produces true godliness. A life transformed is the mystery of godliness and is comprehended only through the revelation of God in Christ. Beyond all question, the mystery from which true godliness springs is great.

## THE DREAD CHAMPIONS

*Having disarmed principalities and powers, He made a public spectacle of them, triumphing over them in it* (Colossians 2:15). The terms used in this verse are all military, and the idea is, that Christ has completely subdued our enemies by His death. A complete victory was achieved by His death so that everything is now in subjection to Him, and we have nothing to fear. Satan and his legions had invaded the earth, dragged its inhabitants into captivity, and subjected them to their evil reign. But Christ, by His death, overcomes the invaders and recaptures those they enslaved. A conqueror returning from a victory displays in a triumphal procession the kings and princes he has taken and the spoils of victory. We should not allow them to set up their dark empire over our souls again, for we are the dread champions.

God is raising prophetic voices that bring the word of the Lord without fear of others, and their souls are aflame with revelation from the throne of heaven. Who could care less about theological voices judging them like Pharisees on their homiletical perfection and exegetical exactitude?

They have not come to scratch the itching ears of Christian pop culture nor sit and listen to lectures by men who have a form of godliness but deny the power. The day of monopoly networks with no relationship with their members and cartel Christian watchdog groups is over. As I once heard Bob Jones say when I was only nineteen years old, "Boy, if you stay in the middle of the river, those dogs can bark all they want, but they will never be able to bite. Remain with the move of God! The move of God is HERE!"

This is the hour of awakening, an hour of outpouring, and the final harvest of souls. We have no time to take our hands off the sickle to hear from those that never helped to plant the seeds of the gospel in us. Where were you when I was born again? The voice of those crying in the wilderness is about to be heard on every street corner in this nation and around the world. The gospel of Jesus Christ will boil from their veins as they preach and demonstrate the power of the kingdom. It is the hour of the prophetic lions! Dare I say that some churches will never open again because they had puppets in the pulpits instead of holy fire baptized prophets. I have no fear of telling the truth because I owe nothing to the establishment or the culture.

I was born free from the religious system, and I am not alone. The standard is being raised for all to see; you have to be blind not to notice what is happening. An army arising in this hour will show the world the true church with power and courage.

*The floods have lifted up, O LORD, the floods have lifted up their voice; the floods lift up their waves* (Psalm 93:3). Yes, there has been a flood in so many ways in the earth: floods of violence, perversion of every kind, pedophilia, sex trafficking, political corruption, genocide, the desolation of war. A flood of every demonic hell-inspired darkness we can imagine has been released.

But the Bible declares that *the enemy has come in like a flood, but the Spirit of the Lord shall lift up a standard against him* (Isaiah 59:19). And Psalm 93:4-5 declares, *The LORD on high is mightier than the noise of many waters, yea, than the mighty waves of the sea. Thy testimonies are very sure: holiness becometh thine house, O LORD, forever.*

We are about to witness one of the greatest tsunami waves of God that the earth has ever seen come crashing upon the earth. In an hour of fearful politicians and voiceless preachers, the wave of revival is about to hit.

The fearless will catch the wave and ride it to the end! I tell you, as a prophet of God, the glamor show is about to be exposed and washed away by the divine *dunamis* power of God that will come crashing in. Everything that has been hidden will be revealed, and people will know the TRUTH. It is not a time of "business as usual" because those days are gone, as well. It is the hour of the dread champions!

## CHAPTER THREE

# WAR OF THE SEEDS,

## PART ONE

*And I will put enmity between you and the woman, and between your seed and her seed. He will crush your head, and you will strike his heel (Genesis 3:15, Berean Study Bible).*

Like a brilliant documentary, the Divine Director exposes the imprints on the biblical narrative of the two seeds at war, a drama between those loyal to Yahweh and then Satan with his minions. Robert Farrar Capon's book *Genesis: The Movie* describes Genesis as an "ecology of opposites": life and death, good and evil, Yahweh and Satan, the serpent and the woman, and the two seeds. The confining moment in the Genesis 3:15 Hebrew text unveils the Messianic weight of these watershed words spoken by Yahweh.

The war clash of the serpent with the woman becomes a stream of enmity amid the plural collective seed comprising all those who love God. Everything narrows into a fatal constriction, resulting in a conspicuous conflict between Satan, the singular serpent, and the Messiah. The woman's singular representative seed and many other seeds through history reflect their loyalty to Yahweh and His kingdom.

Before looking at the keywords in Genesis 3:15, we must look at one Greek word *hū*, meaning "he." There is much theological debate on who *he* is who will crush your head. Some consider Genesis 3:15 as referring not to an individual, particular "savior," but to the sum total of descendants born to both women.

Jeffrey Volkmer, assistant professor of Old Testament at Talbot School of Theology, helps us open the door to an important biblical view. The singularity of translation hints at a Messianic awareness of the one who crushes the head of Satan while others see a collective perspective. Many translations such as the New American Standard, Holman, and the New Living Translation reinforce the messianic reading of Genesis 3:15 by capitalizing the pronoun "He" to make an explicit connection between this verse and Christ the Messiah. But theologians like Mike McKnight prefer a collective sense of "seed" which would equate to something akin to the *Jewish Publication Society's* translation: *I will put enmity between you and the woman and between your offspring [or descendants] and hers [i.e., her "offspring"]; they will strike at your head, and you shall strike at their heal* (JPS, Tanach).[43]

So, does Genesis 3:15, which has long been considered the *protoevangelium* (the "first good news"), not contain a foreshadowing of the Messiah? Now, I can suspend a persuasive hint found in the Hebrew *zera*, which is singular, and we will address it fully. From a broad biblical perspective, we find out that from the "seed" of Seth comes the true "seed" of Genesis 3:15, namely, Jesus, as indicated in the ancestry line in Luke 3:38: the son of Enosh, the son of Seth, the son of Adam, the son of God.

The five keywords in Genesis 3:15 are enmity, seed, crush (bruise), head, and heel. The Hebrew *ebah* means hostility, hatred, and enmity.[44] *Ephraim was a watchman with my God: as for the prophet, a fowler's snare is in all his ways, and enmity (ebah) in the house of his God* (Hosea 9:8).

The Hebrew *zera* means seed, descendants, family, offspring, posterity.[45] *I will establish your seed (zera) forever and build up your throne to all generations* (Psalm 89:4).

The Hebrew word *shûph* means to bruise, crush, strike a blow, which is the same word for head and heel.[46] *For He crushes (shûph) me with a tempest, and multiplies my wounds without cause* (Job 9:17).

The Hebrew word *rōš* means head, leading ones, chief one.[47] *But God will wound the head (rōš) of His enemies, The hairy scalp of the one who still goes on in his trespasses* (Psalm 68:21).

And the Hebrew word *aqeb* means heel, posterior part, rear guard, leave a mark.[48] *Afterward his brother came out, and his hand took hold of Esau's heel (aqeb); so, his name was called Jacob* (Genesis 25:26).

After the tragedy in Genesis 3, a world emerged when evil and sinful behavior appeared to dominate. The world was incurably sick, and the presence of evil provoked appalling results for the human race. Genesis 3 explains how paradise was lost with the consequences of disobedience and God's reaction to the transgression against His command. Genesis 3:15 establishes a cosmic explanation for the world's disorder, Satan, at his diabolical work.

There is no mention of Satan in Genesis 3, only a serpent, either a disguise or a symbol of Satan. Adam and Eve are responsible for their actions and punished accordingly, but their behaviors are inextricably entwined with the serpent's venomous pretense.

God's first act of judgment is also His first promise of salvation through judgment. Enmity is placed between the man and the woman and between the seed of Satan and the seed of the woman. Obviously, judgment falls on the serpent as his head is crushed, but there is also judgment on the seed of the woman as the serpent bruises his heel, but the bearing of the saving seed will be painful. Judgment falls on the man also, as the ground from whose fruit the seed will be for sustenance is cursed, and in painful, sweaty toil, he will labor until he eventually returns to the dust.

You must understand that when Adam and Eve fell into sin, not only were they affected, but all of creation fell, tumbling through a hole of purity, of perfection, into the dark abyss of sin's infection, impacting future worlds. At that moment in human history, the earth collapsed into disarray, but the scriptures are filled with the prophetic promise of transformation, initiating a radical change of the heart.

In the short span of Genesis 3:14–19, God is revealed to be both just and merciful. In the biblical story, God is on display as one who upholds righteousness but offers hope to guilty human rebels. He is the God of justice, rendering a just condemnation for the transgressors. Yet He is also a God of mercy, and so He makes plain that His image-bearers will triumph over the wicked snake.

## THE COLLECTIVE-SINGULAR SEED

The Hebrew *zera* (seed) never occurs in the plural in the Old Testament.[49] But, the singular term can be used "collectively," that is, the singular form is used for both an individual seed or a group of seeds.[50] In the case of humans, it can refer to a single descendant or multiple descendants, as we will illustrate.

Jack Collins, who has advanced studies in biblical languages, has demonstrated through analysis that "when zera (seed) denotes a specific descendant, it appears with singular verb inflections, adjectives, and pronouns."[51] It leads him to conclude that "the singular pronoun hû' (he) in Genesis 3:15 is quite consistent with the pattern where a singular individual is in view."[52]

Building on the collective-singular seed, these potent verses emphasize and confirm Collins' perspective.

> *I will bless you and multiplying I will multiply your descendants (zera) as the stars of the heaven and as the sand which is on the seashore, and your descendants (zera) shall possess the gate of their enemies. In your seed (zera), all the nations of the earth shall be blessed because you have obeyed My voice (Genesis 22:17).*

> *And they blessed Rebekah and said to her: "Our sister, may you become the mother of thousands of ten thousands; And may your descendants possess the gate of those who hate them" (Genesis 24:8).*

The Isaiah text moves from a single to a collective seed, between the individual "seed" and the collective "holy seed." *Yet there will still be a tenth portion in it, and it will again be subject to burning, like a terebinth or an oak Whose stump remains when it is cut down. The holy seed is its stump* (Isaiah 6:13, NASB). According to Isaiah, not all Israel, but the elect remnant alone, is destined for salvation.

God shows unchangeable severity towards sin but covenant faithfulness in preserving a remnant. Isaiah leaves the prophetic legacy to the second half of Isaiah's book, which Paul also alludes to in Romans chapter eleven. *Even so then, at this present time there is a remnant according to the election of grace; And so, all Israel will be saved, as it is written: "The Deliverer will come out of Zion, And He will turn away ungodliness from Jacob"* (Romans 11:6, 26).

As Dempster states, "An oscillation between a group and an individual within the group as its representative is certainly common in the Tanakh."[53] The possibility of an individual or a collective whole being is viewed in how Paul interprets Old Testament texts on the seed. For instance, Paul emphasizes the singularity of the seed: *It does not say, "and to seeds," as to many, but as to one, "and to your seed," which is Messiah* (Galatians 3:16).

But on another occasion, Paul can take the seed text of Genesis 3:15 and apply it collectively to the followers of Christ: "*Now the God of peace will soon crush Satan under your (collective) feet*" (Romans 16:20, emphasis added).[54]

## WAR OF THE SEEDS

Almost immediately after the judgment, God announces there is enmity between the woman's seed and the seed of the serpent. Genesis chapter four narrates the one son who pleased God, Abel, who was slain by one who did not please God. God then judged Cain that He rejected. *Then Cain said to the Lord, "My punishment is greater than I can bear"* (Genesis 4:13). The escalation of hostility is seen in Cain's descendants, *If Cain shall be avenged sevenfold, Then Lamech seventy-sevenfold* (Genesis 4:24), pointing to future generations as representing those whose actions mirror the one who "was a murderer from the beginning." *You are of your father the devil, and the desires of your father you want to do. He was a murderer from the beginning and does not stand in the truth* (John 8:44). It becomes evident through history, even in our times, for those who reject God and live sinful lives.

The sense is not that Cain's line has been physically spawned by Satan, but rather, the Bible describes people figuratively as children of those whose character they emulate.[55] *By this, the children of God are distinguished from the children of Satan: No one who does not do righteousness, neither loves his brother, is from God* (1 John 3:10, Aramaic Bible).

The conflict between Isaac and Ishmael is imagined as enmity between the respective seed—one the seed of the promise and the other a seed of the flesh. And from the two seeds, two nations emerge, and they will be at war forever.

Referring to the "holy seed," the statement that "Sarah received the ability to conceive" should read, "Sarah received power for the birth and foundation of the holy seed," which carries more sway.

> *But God said to Abraham, "Do not be distressed because of the boy and your slave woman; whatever Sarah tells you, listen to her, for through Isaac your descendants (zera seed) shall be named. And of the son of the slave woman, I will make a nation also because he is your descendant (zera)" (Genesis 21:12, 13).*

> *For it is written that Abraham had two sons: the one by a bondwoman, the other by a freewoman. But he who was of the bondwoman was born according to the flesh, and he of the freewoman through promise (Galatians 4:22, 23).*

Egypt's attempt to destroy the male children of Israel also continues this battle between the unbroken lines of descendants. *"When you do the duties of a midwife for the Hebrew women, and see them on the birth stools, if it is a son, then you shall kill him; but if it is a daughter, then she shall live."* So, Pharaoh commanded all his people, saying, *"Every son who is born you shall cast into the river, and every daughter you shall save alive."* (Exodus 1:16, 22 ).

The collective singularity of Israel and their place as the chosen seed can be seen in Exodus 4:23 and the judgment if Pharoah rejects God's word: *And I say to you, send my son that he may serve me, but if you refuse to send him, behold, I am about to kill your son, your firstborn.*

The conflict between the seeds continues throughout the Old Testament and eventually arises as a singular point in the book of Esther. Haman, as an Agagite, was a genocidal enemy of God's people, obsessed with murdering the Hebrews and hanging Mordecai. Dempster writes, "Esther's opposition to Haman continues the major theme running through the narrative, that of the woman against the beast: Eve versus the serpent."[56]

In the oracle of Balaam, he refers to Jacob, being Israel, and their enemy Agag and says, *How lovely are your tents, O Jacob, Your dwellings, O Israel! Like valleys that stretch out, like gardens by the riverside, like aloes planted by the Lord, Like cedars beside the waters. He shall pour water from his buckets, and his seed shall be in many waters. His king shall be higher than Agag, and his kingdom shall be exalted* (Numbers 24:5-7). And now you must understand the issue of Saul's failure to kill Agag (1 Samuel 15).

Once again, the collective seed of Israel is at enmity with another seed of Satan, the Canaanites. Interestingly, the text contends that Israel was defeated under Jabin, king of Canaan, because Israel did what was evil in the sight of Yahweh (Judges 4:1–2). But as usual, after a time of great oppression, the children of Israel cried out to the Lord. Then Deborah, the prophet judge in Israel, told Barak to take ten thousand soldiers and bring them down to the house of Sisera. But Barak only agreed if Deborah, a woman seed, would go with him, and she approved. By the end of the battle, not one soldier was left alive except Sisera.

But God gave the final victory to a Canaanite woman. Jael's "crushing the head" of Sisera is told in Judges 4 and then celebrated in song in Judges five: *Then Jael, Heber's wife, took a tent peg and took a hammer in her hand, and went softly to him and drove the peg into his temple, and it went down into the ground; for he was fast asleep and weary. So, he died.* The seed of the converted woman crushed the head of the Canaanite supreme warrior.

The Jewish midrash praises Jael, wife of Heber the Kenite, and includes many influential women and some who converted: Sarah; Zipporah, wife of Moses; Shiphrah and Puah, Hebrew midwives in Egypt; the daughter of the Pharoah who raised Moses; Rahab, the Canaanite woman who assisted the Israeli spies; and Ruth, the Moabite wife of Boaz; Rebecca and Leah; Esther; and Hannah, mother of the prophet Samuel.[57]

## THE PROPHETS AND GENESIS 3:15 LANGUAGE

Throughout the writings of the prophets, there are definite inferences attached to Genesis 3:15 and the prophetic language as crushing the head of the wicked and elements of hostility, judgment, Messiah, and restoration.

Jeremiah 23 weaves together a tapestry that strikingly shows the threads of the promise of a Davidic ruler with implications of a Messianic restoration of the people and their land. *"Behold, the days are coming," says the LORD, "That I will raise to David a Branch of righteousness; A King shall reign and prosper and execute judgment and righteousness in the earth. 'As the LORD lives, who brought up and led the descendants of the household of Israel back from the north land and from all the countries where I had driven them.' Then they will live on their own land"* (Jeremiah 23: 5, 8 ).

The divine justice established in the council of the Lord required a visitation upon the head of the wicked. *But who has stood in the council of the LORD, that he should see and hear His word? Who has paid attention to His word and listened? Behold, a whirlwind of the LORD has gone forth in fury—A violent whirlwind! It will fall violently on the head of the wicked* (Jeremiah 23:18, 19). The Hebrew word *chuwl* translated "dance."[58]

Thus, the raging whirlwind on the head of the wicked is depicted as being driven by dancing feet, alluding to the crushed heel of Genesis 3:15. That being the case, the justice being visited on the head of the wicked is rendered by the heel of the storm of Yahweh!

This interpretation strengthens with the numerous allusions to Genesis 3:15 peppered through the Old Testament, which they seem to be. For this reason, these Davidic and head-crushing themes are supported by Jeremiah's words reflecting the restoration prophecies in Jeremiah 30.

In the book of Jeremiah, a combination exists between a judgment of the wicked and restoration of God's family. Jeremiah 30:3 is the first verse to illustrate God restoring His people: *For, behold, the days come, saith the Lord, when I will bring back the captivity of my people Israel and Judah said the Lord: and I will bring them back to the land which I gave to their fathers, and they shall be lords of it* (Brenton Septuagint Translation). The dance on the head of the wicked now becomes the dancing seeds of those restored.

For God's people to become what He intended, the enemy must be overcome, and the yoke must be broken for slavery to be removed forever. *"It shall come about on that day," declares the LORD of hosts, "that I will break his yoke from off their neck and will tear off their bonds; and strangers will no longer make them their slaves"* (Jeremiah 30:8, NASB).

The New Testament language fits this Old Testament narrative of deliverance from the enemy, broken yokes, and freedom from slavery.

> *To grant us that we, being rescued from the hand of our enemies, might serve Him without fear (Luke 1:74).*

> *It was for freedom that Christ set us free; therefore, keep standing firm and do not be subject again to a yoke of slavery (Galatians 5:1).*

> *Knowing this, that our old man was crucified with Him, that the body of sin might be done away with, that we should no longer be slaves of sin (Romans 6:6).*

> *Then Israel will no longer serve strangers, foreign rulers who are heathens, but their God Yahveh, and David, the king who will be raised up to them. And they have served their God YHWH, And David, their king whom I raise up to them* (Jeremiah 30:9, LSV).

No king of David's seed has held the scepter since the captivity, for Zerubbabel, though of David's line, never claimed the title of "king." The Son of David, Messiah, as the Targum paraphrases it, "and they shall hearken to, or obey, Messiah the son of David their king,"[59] and as Paul believes, *Now when all things are made subject to Him, then the Son Himself will also be subject to Him who put all things under Him, that God may be all in all* (1 Corinthians 15:28).

These prophetic lines in Jeremiah promise a righteous king who triumphs as the future Davidic ruler. "*Their leader will be one of their own, and their ruler will arise from their midst. And I will bring him near, and he will approach Me, for who would dare on his own to approach Me?*" declares the LORD. "*And you shall be my people, and I will be your God*" (Jeremiah 30:21, 22, Berean Study Bible).

Once again, Yahweh's justice visited upon the head of the wicked is settled by the heel of the storm of Yahweh, whose imagery is reminiscent of Genesis 3:15. Behold the storm of Yahweh—rage goes forth, a tempest excites itself upon the head (rōš) of the wicked ones it shall dance. *Behold, the storm of the LORD has gone out with fury, a whirlwind swirling down upon the heads of the wicked* (Jeremiah 30:23, Berean Study Bible).

Now we find interwoven promises of a Davidic ruler (Jeremiah 30:9, 21) and justice visited upon the head of the wicked (Jeremiah 30:23). Manifestations of His grace always accompany vengeance upon God's adversaries to His people.

Another image of head-crushing is found in Habakkuk 3:13. In a description of the coming of Yahweh in wrath and mercy (Habakkuk 3:2), Yahweh threshes the nations in anger (Habakkuk 3:12). Habakkuk then moves from just wrath to merciful salvation in 3:13, as Yahweh is addressed with the words, *You went forth for the salvation of Your people, to save Your anointed* (mashiach, anointed or Messiah[60]). *You crushed the head of the house of the wicked, laying him bare from head (ros) to toe* (Berean Study Bible).

"From head to toe"—a reference is made to the enemy in the form of a dragon. The serpentine enemy in Habakkuk 3:13 is heightened by the allusion to the description of the snake in Genesis 3:1. The snake is described as "crafty" with the term *'ārûm* in Genesis 3:1. In Habakkuk 3:13, the word *'ārāh* ("lay bare," "make naked") [61]is used to describe the "laying bare" of this creature as in Genesis 2:25, where the man and woman are both "bare," naked, and the Hebrew is *'ārôm* is the same in Habakkuk. It is uncanny for this duplication of the Genesis language to be continuously replicated throughout the scriptures, as you will continue to see.

## THE PSALMS AND GENESIS 3:15 LANGUAGE

The conflict between the seed of the woman and the seed of the serpent emerges again in Psalm 2:1–3: *Why do the nations rage, And the people plot a vain thing? The kings of the earth set themselves, And the rulers take counsel together, Against the Lord and against His Anointed, saying, "Let us break Their bonds in pieces and cast away Their cords from us."*

Yahweh responds to the plotting of the nations with His decree to establish His king on Zion (Psalm 2:4–6): *He who sits in the heavens shall laugh; The Lord shall hold them in derision. Then He shall speak to them in His wrath, and distress them in His deep displeasure: "Yet I have set My King on My holy hill of Zion."*

In 2 Samuel 7:14, concerning King David, the prophet Nathan proclaims, *"God will build a house for my name, and I will establish the throne of his kingdom forever. I will be his father, and he shall be my son."* But Nathan's words are prophetically fulfilled in the Messiah by David's own words: *I will declare the decree: The Lord has said to Me, "You are My Son, Today I have begotten You"* (Psalm 2:7).

Further, the son of Yahweh will break his enemies with an iron rod and dash them to pieces like pottery (Psalm 2:3, 9 ): *Ask of Me, and I will give You The nations for Your inheritance, And the ends of the earth for Your possession. You shall break them with a rod of iron; You shall dash them to pieces like a potter's vessel.* Being on the mark, Psalm 2 connects the smashing of Genesis 3:15 to the Sonship of 2 Samuel 7.

Psalm 68 sings the triumph of God over His enemies for the benefit of His people. In verses 20–22, judgment and salvation are joined together, reflecting back to Genesis 3:15. *Our God is the God of salvation, and to the Lord belong the issues from death. But God will crush (māhas) the head (rō'š) of his enemies, the hairy crown of the one who walks in his guilt* (Psalm 68:20-22).

With David's prophetic poetry, the psalmist writes words of crushing enemies and a seed that will be His throne; again, more imagery from Genesis 3:15.

*I have found My servant David; With My holy oil I have anointed him, the enemy shall have no advantage over him: nor the son of iniquity have power to hurt him. "But I will <u>crush</u> his adversaries before him, and strike those who hate him; His <u>seed</u> also I will make to endure forever, And his throne as the days of heaven"* (Psalm 89: 20, 23, 24, 29 , emphasis added).

As noted in the writings of the prophets and Psalms, the damage is done to the head of the serpent and bruising the heel of the woman's seed from the stomping of the serpent. The woman's seed tramples on the head of the serpent, crushing the serpent's head and incurring damage to their own heel at times. The reality listed in these verses are signs of the application of Genesis 3:15, indicating a war between God's people and the Satanic forces of evil seeking to abort God's purposes. But God has the final word with the enemies of God's people being "trodden down" or "placed underfoot."

## GENESIS 3:15 IN THE NEW TESTAMENT

There are allusions to Genesis 3:15 in the New Testament. For instance, in Luke 10:18–19, Jesus told His disciples, *"I was beholding Satan falling as lightning from heaven. Behold, I have given to you the authority to tread upon snakes and scorpions, and upon all the power of the one who is at enmity."* Jesus portrayed the glorious victory of His disciples by treading upon snakes and overcoming the enemy. And in Romans 16:20, Paul tells the Romans that God will soon crush Satan under their feet.

In Romans 8:20, Paul wrote that the creation (*ktisis*) was subjected to futility. Most scholars think the subjection to futility is the curse of Genesis[62], and the corresponding hope would appear to be the promise of one who would defeat the serpent in Genesis 3:15.[63]

## THE SEED OF THE WOMAN AND THE DRAGON

There are scenes in Revelation 12 influenced by Genesis 3:15, a war between the woman and the dragon. *And the great dragon was thrown out, the ancient serpent, who is called the devil and Satan, deceiving the whole inhabited world. He was thrown down to the earth, and his angels were thrown down with him* (Revelation 12:9, Berean Literal Bible).

John, the seer prophet, describes a conflict between two opposing figures, the heavenly woman and the dragon. In verse nine, John identifies the dragon, and the Greek *Drakon* means one who stares like a dragon or serpent.[64]

But there are three other names attached to the dragon: 'the ancient serpent,' the Greek *archaios Ophis* means the serpent, primal, ancient, and from the beginning; Satan, the Greek *Satanas* means the adversary who opposes another in purpose or act[65]; Deceiver, the Greek *planos* means imposter, wanderer, roving who is misleading and leading into error[66] the whole world, the Greek *oikoumene* means the world, universe, and the whole inhabited earth.[67]

A dragon appears as a woman gives birth to her seed, hoping to devour the child, and clearly, there is enmity between the seed of the woman and the snake.

The woman clothed with the sun, the moon under her feet, and a crown on her head makes one notice the reference to feet and head in Revelation 12:1: *Now a great sign appeared in heaven: a woman clothed with the sun, with the moon under her feet, and on her head a garland of twelve stars.* And she is pregnant with a child and in great pain giving birth, swimming in more Genesis language (v. 2).

And now the enemy of the seed is portrayed as *a dragon, fiery red dragon having seven heads and ten horns, and seven diadems on his heads*

(v. 3). The war of the seeds is rendered as a battle between the woman and the serpent, and the church and Satan.

James Hamilton, a professor of Biblical Studies at Harvard School of Theology, creates a formidable ending to the story. There is enmity between the seed of the woman and the snake. She gives birth to a man child, identified as a descendant of David as referenced in Psalm 2, and child and mother are supernaturally protected from the dragon (v. 5–6): *He shall speak to them in His wrath, And distress them in His deep displeasure: "Yet I have set My King On My holy hill of Zion."*

After a battle in heaven, the dragon is thrown down to earth, and he again pursues the woman and her seed (12:13): *And when the dragon saw that he was cast down to the earth, he persecuted the woman that brought forth the man child.*

The woman and the man child similarly benefit from divine protection (12:14–16): *But the earth helped the woman, and the earth opened its mouth and swallowed up the flood which the dragon had spewed out of his mouth.*

So the dragon leaves pursuit of the singular seed that he might make war on the rest of the collective seed of the woman—those who obey God and hold to the testimony of Jesus (12:17): *And the dragon was enraged with the woman, and he went to make war with the rest of her offspring, who keep the commandments of God and have the testimony of Jesus Christ.*

In Revelation 13:3, we read of a beast with a head that has a mortal wound, and as Beale comments, "Such a wound on the head of the grand nemesis of God's people reflects Genesis 3:15, especially when seen together with Revelation 12:17."[68]

## ODES OF SOLOMON

The "Odes of Solomon" is the earliest known Christian book of verses used as hymns of worship. It dates from before 100 A.D. The authors were perhaps Jewish-Christians, and the originals were in Aramaic. These odes are connected to John's theological writings and associated with the Dead Sea Scrolls. But most likely came from the same community as John but influenced more by the Essenes than John.[69]

Odes of Solomon is one of the earliest interpretations of Revelation 12 and alludes to Genesis 3:15 with Ode 22:5: "He who overthrew by my hands the dragon with seven heads and placed me at his roots that I might destroy his seed."

God was committed to resolving the relational alienation that had set in because humanity had corrupted itself. There is no mention of God satisfying His retributive justice except by "Your right hand destroys his evil venom, and Your hand leveled the Way for those who believe in You" (Ode 22:7).

And God desired to employ His love through Christ to undo the corruption. "Incorruptible was Your way and Your face; You have brought Your world to corruption, that everything might be resolved and renewed" (Ode 22:11). God needed to reassert His relational character of ownership and authority to save the corrupted seeds.

"He who gathers what is in the Middle and throws them to me" (Ode 22:2), to lift humanity out of the depths of sin into the arms of the Beloved.

"He who scattered my enemies, and my adversaries" (Ode 22:3), to eliminate the enemies of the seed. "He who gave me authority over bonds, so that I might unbind them" (Ode 22:4). They were again referencing the woman and the dragon in Revelation 11.

The raising of Christ to God's right hand was followed by placing all things under His feet and making Him, *de facto*, sovereign over all things. These texts powerfully but succinctly describe the enemies of the seed of the woman and "all things" being placed under His feet.

> The LORD said to my Lord, "Sit at My right hand, _Till I make Your enemies Your footstool_" (Matthew 22:44, emphasis added).

> Until _I make your enemies a footstool_ for your feet (Acts 2:35, emphasis added).

> For He must reign till He has _put all enemies under His feet_ (1 Corinthians 15:25, emphasis added).

*He raised Him from the dead and seated Him at His right hand in the heavenly places, far above all principality and power and might and dominion, and every name that is named, not only in this age but also in that which is to come. And <u>He put all things under His feet</u> and gave Him to be <u>head over all things</u> to the church (Ephesians 1:20–22, emphasis added).*

*You have made him a little lower than the angels; You have crowned him with glory and honor and set him over the works of Your hands. You have put all things in subjection under his feet (Hebrews 2:7, 8).*

*Inasmuch then as the children have partaken of flesh and blood, He Himself likewise shared in the same, that <u>through death He might destroy him who had the power of death, that is, the devil,</u> and release those who through fear of death were all their lifetime subject to bondage (Hebrews 2:14, 15, emphasis added).*

*From henceforth expecting till <u>his enemies be made his footstool</u> (Hebrews 10:13, emphasis added).*

## MESSIAH REVERSES THE CURSE

If the books of the Bible were written by and for a remnant of people hoping for this person's coming, we would expect to find various echoes of this promise of God in these texts. But we do find imagery from Genesis 3:15 in biblical texts across both testaments. We have seen the seed of the woman crushing the head(s) of the seed of the serpent, shattered and trampled enemies, dust-eating, defeated enemies, and smashed serpents.

Now Christ's redemption brings a reversal and remedy for the whole disaster of the fall. Above all, Christ brings a remedy for sin, as Romans 3:21-26 and the rest of Romans 8 indicate. But His triumph

ALTARS · 55 ·

will also liberate the larger creation from "futility," that is, the effects of the curse. The creation was originally good, and the futility was imposed only later, at the time of the fall. Hence, there is a genuine basis for believing that God will extirpate futility without destroying the good creation. And that is what Romans 8:21 promises: *the creation itself will be set free from its bondage to decay and obtain the freedom of the glory of the children of God.*

Mark Jones, a teacher at Reformation 21, reflects on the incomprehensible incarnate Christ. It is the "highest pitch of God's wisdom, goodness, power, and glory" (James Ussher). Or, as Goodwin beautifully puts it, "Heaven and earth met and kissed one another, namely, God and man" (Works 2.82). The incarnation should leave us in awe. It is completely incomprehensible.

Even before the catastrophic fall, God eternally decided that the Son should assume a human nature, consisting of a body and soul. As the eternal Son, who has no beginning and no end, He has always known that He would become the incarnate one (i.e., "the enfleshed one").[70]

God sent forth His Son, made of a woman. The descent of the Son in His incarnation into human nature results in the healing of the human spirit as all things in Christ has "resolved and renewed" all things. He healed the fundamental poisoning of human beings by undoing the dragon's venom. By doing this, he freed humanity from its bonds and the enemy's authority, providing the atonement necessary for the healing of the nations.

God prepared a sinless body and fitted Christ with power, wisdom, and the gifts and graces to perform the work of a mediator. After all, the Son needed a body to offer His body. He needed a body so that His resurrection body might be the prototype of our resurrection bodies. God forever identifies with humanity because of the incarnation. Thus, heaven will one day be a "fleshly" place in the New Heavens and New Earth. Not at all "sinful," but certainly a home where we will be truly human because we will be perfectly conformed, in body and soul, to the man, Christ Jesus. *For our citizenship is in heaven, from which we also eagerly wait for the Savior, the Lord Jesus Christ, who will transform our lowly body that it may be conformed to His glorious body, according to the working by which He is able even to subdue all things to Himself* (Philippians 3:20, 21).

> *So, when this corruptible has put on incorruption, and this mortal has put on immortality, then shall be brought to pass the saying that is written: "Death is swallowed up in victory"* (1 Corinthians 15:54).

## CHAPTER FOUR

# WAR OF THE SEEDS,

## PART TWO

Genesis 3:15 is the first glimmer of the gospel, which has a redemptive promise included in the curse. Underneath the dark clouds of deception and rebellion where paradise gained became paradise lost, a light shined through that darkness called *protoevangelium*, the first annunciation of good news. The word is derived from the Greek prefix *proto,* meaning first and *evangelion*, meaning gospel or good news.

The perspective of Genesis 3:15 resolves how you paint the picture of the concluding scriptures, for it is the seed plot of the Bible. The promise of Genesis 3:15 is a seed—a small promise that will eventually grow into the full-blown tree of God's good news, the storyline of scripture. Mark opens his book with these first words: *The beginning of the gospel (euaggelion) of Jesus Christ, the Son of God* (Mark 1:1).

The Hebrew *bâśar* is similar to the Greek *euaggelion* and means to announce or preach the good news.[71] In Isaiah 61:1, the prophet announced the Spirit of the Lord coming upon him with this good news: *The Spirit of the Lord GOD is upon me, Because the LORD has anointed me To preach good news (bâśar) to the afflicted; He has sent me to bind up the brokenhearted, To proclaim liberty to captives And freedom to prisoners.*

*And I will put enmity (open hostility) between you and the woman,*

*And between your seed (offspring) and her Seed; He shall [fatally] bruise your head, And you shall [only] bruise His heel* (Genesis 3:15, AMP). Although interpretations of this verse vary based upon the use of the Hebrew words, most agree that the "enmity" is between "thy seed" (Satan and his followers) and "her seed" (Messiah, who was a descendant of Eve). The concept of Genesis 3:15 being the protoevangelium or "First Gospel" is attributed to St. Irenaeus from his work *Against Heresies*.[72]

"For this end did He put enmity between the serpent and the woman and her seed, they keeping it up mutually: He, the sole of whose foot should be bitten, having power also to tread upon the enemy's head; but the other biting, killing, and impeding the steps of man until the seed did come appointed to trample down his head, which was born of Mary, of whom the prophet speaks: *You shall tread upon the lion and the cobra, The young lion and the serpent you shall trample underfoot* (Psalm 91:13).[73] The Hebrew *darak* means to tread or trample on[74] and the Hebrew *pethen* means venomous snake, adder, cobra.[75] And the Hebrew *tannin* means serpent or dragon.[76]

## IN THE BEGINNING

In the beginning, God created the heavens and the earth—heaven and earth not existing from all eternity but had a beginning. It did not appear by some unexplainable discharge from an indefinable matter but was created by Elohim, an original supreme act by which the universe was called into being. The portrait of God creating a universe within which history evolves according to His purpose and plan is seen in Isaiah 40:21: *Do you not know? Have you not heard? Has it not been declared to you from the beginning? Have you not understood from the foundations of the earth?*

The prophet calls on Israel to consider and honor the Lord, *Who has performed and accomplished it, Calling forth the generations from the beginning? I, the LORD, am the first and with the last. I am He* (Isaiah 41:4, NASB).

The hand of God made the history we now read. *That they may see and know, And consider and understand together, That the hand of the LORD has done this, And the Holy One of Israel has created it* (Isaiah 41:20). At the beginning of the world, Yahweh set in motion a sequence of events that inevitably moved toward His intended end. In the beginning, God established principles He initiated, which remained. *Who has saved us and called us with a holy calling, not according to our works, but according to His own purpose and grace which was granted us in Christ Jesus from all eternity* (2 Timothy 1:9). *In the hope of eternal life, which God, who cannot lie, promised before time eternal* (Titus 1:2, Berean Literal Bible).

## THE INTRODUCTION OF SIN

In the first two chapters of Genesis, two different Hebrew names for God are used: Elohim and Yahweh Elohim. In Genesis 1:1, it reads, *In the beginning, Elohim created the heavens and the earth.* But starting in Genesis 2:4, it is Yahweh Elohim. *These [are] the generations of the heavens and of the earth in their being created, in the day of YHWH God's making the earth and the heavens* (Literal Standard Version).

Hiam Shore, Professor Emeritus at Ben-Gurion University, describes the two names for God, *Elohim,* and *Jehovah* (Yahweh), therefore addressing two separate and logically unrelated concepts of God's visible and seemingly visible presence in His world: By the **law of nature**, revealed in the Hebrew *Elohim* (God) and by **justice combined with grace and loving-kindness**, displayed in the Hebrew *Jehovah* (Yahweh God). The two names relate to two facets of God's presence in the world as the **creator**, who had imprinted the law of nature on the universe and has dominion over all forces of nature, and as a **gracious judge**, source of absolute morality and justice mitigated by love and grace.[77]

By contrast, the serpent and Eve refer only to *Elohim,* the owner of all forces of nature, as they understand the implications; neither appears to be looking for a gracious judge. Only a Jewish teacher could address this issue. By Jewish tradition, God does not punish but only heals and corrects moral distortion of character. It is explicitly conveyed to King David when God addresses his offspring Solomon: "*I will raise up your offspring to succeed you...He is the one who will build a house for my Name...I will be his father, and he shall be my son. When he commits iniquity, I will chase him with the rod of men, and with such plagues as befall the sons of Adam*" (2 Samuel 7:12-14). The correct (literal) translation is: "When he distorts (âvâh[78]) his ways, I will rebuke him with the rod of men." No punishment, just needed correction in the distortions of character. Job makes the point even more bluntly: *I have sinned and perverted that which was straight, and it profited me not* (Job 33:27).

The sin of Adam and Eve was recognizing God as *Elohim* only, aspiring to be *Elohim* by tasting the Tree of Knowledge, consequently leading to discovering the law of nature and domination over nature. The cure was an agonizing battle burdened, and atrocity-weighted human history, only remedied through Christ.

The world as we know it and its human personality is twisted and warped. The material universe clearly witnesses God's existence and power, but His goodness is not as easily seen in a broken world.

Genesis 3:15 is a promise, a message of hope for humanity. God created this world and retained dominion over it, for He will not allow the force of evil to prevail ultimately but will deliver humankind from its grip. God punished our first parents for their disobedience but preserved the divine blessing of future generations as a sign of His mercy. The expulsion of Adam and Eve from the Garden of Eden is alleviated by the hope of an offspring of the woman.

The "cunning" Tempter deflects the woman's attention from the covenantal relationship God had established. In the central scene, the fall reaches its climax. The fatal sequence unfolds rapidly: Eve "saw," "took," "ate," and "gave" (Genesis 3:6), and the series culminates in "he ate." But the forbidden fruit does not deliver what the Tempter promises and instead brings new dark realities, as the covenant Lord had warned.

But the impact of sin created the notion that humanity may have rule over another, and Genesis 4:24 illustrated the chaos in society when each one acted without any restraint. Anarchy led to a civilization in which man's nature was given free expression, and every inclination of the thoughts of man's heart was only evil all the time (6:5). The institution of human government provides but has no guarantee of righteousness.

Adam later explained that he heard God in the garden and was afraid because he was naked. A basic cause of this emotion is awareness of vulnerability because of sin. The behavioral impact of fear leads them down a darkened path as John describes flight away from the light. *And this is the condemnation, that the light has come into the world, and men loved darkness rather than light, because their deeds were evil. For everyone practicing evil hates the light and does not come to the light, lest his deeds should be exposed* (John 3:19, 20).

Men love darkness instead of light because of their sin—fear of being exposed. Often, the human reaction to God's actions and His word is to reject God's word and flee. Sin has wrapped and twisted our perceptions, blinding them from seeing God's love. Instead, a sense of guilt creates a fear of exposure and leads them to flee impulsively from the only source of healing. Thus begins the sinful insurgence in Genesis 6: violence, rebellion, and judgment.

## JUDGMENT

Judgment is initiated in two ways: violation of the divine law of sowing and reaping or God's direct act of judgment. Those laws cannot work any other way than they do. The Bible certainly teaches the concept of sowing and reaping (Galatians 6:7). God will take vengeance on evildoers someday, as noted in Matthew 3:7: *But when he saw many of the Pharisees and Sadducees coming to his baptism, he said to them, "You brood of vipers! Who warned you to flee from the wrath to come?* So, there will be retribution but often delayed for the final judgment. God has a continued and inward aversion to sin and wickedness, being the terrible thing His righteous soul hates. He is not a detached observer. God hates their diabolical work because God cares and sees the events in our world where evil prevails. *And the wicked and the lover of violence, His soul has hated* (Psalm 11:5).

One day, God will judge the world in righteousness and perfect justice. Retribution is coming as seen in Revelation 22:12: *Behold I am coming soon, bringing my recompense with me, to repay each one for what he has done.* Until that day, we are careful not to assume God's blessing or judgment on individuals based on their external circumstances. We trust the Judge of the world always to do what's right. *Far be it from You to do such a thing—to kill the righteous with the wicked, so that the righteous and the wicked are treated alike. Far be it from You! Will not the Judge of all the earth do what is right?* (Genesis 18:25, Berean Study Bible). When the morally wrong break forth, those tender shoots of a corrupted seed will systematically and habitually become workers of iniquity. The blooming sons of iniquity must be destroyed forever. *When the wicked spring up like grass, And when all the workers of iniquity flourish, It is that they may be destroyed forever* (Psalm 92:7).

> *For behold, Your enemies, O LORD, For behold, Your enemies shall perish; All the workers of iniquity shall be scattered (Deuteronomy 28:64).*

But judgment is often echoed with the sounds of scattering people rather than destroying the enemy. *The wise King scatters evil ones and turns a wheel over them* (Proverbs 20:26, Aramaic Bible in Plain English). Sounds of scattering—crushing confederacies and forcing them to flee from the King's presence and the society of the righteous. Turns a wheel over them—the wheel of misfortune has run over them and endured severe punishment, even to death.

> *So the LORD <u>scattered</u> them abroad from there over the face of all the earth, and they ceased building the city. Therefore its name is called Babel, because there the LORD confused the language of all the earth, and from there, the LORD <u>scattered</u> them abroad over the face of all the earth (Genesis 11: 8, 9, emphasis added).*

The sons of God saw that the daughters of man were attractive. And they took as their wives any they chose. Then Yahweh said, "*My Spirit shall not abide in man forever.*" Yahweh's words escort towards a final event because of its horrid sin. God, therefore, decided to send a flood to wipe out humanity. *And God said to Noah, "The end of all flesh has come before Me, for the earth is filled with violence through them; and behold, I will destroy them with the earth"* (Genesis 6:13).

## POWER OF A NAME

In the vast margins of time, the meaning of a name in the Bible was significant unlike some names that had no suggestive meaning. Like Uzziah in 2 Chronicles 26, some names were a spiritual statement: "Yahweh is my strength." Other names, like Joshua, made a proclamation about God: "Yahweh is salvation." In Jewish tradition, a child's name was revealed in the ceremony and was circumcised as a covenant sign. God's ancient people knew that a good name was highly valued, as in Proverbs 22:1: *A good name is more desirable than great riches; to be esteemed is better than silver or gold.* Sometimes a new name has prophetic meaning, and that is why Jacob's name was changed from Jacob to Israel, shifting from Jacob the deceiver to Israel the prince with God.

I've met some people, mostly friends in Africa and even some Indians, who changed their names because they were dedicated to gods or their tribes, which were ungodly. So, the Lord would give them a new name that reflects their new identity in Christ.

The names in the early book of Genesis have great prophetic connotations beginning with Adam, whose Hebrew name means "man of the red earth, which identifies his origins."[79] Abel, son of Adam, means "to breathe."[80] Seth, son of Adam, whose root word means "to set something in place."[81] Enosh, the second son of Seth, means a "weak mortal man."[82] Kenan, the third son of Seth, is difficult to interpret. Abarim Publications' Biblical Dictionary for *Kenan* has six root words: acquire, purchase, reed, fit together, sad song, nest, and make straight.[83] So, one might say that in his nine hundred plus years, he acquired a purchase of a broken reed, trying to put it together, making a straight nest when a sad song emerged.

Mahaleleel, the fourth son of Seth, is a combination of two words that means "the shining one of El." Jared, the fifth son of Seth, means "descent," a going down. Enoch, the sixth son of Seth, means "dedicated."[84]

Methuselah, the seventh son of Seth and grandfather of Noah, means "his death sends." Interestingly, the year Methuselah died, something very big was sent: the flood. Methuselah's name may be a prophecy that on the day of his death, "his death will send" a great surge of water, the flood.[85] Noah, the grandson of Methuselah, means "rest" as we see in Genesis 5:28: *This one (Noach) will bring us rest (nuach) from our work and from the toil of our hands, from the ground which YHWH had cursed.* Noah's role before the flood was as a leader who would guide others to rest, a rest from the toils and troubles of the days previous to the flood.

Now we reach the dark side of Adam's lineage. Cain, a son of Adam, means to acquire or possess something, which is why Eve said, "I have gotten/acquired (*qanah*) a man" (Genesis 4:1). The word means to be empty, often translated as vain or vanity as devoid of substance.[86]

Lamech, son of Cain, is more difficult to determine its meaning, but in the Abarim Bible Dictionary, Lamech means "the striker down, the wild man."[87] He was the first to violate the primeval ordinance of marriage (Genesis 4:18-24). His antediluvian poetry has been called "Lamech's sword-song," not the Song of the Lamb.

In Genesis 4:23-24, Lamech said to his wives, *Adah and Zillah, listen to me; wives of Lamech, hear my words: I have killed a man for wounding me, a young man for injuring me. If Cain is avenged seven times, then Lamech seventy-seven times.*

We don't know the background, but Lamech killed him, which became his song of "shock and awe" and vengeance. Cain's level of angry revenge was vengeance *times seven.* And Lamech's level of retaliation was vengeance *seventy-seven times.* Evidently, he was "rude and ruffianly," fearing neither God nor man. With Lamech, the curtain falls on the lineage of Cain, for we know nothing of his descendants. It is the beginning of a sorrowful rejection of God for their false gods.

## YAHWEH, THE NAME OF GOD

Before opening a look at the interpretive consequences of Genesis 4:26, it is essential to understand the names of God: Yahweh and Elohim. These two names—YHWH and its compound forms and Elohim—cover the majority of mentions when the Hebrew Bible names God.[88] In the Hebrew language, the Hebrew for His name is Yahweh often incorrectly spelled "Jehovah" because there is no "J" in Hebrew or Greek. Yahweh's name appears nearly 7,000 times in the Hebrew Old Testament.[89]

Every English translation, including the freer translations and paraphrases like *The Living Bible*, uses the substitute word "LORD." For instance, Genesis 2:4 is interpreted as "Lord God" in every translation except for the Literal Standard Version's translation, where it is YHWH: *These [are] the generations of the heavens and of the earth in their being created, in the day of YHWH God's making the earth and the heavens* (LSV). The literal Hebrew version of Exodus 20:7 reads, *You do not take up the Name of your God YHWH for a vain thing, for YHWH does not acquit him who takes up His Name for a vain thing* (LSV).

In the Second Temple period, the Tetragrammaton (YHWH) came to be regarded as charged with metaphysical potency and therefore ceased to be pronounced. The translations replaced them with *Adonai*, meaning "Lord," and Greek *kyrios*. Often  *adonai* would later accompany YHVH in written texts as Lord God. It gave rise to the mistaken translation Jehovah or Lord God. Until Jerome, the chief translator who produced the Latin Vulgate, there were Greek manuscripts of translations of the Hebrew scriptures that still contained the divine name in its four Hebrew characters.

Matthew 7:29 reads, *He (Jesus) was teaching them as a person having authority, and not as their scribes.* In the hearing of His faithful apostles, Jesus prayed to YHWH God, saying, *"I have made your name manifest to the men you gave me out of the world... I have made your name known to them and will make it known"* (John 17:6, 26).[90]

In Hebrew, *elohim* can mean "God" or "gods," which takes us to the beginning of sorrow when the people worshiped the gods.

## BEGINNING OF SORROW, WORSHIP OF THE GODS

> *And as for Seth, to him also a son was born; and he named*
> *him Enosh. Then men began (châlal) to call on the name of*
> *the Lord (Genesis 4:26).*

*Seth also fathered a son, whom he named Enosh. At that time, profaning*
*the name of the LORD* (Yhvh) *began* (Genesis 4:26, ISV). The Hebrew
*châlal* different meanings are profane, pollute, defile, bow drilled, and
open a wedge.[91]

Combining the two theological interpretations, profaning the name of the Lord and beginning to seek the Lord, we can design a pathway in two directions: serving Yahweh and worshiping other gods. If a theologian goes down this road, the narrow road of Seth's lineage, then the Bible scholars must admit there were only two names mentioned who believed in and were loyal to Yahweh. There was no community of people devoted to Yahweh Elohim, but only the small generational line of Seth, Enoch, and Noah who followed Yahweh.

Enoch was the seventh generation through the line of Seth, and *Enoch habitually walks with God, and he is not, for God has taken him* (Genesis 5:22, NSV). And in Jude 14, 15, Enoch prophesied judgment on the ungodly acts of wickedness.

Enoch, the seventh from Adam, also prophesied about them: "Behold, the Lord is coming with myriads of His holy ones to execute judgment on everyone, and to convict all the ungodly of every ungodly act of wickedness and every harsh word spoken against Him by ungodly sinners" (Berean Study Bible).

And in the Book of Enoch 1:1-3, he spoke words that would bless the righteous elect: "The words of the blessing of Enoch, wherewith he blessed the elect and righteous, who will be living in the day of tribulation when all the wicked and godless are to be removed. And he took up his parable and said Enoch a righteous man, whose eyes were opened by God, saw the vision of the Holy One in the heavens, which the angels showed me, and from them, I heard everything, and from them, I understood as I saw, but not for this generation, but for a remote one which is for to come."[92]

But there is another darker side to this advanced godless society. It is typical of every people or group which rejects God to the point of being abandoned by God, a community where *the wickedness of man was great in the earth, and that every intent of the thoughts of his heart was only evil continually* (Genesis 6:5). So prevalent was evil in the world of Cain that *the Lord was sorry that He had made man on the earth, and He was grieved in His heart* (Genesis 6:6). It was a world so calloused that it could for 120 years reject the preaching of Noah and ignore the recorded warnings of Enoch.

The poet has rightly observed, "The saddest words of tongue or pen, are these four, `It might have been.'"[93b] By this standard, the failure of Cainite society was indeed sad. No man sins unto himself, and when a man removes God from his life, he also robs future generations of their potential spiritual heritage. This principle is particularly evident in the experience of Cain when the lives of representatives of the seventh generation are compared.

From the Ancient Hebrew Lexicon, the root of *chalal* is the bow drill or wedge, used to make an entrance so it might be split and weakened. **To profane** something sacred is to weaken its sanctity in the eyes of the people commanded to hold it sacred.

In Genesis 4:26, men began to profane in Genesis 1-11, and the following history reveals how society was weakened: *Men profanely began to call themselves by the name of YHVH, or take upon themselves titles and attributes of Deity*. As a result, the wickedness testified in chapters five through six increased and became great. Effect: the individual integrity of man was weakened.

In Genesis 6:1-4, men profanely began to multiply their daughters, not as children to be cherished and raised to feminine maturity as helpmates and mothers of their own house, but as objects to be bartered for the use of the wealthy elite in possibly the first instance of human trafficking in the history of the world. Effect: the father and family bond was weakened.

In Genesis 9:20, Noah profanely began to plant a vineyard, resulting in the first instance of drunkenness related in scripture. [93]

In Genesis 11:6, the people at Babel profanely began to build the tower rather than obey God and disperse to their assigned borders, which weakened the peace between national neighbors and introduced warfare into the human experience. Result: peaceful co-existence between the global family of nations was weakened.[94]

In Exodus 12:12, Yahweh declared, *"I have passed over through the land of Egypt during this night, and have struck every firstborn in the land of Egypt, from man even to beast, and I do judgments on all the gods of Egypt; I [am] YHWH"* (LSV). *The Egyptians are burying those whom YHWH has struck among them, every firstborn, and YHWH has done judgments on their gods* (Numbers 33:4).

Egypt has gods, but Yahweh defeats all gods. The first commandment is *"You shall have no other gods before me"* (Exodus 20:3).

In Deuteronomy 4:19, the Israelites are forbidden from worshiping gods that the other nations worship: *And lest you lift your eyes to the heavens, and have seen the sun, and the moon and the stars, all the host of the heavens, and have been drawn away, and have bowed yourself to them and served them, which your God YHWH has apportioned to all the peoples under all the heavens.*

In Deuteronomy 4:19, the Israelites are forbidden from worshipping "the sun, the moon and the stars, all the host of heaven . . . [which] Yahweh your God has allotted to all the peoples everywhere under heaven." In other words, they were told not to worship other gods, not because those gods did not exist, but because they were supposed to rule other peoples, not Israel. The Psalms explode with such evidence.

> *Among the gods, there is none like You, O Lord; Nor are there any works like Your works (Psalm 86:8).*

*For the LORD is great and greatly to be praised; He is to be feared above all gods (Psalm 96:4).*

*For the LORD is the great God, And the great King above all gods (Psalm 95:3).*

## DEMONS, EVIL SPIRITS, IDOLS, AND GODS

The false gods mentioned in the scriptures were worshiped by the people of Canaan and the nations surrounding the promised land. Still, one wonders if these idols were fabricated imaginary deities or possessed supernatural power? Few attempts have been made to create a doctrine of demonology in the Old Testament instead of a clearer view of Satan and demons in the New Testament.

But it is evident that they exist and have influenced ungodly nations and impacted Israel. Demons are mentioned a few times in the Old Testament, but many more are references to evil spirits. Bible scholars are convinced some of these spiritual beings could do amazing acts because they were evil spirits disguised as gods. There is a clear connection in the Bible between idols and demons. Paul makes this link in 1 Corinthians 10:20: *Rather, that the things which the Gentiles sacrifice they sacrifice to demons and not to God, and I do not want you to have fellowship with demons.*

The demons mentioned in the Old Testament are of two classes, the "se'irim" and the "shedim."[95] The se'irim ("hairy beings"), the Israelites sacrificed in the open fields. *And they shall no longer offer their sacrifices to the goat demons* (se'irim) *with which they play the prostitute. This shall be a permanent statute to them throughout their generations* (Leviticus 17:7, NASB). And in Isaiah 13:21, an oracle of Babylon in which God will overthrow Babylon like Sodom and Gomorrah, leaving empty spaces of demons. *But wild animals will lie down there, and its houses will be full of howling creatures; there ostriches will live, and there goat-demons will dance.*

*But Jeshurun became fat and kicked—You have become fat, thick, and obstinate—Then he abandoned God who made him, And rejected the Rock of his salvation. They made Him jealous with strange gods; With abominations they provoked Him to anger. They sacrificed to demons (shedim), who were not God, To gods whom they have not known, New gods who came lately, Whom your fathers did not know (Deuteronomy 32:15-17).*

Jesurun is a title for Israel, which means the upright one, which signifies what Israel was called to be. But the righteous-nation conducted themselves through various acts of rebellion, murmuring, and idolatrous apostasy. Israel excited Jehovah's jealousy through strange gods, and they provoked Him by their abominations. The Deuteronomy Hebrew text uses synonymous parallelism, a poetic literary device involving two or more lines communicating the same idea using different words.[96]

Israel continued their unholy sacrifices when it was the will of God they should cease, but offering to demons, not to God, under the instigation of Satan. Jesus said that the Jewish leaders were of their father the devil and listened to his desires (John 8:44). Israel chose to reject the law and established their form of righteousness, offering sacrifices to the *shedim* gods and not to God, which is equal to trampling under the Son of God as an insult to the Spirt of grace (Hebrews 10:29). The false gods contrast with the true God, the "Rock."

Unless you study the scriptures, looking at biblical language, you will miss the hidden elements in such a beautiful prayer in Psalm 90: *He who dwells in the secret place of the Most High Shall abide under the shadow of the Almighty. I will say of the Lord, "He is my refuge and my fortress; My God, in Him I will trust"* (v. 1, 2).

Professor Matthias Henze, who has a Ph.D. in Hebrew Bible and Early Judaism from Harvard's Department of Near Eastern Languages and Civilizations, wrote that the interpreters xPsalm 90. Because there is no line at the top of that psalm, one believed it was a prayer of worship or psalm of refuge before entering the Temple or just the psalmist declaring with confidence that what God has done, He will do for others.[97]

But we arrive at the main point in verses five and six, so read, *You shall not be afraid of the terror by night, Nor of the arrow that flies by day, Surely He shall deliver you from the snare of the fowler And from the perilous pestilence. Nor of the pestilence that walks in darkness, Nor of the destruction that lays waste at noonday.* The two clauses, an arrow that flies by day and a snare of the flower, form a single sentence, arranged in perfect symmetry, and introduced by the assurance formula, "You shall not fear."

The German theologian and Bible scholar Erich Zenger (1939–2010) writes, The psalm evokes the chaotic, lowering danger of death by having it act as personified powers of evil that practice their wickedness night and day.[98]

The pestilence (*mid·de·ḇer*: plague), which already appeared in verse 3, and the "destruction" (*qeṭeḇ*: pestilence, plague) are both deadly epidemics. The use of "pestilence" occurs four times in the Hebrew Bible (Psalm 91:6; Deuteronomy 32:24; Isaiah 28:2; Hosea 13:14), while "plague" is attested more than fifty times, as the fifth plague in the exodus story (Exodus 9:3). From ancient times to the present, many interpreters have understood the two perils in verse 6 not to be epidemics but rather evil spirits or demons.[99] The Brenton Septuagint interprets verse six as "{nor} of the {evil} thing that walks in darkness; {nor} of calamity, and the evil spirit at noon-day."[100]

In direct response to the threat of demons in verses 5-6, the author describes divine support protecting the faithful. For those who put their trust in Yahweh, He will command "His angelic messengers" to watch over and protect you "in all your ways, even if you stumble." *Because you have made the Lord, who is my refuge, Even the Most High, your dwelling place, No evil shall befall you, Nor shall any plague come near your dwelling; For He shall give His angels charge over you, To keep you in all your ways. In their hands, they shall bear you up, Lest you dash your foot against a stone* (vs. 10-13).

In verse 13, the faithful ones will be sheltered from wild beasts and tread on the evil ones. *You shall tread upon the lion and the cobra* (*pethen:* venomous serpent).[101] *The young lion and the serpent (Tannin: serpent, dragon)*[102] *you shall trample underfoot*, which is the language associated with demonic evil spirits.

The intrusion of demons still happens today. When I was in Nepal years ago, I went to the all-seeing eye in Katmandu, and the idols were massive in size. I walked into one of the temples, and the idol was as big as a building. And there were hundreds of people in there worshiping this massive idol. So, when you looked at its eyes, the eyes would move inside. There was a living demonic entity inside that statue.

The Bible backs up the reality of experiences associated with deceiving spirits, demons, angels of light, and counterfeits for the true Spirit of God: *Now the Spirit expressly says that in latter times some will depart from the faith, giving heed to deceiving spirits and doctrines of demons* (1 Timothy 4:1-2, NIV).

Like the Gentiles, there will be those who will sacrifice to demons. *Rather, that the things which the Gentiles sacrifice they sacrifice to demons and not to God, and I do not want you to have fellowship with demons. You cannot drink from the cup of the Lord and from the cup of demons, too. You cannot eat at the Lord's Table and at the table of demons, too* (1 Corinthians 10:20-21).

And these people are false apostles with a disguise like Satan transformed himself into an angel of light. *For such are false apostles, deceitful workers, transforming themselves into apostles of Christ. And no wonder! For Satan himself transforms himself into an angel of light* (2 Corinthians 11:13-14).

## THE BOOK OF ENOCH

One of the most important apocryphal works of the Second Temple Period is Enoch. According to the biblical narrative (Genesis 5:21-24), Enoch lived only 365 years (far less than the other patriarchs in the period before the Flood). Enoch "walked with God; then he was no more for God took him." The original Aramaic version was lost until the Dead Sea fragments were discovered.[103]

The **First Book of Enoch,** also called **the Ethiopic Book of Enoch, comes from a previous Greek translation made in Palestine,** in the original Hebrew or Aramaic. Though it is not considered canonical, most scholars still accepted and honored it.

R.H. Charles, an Irish Anglican theologian, is a biblical scholar known particularly for his translations of apocryphal books, including the Book of Enoch. "The Book of Enoch was extant centuries before the birth of Christ and yet is considered by many to be more Christian in its theology than Jewish. It was considered scripture by many early Christians. The earliest literature of the so-called 'Church Fathers' is filled with references to this mysterious book" (R.H. Charles, *The Book of Enoch*). Charles also had this direct comment on certain Church Fathers: "Second and Third Century 'Church Fathers' like Justin Martyr, Irenaeus, Origin, and Clement of Alexandria all use the Book of Enoch. Tertullian even called the Book of Enoch 'Holy Scripture.'"[104]

Eusebius highly recommended the Book of Enoch for his book *Church History* (AD 330), mentioning that the Apocalypse of John was accepted as a canonical book and rejected at the same time. We can use the book of Enoch as historical just as if we were to read the book of Job. Though we don't look at them as canonized, most people accept them as legitimate historical facts. Of all the church fathers, only Tertullian didn't agree to include it.

The Book of Enoch found popularity among Jewish communities in the Second Temple Period, which was during Jesus' time. It is rich in themes that New Testament writers either presupposed or borrowed, and Jude wrote about angels who left their abode. *"And the angels who did not keep their proper domain, but left their own abode, He has reserved in everlasting chains under darkness for the judgment of the great day* (Jude 1:6).

## NEPHILIM, WATCHERS, AND THE REBELLION

The Book of Enoch is composed of various monumental works. *The Book of Watchers* is the first thirty-six chapters of the Book of Enoch, telling the story of fallen angels who took wives, created the Nephilim, and taught advanced technology to humankind, ultimately leading to the great flood and their destruction. Mount Hermon is where the *Grigori,* a transliteration of the Greek *egrégoroi* meaning watchers, appears in the Book of Enoch.

Though a noncanonical Jewish text, the Book of Enoch remains popular because of the broadened view of the Nephilim activity of fallen angels coming to give birth from human women, which they were afraid of the price they would pay.

The Watchers were angels dispatched to earth to watch over the people. Soon, they began to lust for the human women they saw, and at the prodding of their leader, Samyaza, they defected en masse to marry and live among humanity. The children produced by these relationships are the Nephilim, savage giants who pillaged the earth and endangered humanity. The Hebrew word *neflim* is directly translated as "giants"[105] or taken to mean "the fallen ones" from the Hebrew *nephal*, "to fall."[106]

"And it came to pass when the children of men had multiplied that in those days were born unto them beautiful and comely daughters. And the angels, the children of the heaven, saw and lusted after them, and said to one another: 'Come, let us choose us wives from among the children of men and beget us children.' And Semjaza, who was their leader, said unto them: 'I fear ye will not indeed agree to do this deed, and I alone shall have to pay the penalty of a great sin' "[107](Enoch 6:1-4).

So, they made a covenant of agreement never to desert the scheme and stick together and then swooped down upon Mount Hermon. And they all answered him and said: "Let us all swear an oath, and all bind ourselves by mutual imprecations not to abandon this plan but to do this thing. Then sware they all together and bound themselves by mutual imprecations upon it. And they were in all two hundred; who descended in the days of Jared on the summit of Mount Hermon, and they called it Mount Hermon, because they had sworn and bound themselves by mutual imprecations upon it. And these are the names of their leaders: Samlazaz, their leader, Araklba, Rameel, Kokablel, Tamlel, Ramlel, Danel, Ezeqeel, Baraqijal, Asael, Armaros, Batarel, Ananel, Zaqiel, Samsapeel, Satarel, Turel, Jomjael, Sariel. These are their chiefs of tens" (Book of Enoch 6:4b-8).[108]

The angels of Yahweh are greatly concerned over the vengeance killing, shedding of blood, and the lawless activity. Enoch 9:1-2 says, "And then Michael, Uriel, Raphael, and Gabriel looked down from heaven and saw much blood being shed upon the earth. All lawlessness being wrought upon the earth. And they said one to another: 'The earth made without inhabitant cries the voice of their cryingst up to the gates of heaven.'"[109]

Hence, they enter into the divine council, presenting their case before the Holy One because of their unrighteousness and revealing heaven's secrets. "'Bring our cause before the Most High,' And they said to the Lord of the ages: 'Lord of lords, God of gods, King of kings, and God of the ages, the throne of Thy glory (standeth) unto all the generations of the ages, and Thy name holy and glorious and blessed unto all the ages! Thou hast made all things, and power over all things hast Thou: and all things are naked and open in Thy sight, and Thou seest all things, and nothing can hide from Thee. Thou seest what Azazel hath done who hath taught all unrighteousness on earth and revealed the eternal secrets which were (preserved) in heaven, which men were striving to learn'" (Enoch 9:3b-6a).

As Yahweh Elohim observes the activity of the fallen angels, He arrives at a place where His toleration has ended with the Nephilim and the wicked humans on the face of the earth. *So the LORD said, "My Spirit will not contend with man forever, for he is mortal; his days shall be 120 years"* (Genesis 6:3, Berean Study Bible).

So, the situation reached the final tipping point with the fallen angels and human daughters giving birth to them and the emergence of the Nephilim. The mystery of iniquity stretches out to the last moment when days are numbered and judgment made. But first, a warning to Noah. "Then said the Most High, the Holy and Great One spake, and sent Uriel to the son of Lamech, and said to him: 'Go to Noah and tell him in my name "Hide thyself!" and reveal to him the end that is approaching: that the whole earth will be destroyed, and

a deluge is about to come upon the whole earth, and will destroy all
that is on it. And now instruct him that he may escape and his seed
may be preserved for all the generations of the world'" (Noah 10:1-3).

## MOUNT HERMON

Mount Hermon was called Senir by the Amorites and Sirion by the
Sidonians (Deuteronomy 3:9). The mountain served as the land's
northern boundary promised to the Israelites (Deuteronomy 3:8). It
was also known as Mount Siyon (Deuteronomy 4:48).

The Canaanites used the high places of Mount Hermon, refer-
ring to the mountain as Mount Ba'al-Hermon (Judges 3:3). According
to the Encyclopedia Britannica, Hermon means "Forbidden Place."
Jerome (4th-century translator of the Latin Vulgate Bible) interpreted
Hermon as "anathema." Mount Hermon was the port of entry for the
Watchers who corrupted the human race in the days of Noah.[110]

However, Psalm 89:12 speaks of God's creation of Mount Tabor and
Mount Hermon, covering the north and south of Israel, with songs of
joy because of Yahweh's creative work: *The north and the south, You
have created them; Tabor and Hermon rejoice in Your name.* The author
of Psalm 133 wrote poetically of the "dew of Mount Hermon" falling
on Mount Zion, while the Song of Solomon 4:8 sings of the lover's
bride descending from *"the summit of Hermon, from the lions' dens and
the mountain haunts of the leopards."*

When the rebel Watchers first meet upon Mount Hermon orga-
nizing their secret society of 200 members, Samyaza, the recognized
leader, initially doubted the recruits' resolve to disavow heaven. So,
the plan was to secure dark alliances and clandestine oaths sworn
under penalty of death, thereby binding themselves to that treachery
whereby they would use their heaven-acquired knowledge to create a
counterfeit religion on earth to satisfy their lusts and carnal desires.[111]

*"And all the others together with them took unto them-
selves wives, and each chose for himself one, and they began to go in unto them and to defile themselves with them,*

*and they taught them charms and enchantments, and the cutting of roots, and made them acquainted with plants"* (Enoch 7:1, 2).[112]

*"And Azazel taught men to make swords, and knives, and shields, and breastplates, and made known to them the metals of the earth and the art of working them, and bracelets, and ornaments, and the use of antimony, and the beautifying of the eyelids, and all kinds of costly stones, and all 2 coloring tinctures"* (Enoch 8:1, 2).[113]

*"Semjaza taught enchantments, and root-cuttings, 'Armaros the resolving of enchantments, Baraqijal (taught) astrology, Kokabel the constellations, Ezeqeel the knowledge of the clouds, Araqiel the signs of the earth, Shamsiel the signs of the sun, and Sariel the course of the moon"* (Enoch 8:3).[114]

*"Amidst all this, there arose much godlessness, and they committed fornication, and they were led astray, and became corrupt in all their ways"* (vs. 2, 3).[115]

These weapons of destruction created by the Watchers are also mentioned in other places that reflect the implementation of their reprehensible evil work, as in Ezekiel 9:1, 2: *Then I heard Him call out in a loud voice, saying, "Draw near, O executioners of the city, each with a weapon of destruction in hand." And I saw six men coming from the direction of the Upper Gate, which faces north, each with a weapon of slaughter in his hand. Another man clothed in linen was with them who had a writing kit at his side. And they came in and stood beside the bronze altar.* But then God told the man in a linen cloth to mark the forehead of those grieving the detestable things they did (vs. 3, 4). So, God sent His messengers to kill those throughout the city (v. 7).

Jesus spent a great deal of time interacting with and teaching the disciples. After six days in the neighborhood of Caesarea Philippi,

He took Peter, James, and John to a high mountain, probably Mount Hermon, a short distance from Caesarea Philippi.

When reaching the top of the mountain, Jesus introduces them to the dark cloud of transfiguration. "He appeared in *another form* unto two of them." The word implies more than a change of mere outward semblance. The words *as the light* hint that the transfiguration took place at night, which is also rendered probable by the statement of St. Luke that the three apostles were "heavy with sleep."[116] In that act of communion with His Father, the divine glory flowed out into visible brightness in transcendent wonder.

In the middle of the transfiguration, Moses and Elijah talk with Jesus. As you would expect, a bit overwhelmed by the intensity of the moment, Peter blurts out, *"Let us make here three tabernacles: one for You, one for Moses, and one for Elijah"* (Matthew 17:4).

*While he was still speaking, behold, a bright cloud overshadowed them, and suddenly a voice came out of the cloud, saying, "This is My beloved Son, in whom I am well pleased. Hear Him"* (Matthew 17:5). A luminous cloud overshadows them, casting a kind of light and shade over their forms to make it less clear than they were before the cloud intervened. At Jesus' baptism, God confirmed their relationship, but it seems more directed to the disciples on the mountain, preparing them for the coming trauma of the crucifixion and death. "Hear ye Him" gained a new significance.

The hope for an apocalyptic cleansing of evil during the flood did not happen because corruption continued. Still, the book of Revelation describes the final conflict with the crushing of the Satanic forces of evil. Evil abounds, regardless of when or where. The smoke of Satan does not stop discriminating: in middle-age feudal systems, the 21st-century cyber world, posh suburbs of major cities, poor slums spanning the globe, and organized crime activity. Not even the decency of organized religion is spared. In endless places and abundant ways, evil thrives, bringing violent floods of suffering, murder, abortion, destruction of property, human trafficking, torture, wars, and chaos.

There are also enemies that demonic entities use as spiritual weapons to war against you and your family. But our weapons are not carnal. The Holy Spirit moves with spiritual weapons, not of the flesh. When Paul speaks of the flesh, he's talking about a realm of corruption but will not enter because Paul says that flesh and blood cannot inherit the kingdom of God; neither doth corruption inherit incorruption (1 Corinthians 15:50).

In 2 Corinthians 10:4, Paul said, *the weapons of our warfare are not carnal but mighty in God for pulling down the stronghold.* And the weapons of our war are not fleshly weapons of force, wealth, violence, corruption, and unjust infringements. But the spiritual weapons are powerful and effective through the blessing of God and the influences of Messiah's grace and Spirit to the edification of saints, the defense of truth, the confutation of error, the destruction of Satan's kingdom, and the advance of God's kingdom.

## THE WIND AND THE GLORY

God will deal with His enemies, and like a mighty wind, Yahweh will raise a standard of holiness, righteousness, justice, and love. His glory will be revealed from the rising sun. *According to their deeds, accordingly, He will repay, Fury to His adversaries, Recompense to His enemies; The coastlands He will fully repay. So shall they fear The name of the Lord from the west, And His glory from the rising of the sun; When the enemy comes in like a flood, The Spirit of the Lord will lift up a standard against him* (Isaiah 59:18, 19).

The Septuagint reads, "for the wrath of the Lord shall come as a mighty river, it shall come with fury." And the Tanakh says, "For distress will come in like a flood, Which the breath of the LORD driveth." When the world reaches its lowest ebb, a forceful furious wind will blow from the breath of Yahweh, driving out the enemy. And the Spirit of the Lord will lift a standard for the truth, and by the power of His grace, the kingdom of Jesus shall be revealed in fullest glory.

*But where sin increased, grace increased all the more* (Romans 5:20). In Bonhoeffer's book, *The Cost of Discipleship,* he defined "cheap grace" as "the preaching of forgiveness without requiring repentance, baptism without church discipline. Communion without confession. Cheap grace is grace without discipleship, grace without the cross, grace without Jesus Christ." Costly grace is the treasure hidden in the field; for the sake of it, a man will gladly go and sell all that he has. It is the pearl of great price to buy which the merchant will sell all his goods. It is the kingly rule of Christ![117]

The two thrones of grace and glory: *Let us, therefore, come boldly unto the throne of grace, that we may obtain mercy, and find grace to help in time of need* (Hebrews 4:16) and *When the Son of man shall come in his glory, and all the holy angels with him, then shall he sit upon the throne of his glory* (Matthew 25:31).

The grace of God is an empowering presence enabling us to walk in righteousness and overcome the forces of evil; it has to do with our being and doing. *For you, brethren, have been called to liberty; only do not use liberty as an opportunity for the flesh, but through love serve one another* (Galatians 5:13). God calls the church to a higher standard empowered by the Spirit. The higher standard is a life of sanctification and consecration, the righteous and holy life pleasing to God. It requires a renewing, a changing of the heart, by grace, and for His glory.

> *We have seen his glory, the glory of the one and only Son, who came from the Father, full of grace and truth; And of His fullness, we have all received, and grace for grace (John 1:14, 16 ).*

What began with the serpent and Watchers ends with glory, grace, and the rising sun of the Messiah's glorious kingdom, and of the greatness of His government and peace, there will be no end (Isaiah 9:7).

## CHAPTER FIVE

# ALTARS AND GODS

*For a while, I was passing through and examining the objects of your worship, and I also found an altar with this inscription, "TO AN UNKNOWN GOD." Therefore, what you worship in ignorance, this I proclaim to you (Acts 17:23).*

In antiquity, altars were an indispensable part of the worship of the gods that it seemed impossible to conceive of the worship of the gods without altars. Thus, we have the amusing syllogism, a coinciding of two truths in Lucian rhetoric (a Syrian famous for his quips): εἰ γὰρ εἰσὶ βωμοί, εἰσὶ καὶ θεοί· ἀλλὰ μὴν εἰσὶ βωμοί, εἰσὶν ἄρα καὶ θεοί, which means, "For if there are altars, there are also gods. But there certainly are gods; then there are gods too." Almost every religious act was accompanied by sacrifice. It was often necessary to provide altars on the spur of the moment. They were then constructed of earth, sods, or stones, collected on the spot, but when the occasion was not sudden, they were built with regular courses of masonry or brickwork.[118]

In ancient Greek religion, they worshiped the gods and their heroes, and the practices became an ancestral cult of worshiping the dead, which remains in many eastern cultures. Their cult worship included sacrificing animals and blood lust in war influenced by demons. A hero was more than human but less than a god, and various supernatural figures (demon idols) came to be assimilated into the class of heroes.[119]

Two key Greek words reflect the altars of gods, including *eschara* and *bothros*. These words properly signify any elevation but came to be applied to an elevation used to worship the gods, and hence an altar. *Eschara* is a low-lying altar used in burnt offerings for heroes, demi-gods, and spirits. If *eschara* is to be understood as the place for the fire, then some of the medal *eschara* mentioned in the inscriptions may refer to such metal sheets or pans protecting the upper surfaces of the altars. The metal *eschara* must have rested on appropriating assumptive bedding of clay or plaster, which would have further protected the stone from the heat.[120]

The Greek *bōmos* is an elevated place, place on which to offer a sacrifice, an altar, and is mentioned in Acts 17:23. Six hundred years before Christ, there was a remarkable altar raised in Athens in a time of pestilence in honor of the unknown god which had granted them deliverance. Diogenes Laertius says that Epimenides restrained the epidemic in the following manner: "Taking white and black sheep, he led them to the Areopagus, and there permitted them to go where they would, commanding those who followed them to sacrifice to a god who had the power of averting the plague, whoever he might allay the pestilence."[121] Paul saw the altar to the unknown god years later, and it became a launching pad to preach the gospel.

The meaning of the term *bothros* is a hole, trench, or pit dug in the ground. It also gives the explanations "hollow," "grave," and "ritual pit for offerings to the subterranean gods." The *bothroi* used for ritual purposes is characteristic of the cult of the heroes, the deceased, the divinities, and the sanctuaries of the gods.[122]

Correct use of the language has been claimed that *bothros* was distinguished from *eschara*. A *bothros* was a sacrificial pit, a hole in the ground into which libations were poured, the most prominent being the blood of the sacrificial victims. Sacrifices could also be burnt in the *bothros* pit. The pit could be freshly dug for each occasion or be a permanent construction, which sometimes was raised above the ground level, such as the *bothroi* found in the sanctuaries of deities.[123]

## BUILD AN ALTAR TO YAHWEH

*From there he (Abram) moved on to the hill country east of Bethel and pitched his tent, with Bethel on the west and Ai on the east. He <u>built an altar to Yahweh</u> there, and he called on the name of Yahweh (Genesis 12:8, Holman Bible, emphasis added).*

The Hebrew *mizbeach* is from a verbal root meaning "to slaughter." Greek renders this word as *thusiasterion*, "a place of sacrifice." The altars were places to make sacrifices to God, and the sacrifice was the essential act of external worship. The sacrificial act moved the offering from the profane to the sacred, visible to invisible. By this action, the worshiper sealed a contract with God.[124]

*The land of Canaan was inhabited by the Canaanites who did not know Yahweh and worshipped other gods, practiced witchcraft, and all kinds of other ungodly practices. The altars to the gods they worshipped attracted dark spirits and gave these spirits legal authority over the land. The land of Canaan was under another spiritual principality.*

*Abram contended with this spiritual darkness by building altars to Yahweh, preparing the land spiritually for change by possessing the enemy's gates. Abram's altars drew the presence of Yahweh and broke the powers of darkness. They were like lighthouses in the spiritual realm, declaring that the spiritual authority and atmosphere altered everything in favor of the Lord Jehovah.*

Abram was taking territory from the forces of darkness and claiming it for the kingdom of YHVH. It is the essence of spiritual warfare. We don't exist in a spiritual vacuum, *for we are marked spiritually by what goes on in our area and where we live. There is no neutral ground; it is either part of the kingdom of YHVH or the kingdom of darkness. We are fighting a spiritual battle, fighting for territory. Territory equals influence, and if we lose land, YHVH's kingdom loses influence.*[125]

> *Then Jacob awoke from his sleep and said, "Surely the*
> *Lord is in this place, and I did not know it." And he was*
> *afraid and said, "How awesome is this place! This is none*
> *other than the house of God, and this is the gate of heaven"*
> *(Genesis 28:16, 17).*

Jacob came to "a certain place" and named it Bethel. It is not the first time he called it that name, for Abraham also worshipped God at Bethel, the name already existing. The place where Abraham previously built an altar to YHVH was the place of Jacob's encounter with God (Genesis 12:8). Abraham's altar created a gateway to heaven, and Jacob saw it in his dream. "*When Jacob came to that certain place (Bethel), we are told that he lighted upon 'the place.' The Hebrew maqom, like the cognate Arabic maqam, denotes a sacred place or sanctuary. The maqom was undoubted that Abraham had sacrificed East of Bethel.*"[126]

This gateway to heaven was first established by Abraham when he called on Yahweh's name at that place. Jacob experienced this gateway in a dream. When we call upon Yahweh's name, which means to worship Him and pray to Him, a prayer altar is established, forming a gateway into the heavenly spaces.

## ALTARS, GATES, AND COVENANTS

The foundation of any kingdom is composed of three things: gates, altars, and covenants.

Wherever there is a throne, there is an altar. And where there is an altar, there is a gate founded on covenants. So, we will start with plunging into the subject of gates. The study of scripture and history teaches us how gates are crucial parts of any kingdom's foundation, especially since the medieval gates were critical to protecting cities. Gateways, like all openings, were seen as weak points in any defensive fortress.

For this reason, defenders tended to take simple precautions, minimize the number of gates, and provide additional defense for gateways. As entrance points into the particular castles and the kingdoms, they needed fortified gates. There are two other things to consider concerning gates: protecting from satanic forces seeking to intrude and squashing the fortress gates of our enemies.

One of the most interesting aspects of the early Jesus community was how dynamic and quickly it expanded beyond its initial base in Jerusalem. Following Jesus' resurrection and before His ascension, He gave the following command to His followers: *"But you will receive power when the Holy Spirit has come upon you; and you will be my witnesses in Jerusalem, in all Judea and Samaria, and to the ends of the earth"* (Acts 1:8).

This statement became the marching orders for the life and work of the early church to advance into the world, establishing a fortress against the enemy and tearing down strongholds. With Paul's arrival on the scene, the apostolic missionary expanded the church into the Gentile world, which created the opportunity to preach the gospel but with resistance and persecution by those who embraced their altars and gods.

Before Christianity was fully formed in those distant places, the ground had to be cleared of local cult places, temples, statues, and altars in honor of God. The disciple Bartholomew became a great apostolic leader who opened doors to many nations. Although there are no traces of the ancient apostle, the Acts of Bartholomew reveal many truths that are biblically accepted, especially his travels to Armenia, Asia Minor, and India to plant the church and attack the enemy.

In the *Passio Bartholomaei,* there are mentions of his apostolic adventures in those nations. Upon his arrival, Bartholomew immediately enters into combat with the local godhead Astaroth. The cult of this god takes shape in awe of an image or statue (*idolum*) of the god, placed in Astaroth's temple. The idol is presented as the dwelling place of the godhead, who claims to heal the sick as a response to the people's sacrifice. Thus, the godhead's temple is a place for sacrifice and veneration and a healing spot: the ill stand around the godhead's image. In the *Passio*, Astaroth's "healing practice" is presented as a delusion: it is the godhead itself that makes the people ill to bind them to his cult and power. This truth about Astaroth is later made public by Bartholomew, who forces the godhead to confess its incapacity to heal the people genuinely. Once the apostle has revealed the godhead's true nature to the people, they are all too willing to destroy with their own hands the old cult place and replace it with a church.[127]

Every battle fought is usually won or lost at the city's gates. *In that day, the LORD of hosts will be for a crown of glory and a diadem of beauty to the remnant of His people, for a spirit of justice to him who sits in judgment, and for strength to those who turn back the battle at the gate* (Isaiah 28:5, 6).

## POSSESSING THE GATES

There is never a time in your Christian walk when there is no resistance because the enemy is always there, tempting to crush your faith in God. But when we possess and fortify the gates, eliminating a satanic entrance, we access the entire territory and not just one particular structure. We may feel weary and tempted to give up when the battle is long. But these are the moments when we must remember that by the strength of the Lord, we establish heavenly gates of resistance. But there are realms in the spirit where the enemy is trying to occupy our space, and that is when we have been called to execute judgment and clear that space and possess the gate of our enemies.

> *Blessing I will bless you and multiplying I will multiply your descendants as the stars of the heaven and as the sand which is on the seashore; and your descendants shall possess the gate of their enemies (Genesis 22:17).*

> *And they blessed Rebekah and said to her: "Our sister, may you become the mother of thousands of ten thousands; And may your descendants possess the gates of those who hate them" (Genesis 24:60).*

Possess the gates—physical gateways represent the spiritual gateways, first the physical and then the spiritual. We must possess our gates, not allowing gates to slip into the enemies' hands, because we are at war with satanic forces. Controlling the gates requires taking control of every facet of our lives: spiritual awareness, our thinking, finances, social values and connections, decisions, government and laws, and our physical protection.

## FOUR KEYS OF SPIRITUAL WARFARE

Number one is to know and locate your enemy and deal with warfare at the gate, the prince of the power of the air. Paul describes Satan as the prince of the power of the air, a prince only because there can only be one King, and Yahweh is His name. *And you were dead in the trespasses and sins in which you once walked, following the course of this world, following the prince of the power of the air, the spirit that is now at work in the sons of disobedience* (Ephesians 2:1, 2, ESV). Satan has authentic power and should not be ignored, and we must locate his activity. We know that we are of God, and the whole world lies *under the sway of* the wicked one (1 John 5:19).

God did not reveal all of the whys and whens concerning Satan's rule, but He has made it clear that there is only one way to escape the power of Satan's dominion, and that is through His Son, Jesus. *He has delivered us from the power of darkness and conveyed us into the kingdom of the Son of His love* (Colossians 1:13). And we have been called to release others from their power *to open their eyes, and to turn from darkness to light, and from the power of Satan unto God* (Acts 26:18).

Even now, the enemy is trying to come through your gate, but you must take possession, take territory for God's kingdom, and push through to rout and execute judgment upon the realms of darkness. And this comes to prayer, and God will begin to reveal things to you. Constantly, things occur that cause spiritual warfare, but we respond with power from God and use the weapons of our warfare in Christ.

Although Satan has power and authority running to and from throughout the earth, seeking whom he can destroy, *God raised us up with Christ and seated us with Him in the heavenly realms in Christ Jesus*

(Ephesians 2:6). Prayer in the heavenly is a powerful weapon to locate satanic activity and to shred those demonic gates with spiritual power. You are already losing the battle as long as you're trying to break through into the heavens. You must make war from where you're seated in the heavenly places.

Number two entails locating Satan's source of strength. *Or how can one enter a strong man's house and plunder his goods unless he first binds the strong man? And then he will plunder his house* (Matthew 12:29). In this parable, the "strong man" is Satan. The "house" is the territory subject to him, either the world or the spirits of individual men. The "goods" or "instruments of armored weapons," as stated in Luke 11:22, are the demons or subordinate powers of evil by which he maintains his dominion. The "binding of the strong man" is the assessment given to the tyranny of Satan by emancipating the possessed sufferers from their slavery; the "spoiling of the house" implies the final victory over him.

Jesus is the One who was and is stronger than the strong man. He is the only One who can bind the strong man and rescue us from his clutches. *Now is the judgment of this world; now shall the prince of this world be cast out* (John 12:31). And it is our responsibility to enforce what Christ has accomplished.

Then number three is where the enemy channels his power, possibly with an altar. It could be an altar that involves a covenant. It could even be a particular device or in the natural. Or the enemy can use a person who operates through the occult by channeling the power to bring a curse that harms you or your family. And then take an assessment of your enemy's strength relative to yours. And then you take an appraisal through the word of God and take control, whether it's a witch, a warlock, a Satanist, or even someone that is a shape-shifting devil. The apostle Paul had a demonic message sent to buffet his flesh. *Lest I be lifted up by the abundance of revelations, a thorn for my flesh was handed over to me, an Angel of Satan to buffet me, lest I be lifted up* (2 Corinthians 12:7). Paul was working at such an apostolic level with dominion over the enemy that a satanic angel had to counter his work by buffeting him. The Greek *kolaphizó* means to beat as with a fist, harshly and roughly treated, and tormented. The false apostles and prophets made many false accusations against them, a thorn in his flesh. The suffering and abuse Paul experienced by religious leaders and the sectarian Gentiles were all instigated by satanic forces. But their attempts were futile, and Paul's actions and the heavenly resistance to demonic forces sent the evil ones scrambling because of his great success.

## BREAKING THE GATES OF HELL

In one of those private moments, Jesus asked the disciples a penetrating question requiring thought. Caught in a moment without an answer, they turned to the opinions of others rather than speaking from their heart. While the others were talking, Peter quickly grasps a revelation of Christ and blurts it out with confidence.

> Simon Peter answered and said, "You are the Christ, the Son of the living God." Jesus answered and said to him, "Blessed are you, Simon Bar-Jonah, for flesh and blood has not revealed this to you, but My Father who is in heaven. And I also say to you that you are Peter, and on this rock I will build My church, and the gates of Hades shall not prevail against it. And I will give you the keys of the kingdom of heaven, and whatever you bind on earth will be bound in heaven, and whatever you loose on earth will be loosed in heaven" (Matthew 16:16-19).

The Jews expected to know the Messiah by His external splendor, pomp, and power as a man. But Peter did not receive the truth from scribes' teaching, but by a revelation from the Father. It was as if Peter was led through the veil of Jesus' human nature to recognize the divine, requiring faith and divine revelation. Peter was a rock of revelation and stability, and upon this rock of revelation and confession, the church will be built. But the Rock is Christ, and the gates of hell cannot prevail against Christ and His church, though there will be some who stumble and fall. Concerning a little "rock" of pagan values and dead idolatry prominent in Caesarea Philippi, Jesus was saying that His church would replace those ungodly altars and gates with the kingdom church.

Having the key means the power of access, an emblem of authority to bind the demons and loose those bound by the enemy. The resistance to demonic gates involves binding and loosing. The expressions "bind" and "loose" were common to Jewish legal phraseology meaning to declare something forbidden or allow it. The Greek *déō* means to bind, fasten with chains, throw into chains, and prohibit. It can mean Satan's binding, employing a demon as his messenger, and implies binding Satan's power, preventing his diabolical efforts.[128]

The Greek *lýō* means to loose one bound, unbind, release from bonds, set free one bound with chains, loosen, undo, dissolve anything tied, or compacted together, deprive of authority, and overthrow, to do away with.[129]

## POWER OF PRAYER AND BREAKING GATES

*But at midnight, Paul and Silas were praying and singing hymns to God, and the prisoners were listening to them. Suddenly there was a great earthquake so that the foundations of the prison were shaken, and immediately all the doors were opened, and everyone's chains were loosed (Acts 16:25-27).*

*Now, in the same way, the Spirit also helps our weakness; for we do not know what to pray for as we should, but the Spirit Himself intercedes for us with groanings too deep for words (Romans 8:26).*

*For he who speaks in a tongue does not speak to men but to God, for no one understands him; however, in the spirit, he speaks mysteries (1Corinthians14:2, NASB).*

*With every prayer and request, pray at all times in the Spirit, and with this in view, be alert with all perseverance and every request for all the saints (Ephesians 6:18).*

*To another different kinds of tongues, to another the interpretation of tongues. But one and the same Spirit works all these things, distributing to each one individually as He wills (1 Corinthians 12:10, 11).*

We won't know the power of prayer until we pray and do not wish because our God is not a genie. John Wesley, the revivalist, said, "God does nothing but by prayer, and everything with it." The greatest battles are won when you pray, and when your prayers become habits, miracles become a lifestyle. Billy Sunday, a baseball player for the White Sox who became an evangelist, said, "If you are a stranger to prayer, you are a stranger to the greatest source of power known to human beings."

When you pray in the spirit, you are praying creative revelation ascending into the atmosphere of things you do not know, but it returns as a revelation from God. *Call to Me, and I will answer you, and tell you [and even show you] great and mighty things, [things which have been confined and hidden], which you do not know and understand and cannot distinguish* (Jeremiah 33:3, LSV).

Sometimes, as you minister to the Lord and pray in tongues, you suddenly begin to interpret what you were saying in the spirit realm. Whatever revelation you receive will be backed by the word of God. There is no vacuum in the realm of the spirit, but it depends on what fills the room. When you empty a glass of water, that glass is not empty, for there are air molecules of different gases, things you cannot see.

So, in the spiritual realm, things exist, but we do not always see. But when we call on the Lord in prayer, He will answer and reveal mysteries. *But God has revealed them to us through His Spirit. For the Spirit searches all things, yes, the deep things of God. Even so, no one knows the things of God except the Spirit of God. Now we have received, not the spirit of the world, but the Spirit who is from God, that we might know the things that have been freely given to us by God* (1 Corinthians 2:10-12). When praying in the Spirit, the supernatural world becomes clearer.

This power of prayer and the infusion of the Holy Spirit with our spirit brings illuminating revelation that empowers us to possess the enemy's gates and bring them down to destruction. That ground now belongs to Yahweh Elohim, and there we build altars to the Lord in those places once inhabited by demons. As Paul did among the Gentiles, so should we do in our times.

## GATEWAYS OF THE SPIRIT, SOUL, AND BODY

*And the same God of peace consecrate you perfectly compete; and your whole spirit and soul and body be kept faultless to the arrival of our Lord Jesus Christ (1 Thessalonians 5:23, Young's Literal Translation).*

As stated, gateways are spaces of authority where dominion is applied. Whatever controls life's gateways exercises authority, command, and control over you, whether you, the enemy, or God. Unfortunately, those who have inadvertently given demonic forces legal access and rights to sit in those gateways can dominate, but you must take back the authority by violent force. *The kingdom of heaven suffers violence, and violent men take it by force* (Matthew 11:12b).

Through our bodies, we perceive the physical world using the five senses — the senses of sight, hearing, taste, smell, and touch, the gateways of the body. And what happens in the body will affect the soul. For instance, something you see can trigger an ungodly thought or a song you hear that initiates an emotion. There are five gates into your soul, and any one of those gates can produce something that affects you spiritually or can affect you in an ungodly way, which becomes a gateway for the enemy of your soul. *The lamp of the body is the eye. If therefore your eye is good, your whole body will be full of light. But if your eye is bad, your whole body will be full of darkness. If, therefore, the light in you is darkness, how great is that darkness?* (Matthew 6:22, 23).

The gateway to the soul is the mind, will, and emotions, and whatever is in control determines their mood, lust, love, compassion, or desires. Letting your sinful nature control your mind leads to spiritual death. *The mind governed by the flesh is hostile to God; it does not submit to God's law, nor can it do so* (Romans 8:7). The soul's gateway can also be affected by demons or the deceitful plots of the enemy if you listen, as it was with Adam and Eve. So, the battle not against flesh and blood. *Our struggle is not against flesh and blood, but against the rulers, against the authorities, against the powers of this dark world, and against the spiritual forces of evil in the heavenly realms* (Ephesians 6:12). Watchman Nee says, "The soul stands between the spirit and the body, binding these two together. The work of the soul is to keep these two in their proper order so that they may not lose their right relationship."[130]

The gateways of the spirit are doors to the supernatural world and the presence of God. The Holy Spirit has accessed through the gate into the human spirit, and the Spirit within us fortifies our soul, giving us strength to obey God's will and resist sin. The Spirit inclines our hearts towards God's desires and brings revelation while quickening our spirit, creating a passion for the spiritual realm and the presence of God.

Watchman Nee says that the body is like the outer court, occupying an external position with its life visible to all. Here man ought to obey every commandment of God. The soul resembles the Holy Place, for it is amply enlightened with many rational thoughts and precepts, much knowledge and understanding concerning the things in the conceptual and material world. The spirit is like the Holy of Holies. It is the most sacred spot, where the four corners of the temple converge and rest. However, before the fall of man, the soul, despite its many activities, was governed by the spirit. And this is the order God still wants: first the spirit, then the soul, and lastly, the body.[131]

## STORIES OF GATES AND ALTARS

I remember this story when I was in Tulsa to minister at a church called Rivergate, which is interesting. While in the hotel room, I was getting ready for my friend to pick me up for dinner. As I waited, I was praying the spirit when suddenly the phone in my hotel room started ringing. I thought that was very strange, but assumed the pastor was waiting for me in the lobby. But that seemed weird also because he could have sent me a text message. I picked up the phone expecting to hear the pastor's voice saying, "Charlie, we're ready for you to come downstairs to head for supper."

But that's not what happened. After saying hello, a witch was on the other end of the phone, speaking in demonic tongues and hurling curses at me. She told me that she knew I was in town for the meeting and wouldn't tell me her title but supposedly was one of the top witches. Then she said, "I felt the moment I knew you were here; I would come to your meeting tonight to kill you."

I burst out laughing over the phone, and then I said, "You don't have the power to kill me because I have dealt with higher Celtic witches and warlocks than you." Then I told her that she was a North American witch and there was nothing like her that I had dealt with before. I could tell that I was talking in a demonic tongue, so I began mocking her, letting her know that the witches in the States are nothing to be compared to real witches in Africa. And I followed that up, saying, "You wouldn't even be eligible for ordination as a witch, and your witchcraft is kindergarten compared to the things I faced before."

Continuing to mock her, I said that the witchcraft in Africa is strong but what I dealt with in Southeast Asia is superior to what she might do. Ridiculing her, I said, "If you are so powerful, you could have projected yourself into my bedroom instead of calling me on the phone, you vile devil. You are not going to kill me. I'm going to pray for God's mercy to be upon you. If you don't repent, then every curse you spoke over me will return on you, and you will be dead before the end of the week."

After ending that conversation, I called the front desk and asked them why they put that call through to me, and they responded by saying a call never went through to you. I ended the call by saying a devil was on the other end saying horrible things. It is important to understand and be sensitive to the demonic realm and bravely confront them and deliver them or drive them away, as Jesus and Paul did.

## IMMIGRATION POSTS, SPIRITUAL VISAS, AND EMBASSIES

As there are natural gates, spiritual gates are like an immigration place allowing access depending on acceptance. Immigration spaces in the spirit realm have ports of entry like one entering other nations. These posts are spiritual gates to the spiritual realms, checkpoints determining who may enter.

Some gates represent embassies. That's why I call it spirit embassy. You are not meant to be a spectator but a participant in a supernatural exchange. And there are gates in the spirit realm where there are embassies, and there can be timestamps on those places where God has called you to enter a nation. When God grants access by a spiritual visa, you have access to the world. As ambassadors in God's embassy, we become the voice to the world. As God called Paul, so He will call you into your special place to speak. *Then God said to me, "Depart, for I will send you far from here to the Gentiles"* (Acts 22:21).

As it is in the earthly realm, it is in the spiritual realm, as Paul declared: *Blessed to be the God and Father of our Lord Jesus Christ, who has blessed us with all spiritual blessing in having places in Christ* (Ephesians 1:3).

Now take the heavenly places out and call it heavenly embassies, in Christ. So, there are rooms, heavenly embassies, spaces in the realm of the spirit. There are gates that you go through that are spiritual places that when you go, you have access through Christ, but you have to go in Christ.

To enter another country, you need a visa to visit that country, or you have to become an ambassador who abides there with national authority, and so it is in the spirit realm. Nehemiah is the first to mention in the Bible about needing a visa. *Furthermore, I said to the king, "If it pleases the king, let letters be given to me for the governors of the region beyond the River, that they must permit me to pass through till I come to Judah, and a letter to Asaph the keeper of the king's forest, that he must give me timber to make beams for the gates of the citadel which pertains to the temple, for the city wall, and for the house that I will occupy." And the king granted them to me according to the good hand of my God upon me* (Nehemiah 2: 7, 8).

Your physical passport may state that you are American, German, French, or Japanese, but you cannot access the spiritual realm unless you have a heavenly passport. As God's ambassadors, we enter the world to advance God's kingdom. Jesus told us that we are not of this physical world, but belong to the spiritual world (John 15:17).

God wants you to carve out space and make it home as if you would go to a foreign nation. When Americans step on the grounds of a foreign country, then they are no longer in America. As an ambassador of Christ, when you go to a foreign land, you bring the kingdom of God with you, and you have access to that spiritual embassy where no weapons formed against you will prosper. Spiritual blessings await you in those heavenly embassy gates where decision-making occurs.

## ALTARS, GATES, AND THRONES

Thrones, gates, and altars are symbols of legal authority over a kingdom. Thrones stand over altars and gates, and the one who sits upon the throne has the actual power behind the altar, where strongholds must be eliminated. We have to destroy the demonic throne and the authority behind the altar. Thrones are set up through decrees and ordinances, so our decisions are important and cannot be taken lightly.

We live in a world of thrones with unseen altars seeking to destroy the spiritual foundations God intended, but our battle is not against flesh and blood. *Because to us the wrestling is not against blood and flesh, but against the rulers, against the authorities, against the cosmic powers of this darkness, against the spiritual forces of evil in the heavenly realms* (Ephesians 6:12, Berean Literal Bible).

Two altars were used in the tabernacle service: the brazen altar or altar of burnt offering, which stood inside the court at the gate, and the golden altar or altar of incense, which stood in the Holy Place immediately in front of the veil. The fire that consumed the sacrifice on the brazen altar was the same fire brought to the golden altar to cause the sweet perfume of the incense to ascend to Jehovah. *Then he made the altar of incense of acacia wood: a cubit long and a cubit wide, square, and two cubits high; its horns were of one piece with it. You shall also set the altar of gold for the incense before the ark of the Testimony and put up the screen for the door of the tabernacle* (Exodus 40:5, 6, emphasis added).

The book of the covenant in Exodus is related to the Jewish people's tabernacle, temple, and worship practices. God commanded these covenant codes to the people of God as ways to obey and honor Him. One of the covenant codes is instruction on building altars.[132] The rules for the building of altars must have been old and accepted and are consistent with the construction of the altar of the tabernacle court. *You shall make an altar of earth for Me, and you shall sacrifice on it your burnt offerings and your peace offerings, your sheep and your oxen; in every place where I cause My name to be remembered, I will come to you and bless you. And if you make an altar of stone for Me, you shall not build it of cut stones, for if you wield your chisel on it, you will profane it* (Exodus 20:24, 25, NASB, emphasis added).

But there comes a time when the abominable idols must be turned down. So, there was a time in Israel's story when the Spirit of God came upon Azariah, the son of Oded, and he went out to meet King Asa with the prophecy of Oded leading to restoring the altar. *And when Asa heard these words and the prophecy of Oded the prophet, he took courage, and removed the abominable idols from all the land of Judah and Benjamin and from the cities which he had taken in the mountains of Ephraim; and he restored the altar of the LORD that was before the vestibule of the LORD* (2 Chronicles 15:8, emphasis added).

Instances arise when religious leaders must weep at the altar when it appears God has forsaken them. *Let the priests, who minister to the LORD, Weep between the porch and the altar; Let them say, "Spare Your people, O LORD, and do not give Your heritage to reproach, That the nations should rule over them. Why should they say among the peoples, 'Where is their God?'"* (Joel 2:17).

Occasionally those of wisdom must take their stand, and at this particular time, they were on the high mountain crying at the gates. *She takes her stand on the top of the high hill, Beside the way, where the paths meet. She cries out by the gates, at the entry of the city, At the entrance of the doors* (Proverbs 8:2-3, emphasis added).

In Revelation 21, there are gates on high mountains with the angels present, and the gates have names. *She had a great and high wall with twelve gates, and twelve angels at the gates, and names written on them, which are the names of the twelve tribes of the children of Israel* (Revelation 21:12, emphasis added).

When you enjoy favor with the king, the ungodly ones will seek to destroy you, so what do you do? You sit at the king's gate who is on his throne, and he will give you favor. *In those days, while Mordecai sat within the king's gate, two of the king's eunuchs, Bigthan and Teresh, doorkeepers, became furious and sought to lay hands on King Ahasuerus. So, the matter became known to Mordecai, who told Queen Esther, and Esther informed the king in Mordecai's name. And when an inquiry was made into the matter, it was confirmed, and both were hanged on a gallows, and it was written in the book of the chronicles in the presence of the king* (Esther 2:21-23, emphasis added).

There are times when the life of a prophet is not too exciting. Religious people can be a serious frustration. Jeremiah's prophetic words created a bombardment of retaliation from the religious leaders and prophets. So, the religious group dared to sit at *the gate of the Lord*, seeking to kill the prophet.

> *So, the priests and the prophets and all the people heard Jeremiah speaking these words in the house of the Lord; Why have you prophesied in the name of the Lord, saying, 'This house shall be like Shiloh, and this city shall be desolate, without an inhabitant?" And all the people were gathered against Jeremiah in the house of the Lord. The officials of Judah heard these things; they came up from the king's house to the house of the Lord and sat in the entrance of the New Gate of the Lord's house* (Jeremiah 26:7, 9, 10, emphasis added).

But there are times when the prince and people are on your side. So, the princes and all the people said to the priests and the prophets, *"This man does not deserve to die. For he has spoken to us in the name of the Lord our God"* (Jeremiah 26:16).

The crown of pride exists in the soul of pompous arrogance but is dissimilar to the crown of glory where the Lord reigns with His army as King and shall guard and defend the remnant of His people. *The crown of pride, the drunkards of Ephraim, Will be trampled underfoot; In that day the Lord of hosts will be For a crown of glory and a diadem of beauty To the remnant of His people, For a spirit of justice to him who sits in judgment, And for strength to those who turn back the battle at the gate* (Isaiah 28:5, 6, emphasis added).

Those who sat upon the bench of justice were propelled back—turning the battle at the gate—they repelled their foes from their gates but drove out the gates of their cities. And the messenger said to David, *"Surely the men prevailed against us and came out to us in the field; then we drove them back as far as the entrance of the gate"* (2 Samuel 11:23, emphasis added).

The Hebrew *Qadash* means to be treated as holy, honor, hallow, observed as sacred, and set apart.[133] When God told them to **honor the Sabbath,** He told them to *consider the rest sacred.* "The term 'Sabbath' is derived from the Hebrew verb 'to rest or cease from work.'"[134] Obviously, and tragically, Judah and Jerusalem did not return to the Sabbath at Jeremiah's word, and they faced the severe judgment of God by burning the gates.

> *Say to all the people, "Listen to this message from the LORD, you kings of Judah and all you people of Judah and everyone living in Jerusalem. This is what the LORD says: Listen to my warning! Stop carrying on your trade at Jerusalem's gates on the Sabbath day. Do not do your work on the Sabbath but make it a holy day. I gave this command to your ancestors. But if you do not listen to me and refuse to keep the Sabbath holy, and if on the Sabbath day you*

*bring loads of merchandise through the gates of Jerusalem just as on other days, then I will set fire to these gates. The fire will spread to the palaces, and no one will be able to put out the roaring flames" (Jeremiah 17:20-22, 27).*

## JOB AT THE CITY GATES

*As I was in the prime of my days, When the friendship of God was over my tent; When the Almighty was yet with me, and my children were around me; When my steps were bathed in butter, And the rock poured out for me streams of oil! When I went out to the gate of the city, When I took my seat in the square, The young men saw me and hid themselves, And the old men arose and stood. The princes stopped talking and put their hands on their mouths; The voice of the nobles was hushed, and their tongue stuck to their palate. For when the ear heard, it called me blessed, and when the eye saw, it gave witness of me (Job 29:4-7, NASB).*

Exactly when the book of Job was written remains something of a mystery, but there is no doubt it is the oldest book in the Bible. Job is over four hundred years older than Genesis, meaning that Job is the sole drama in the Bible and the oldest book by far, making it extremely fascinating. While the themes found in Job are common across the ancient world, the language is not. Job is written in Hebrew, which is even older than the ancient Hebrew that makes up most of the Old Testament.

The language used in Job is not even usually referred to as ancient Hebrew. Instead, it is called "Paleo-Hebrew." The Paleo-Hebrew script is found in Canaanite inscriptions from biblical Israel and Judah. It is considered the script used to record the original texts of the Hebrew Bible due to its similarity to the Samaritan script, as the Talmud stated that the Samaritans still used the Hebrew ancient scripts.

The book also contains Syriac and Arabic expressions that point to a period between 1900 and 1700 B.C. when the Semitic tribes had not yet separated into speaking separate Syriac, Hebrew, and Arabic dialects. Instead, they still shared a common language.[135]

These verses give us a historical perspective on the ancient language spoken by Job. We know that Job is the oldest book in the Bible and that the elders sat at the gates, but there is a diversity of spiritual perception of ancient gates. A spiritual sense was also attached to the use of "gate." Righteous worshippers were invited to enter or come into Yahweh's gates with thanksgiving (Psalm 100:4). The temple was seen as Yahweh's abode, enthroned among His covenant people. The invitation to enter the gates of Yahweh's dwelling would suggest that you will have gained access to Him (Psalm 118:19-20).

The city gate held an important social and administrative role of the elders who sat at the gate to decide cases in the culture of ancient cities. Instructional and prophetic messages were also delivered at the city gates in ancient Israelite society.[136]

It is all true in scriptures concerning the city gates, but in this case, I think Job's words concerning the city's gate have a profound spiritual connotation based upon his use of language. Job started the dialogue—the friendship of God was over my tent—using the language of the Tent of Meeting and the secret place of Yahweh. And the flame over his head, the oil and the butter indicate more than a city gate; it was personal.

Flame over his head, which is the fire of the Holy Spirit—*When the Lord has washed away the filth of the daughters of Zion and purged the bloodshed of Jerusalem from her midst, by the spirit of judgment and the spirit of burning* (Isaiah 4:4). In that secret space, you see what others don't see. The fire over Job empowered him to make spiritual judgments that burn away the waste.

Bathed in butter—In Job 20:17, he says, *He shall not see the rivers, the floods, the brooks of honey and butter.* You shall not see—describes something spiritually hidden. But things spiritually hidden are revealed by God. *For nothing is hidden that will not be made manifest, nor is anything secret that will not be known and come to light* (Luke 8:17).

*He reveals deep and hidden things; he knows what is in the darkness, and the light dwells with him* (Daniel 2:22). The secret knowledge of God's word (butter) and His law (honey) shall he study (eat) that he knows to refuse evil and choose good. *Butter and honey shall he eat that he may know to refuse the evil and choose the good* (Isaiah 7:15).

Streams of oil—the metaphor of oil—the visible and tangible liquid poured upon and absorbed by a human being—relates to the invisible presence and action of the Holy Spirit. And the biblical associations of oil with light in oil lamps reflect the Spirit's work to reveal and illuminate God and His word.

When Job and other gifted ones live in the spirit and sit at the gates, decision-making occurs in the spirit realm. Gates are where transactions are seen, like Job and other judges in the Bible. Besides being part of a city's protection against invaders, city gates were the central activity in biblical times. Important business transactions were made at the city gates, the court was convened, and public announcements were heralded. Accordingly, it is natural that the Bible frequently speaks of "sitting in the gate" or of the activities at the gate.

Abraham engaged in an exemplary negotiation to buy a burial plot when Sarah died. He conducted the negotiations openly and honestly in the presence of witnesses, taking due care of the needs of both himself and the seller. Abraham initiated the request for a real estate transaction. The local Hittites freely offered a choice tomb. Abraham balks, asking them to contact a certain owner of a field with a cave appropriate for a burial site so that he could buy it for the "full price." Ephron, the owner, overheard the request and offered the field as a gift.

> *Now Ephron dwelt among the sons of Heth; and Ephron the Hittite answered Abraham in the presence of the sons of Heth, all who <u>entered at the gate of his city</u>, saying, "No, my lord, hear me: I give you the field and the cave that is in it; I give it to you in the presence of the sons of my people. I will give it to you. Bury your dead!" Then Abraham bowed himself down before the people of the land, and he spoke to Ephron in the hearing of the people of the land, saying, "If*

*you give it, please hear me. I will give you money for the field; take it from me, and I will bury my dead there." And Ephron answered Abraham, saying to him, "My lord, listen to me; the land is worth four hundred shekels of silver. What is that between you and me? So, bury your dead." And Abraham listened to Ephron; and Abraham weighed out the silver for Ephron which he had named in the hearing of the sons of Heth, four hundred shekels of silver, the currency of the merchants.... So, the field and the cave in it were deeded to Abraham by the sons of Heth as property for a burial place (Genesis 23:10-16, 20, emphasis added).*

The story of Ruth and Boaz is another story of negotiating a transaction at the city gates to assist Naomi and Ruth. *Now Boaz went up to the gate and sat down there, and behold, the close relative of whom Boaz had spoken came by. So, Boaz said, "Come aside, friend, sit down here." So, he came aside and sat down* (Ruth 4:2). As was traditional, the city gate was where business took place and where the city's elders met to make decisions and act as judges. Elimelech's land was for sale, and the closest relative had the first right to buy it and thought it was a good deal until he heard more.

He realized that whoever bought it would be obliged by custom to take Ruth the Moabitess as wife to beget a son for the dead husband. Learning of this, he declined and granted Boaz permission to take his place, at which Boaz announced to the elders that he would be purchasing Elimelech's land and marrying Ruth to bear sons to perpetuate their names. And to confirm the deal, one man took off his sandal and gave it to the other, which was a confirmation in Israel (Ruth 4:7).

## CHAPTER SIX

# GATES, DOMINIONS, AND CHANGING ATMOSPHERES

*Still round the corner, there may wait*
*A new road or a secret gate,*
*Through shadows to the edge of night,*
*Until the stars are all alight*
*(J. R. Tolkien's Lord of the Rings)*[137]

Tolkien made it clear that Lord of the Rings was not an allegory, but he implanted symbols using biblical concepts underlying the narrative, including the battle of good versus evil, the triumph of humility over pride, and the activity of grace, as seen with Frodo's pity toward Gollum. The work includes the themes of death and immortality, mercy and compassion, resurrection, salvation, repentance, self-sacrifice, free will, justice, fellowship, authority, and healing.

Lord of the Rings focuses on middle-earth, mirroring the Genesis story in Eden. In the book, the elves articulate the creation story in which the "One," who represents God, designs the sounds of creation. God's intention comes with a powerful and alluring gift. This gift is free will. At the story's beginning, the free will he creates is embodied by rings he gives to his creation. Like the Trees of Good and Evil, the rings bring great temptation for those in their particular worlds, and Melchor possessed the ring but fell, and his name was changed.

This opening corresponds to the account of Lucifer. Lucifer, being at the height of the angelic choir, experienced a dramatic and deadly fall. While Lord of the Rings shows the physical destruction caused by the ring, the Christian story identifies the immaterial destruction of the soul by sin. Within the Lord of the Rings narrative, there are many gates. Some lead to dangerous places, and others are places of protection from the evil ones in Middle Earth. There was the Black Gate, the Great Gate, the Forest Gate, the East Gate, and the Front Gate. The Black Gate was the fortified gate into hell. The Front Gate was the place of resistance against the evil ones in Lord of the Ring. And many battles were won, and Gandalf, the voice of angels, was a warrior angel with great wisdom to assist them in their world, as God sent His angels as messengers, providing information and support to God's people.

## PORTALS AND GATEWAYS

When considering how gates function, we understand how important it was for a city or community to possess its own gateways. If their enemy had possession, the enemy would be able to control every facet of their lives. Spiritual gates are passageways to enter or exit from destinations, like in the Lord of the Rings.

Doors are portals, an entrance into a different place. Like the doors in your home, each door leads you to other rooms with different purposes. The front door is the door of access and protection. The door into the dining room is a door of nourishment, and the door into the living room is the place of conversation and enjoying the presence of others. The bedroom is the place of rest and dreams. So, it is in the spiritual realm; the doors are portals into the supernatural realm that guides you to different places, gaining supernatural insight and unique prophetic intention.

*Blessed is the man who listens to me, watching daily at my gates, wait-*

*ing at my doorposts for whoever finds me finds life And obtains favor from the LORD* (Proverbs 8:34, 35). He who listens will be deeply enriched in the presence of God, but he who does not listen remains a fool and ignorant of God's heart and ways. *For God alone, my soul waits in silence* (Psalm 62:10). *He that has an ear let him hear what the Spirit says* (Revelation 3:22).

He who listens will learn. As a student sitting at the door to the classroom is eager to learn, the hungry soul will position themself at a place where wisdom is given and revelation unveiled.

God commands us to watch, wait, and search for Him at the gates, waiting for teachable moments in God's presence with opportunities to learn from God. And if you find Him, you find life and favor. Amos reiterates Solomon's words, *"Seek Me and live!"* (Amos 5:4).

In Psalm 78:23-25, *God opened the doors of heaven and fed the Hebrews in the desert the food of angels* (emphasis added). He commanded the clouds from above, opened the doors of heaven, and had rained down manna upon them to eat, and had given them of the corn of heaven, and man did eat the angels' food, meat to the full.

## DARK GATES OF SUPERNATURAL ACTIVITY

Before she was born again, my grandmother was involved in the occult, so I had not desire to enter certain rooms in her house. Even at a young age, I felt spiritually sensitive and could feel weird things, and although I couldn't see them, something wasn't right.

In late 1865, during the early days of the Reconstruction Era, the city founded the first Ku Klux Klan (KKK) by six Tennessee veterans of the Confederate Army. They established the KKK in Pulaski on December 25, 1865, creating a secret white society. The white insurgents were determined to maintain and fight secretly against the political advancement of freedmen and sympathetic whites. KKK members often attacked their victims at night to increase the intimidation with threats and assaults. Other incidents of racial violence against blacks also took place. The Pulaski riot was a race riot initiated against blacks in Pulaski in the winter of 1868 in Davidson County.[138]

The gates and altars of human sacrifice by lynching African Americans were instituted by demonic forces and acted on by racists who were possessed with anger and violent spirits.

There are places where the African Americans were lynched from trees creating a gate of oppression that influenced the town. As a young man, I remember my father did lots of prayer walks, and he and his friend would go to places to pray for healing and cleansing of the atmosphere.

I grew up on a Confederate army military base in Tennessee, filled with history there. My dad would go to different high places in the city to do spiritual mapping to identify territorial spirits. They would plead the blood of Jesus over these areas because they wanted to see revival break out in their towns. And a great move of God happened when I was a kid in Pulaski, Tennessee, and in Columbia, Tennessee.

They were releasing the presence of God in these specific places. Even in my home as a kid, I'd wake up at two or three o'clock in the morning with my dad praying in a certain part of our house, and you could feel the presence of God. The atmospheric conditions created and dispensed manifestations. It became obvious that the spiritual environment creates conditions for releasing spiritual manifestations. Prayer changes the atmosphere!

## TENT GATES AND PRAYER

I remember a man so enamored by the revelations he received that you could fill a room with the glory of God. As a result of glory manifestations, he set up a tent inside his home and said he would fill his tent with God's glory. But that was only the beginning because he decided once his room was filled, he would move to the street, and the tent was filled with God's glory. And then he passionately filled the whole city with God's glory. He would pray for hours in that little glory tent.

Then I started spreading it out into the neighborhood and praying every day, entering the realm of the Spirit. You fill the once empty space when you connect to the spirit realm. And prayer changed the atmosphere. Prayer is downright powerful, and when men and women pray, amazing things will happen.

Paul said that he prayed without ceasing. Smith Wigglesworth said that he never went thirty minutes without prayer. Watchman Nee said that our prayers lay down the tracks on which God's power can come. Like a mighty locomotive, His power is irresistible but cannot reach us without the rails of prayer.

Hannah was deeply distressed, and as she prayed, she wept bitterly (I Samuel 1:10, ESV). *God's wisdom is something mysterious that goes deep into the interior of his purposes* (I Corinthians 2:7, The Message Bible). Jesus often went into a private place to pray to strengthen Him in those troubling times. I encourage you to establish a space to pray dedicated to the glory of God so heaven can come down.

## GATES OF THE SOUL AND BODY

Consider your body as an allegory where it is a city with gates that watch over the entrances and exit to that city. The gates are our senses and soul through which things can enter, influencing you spiritually. In this story, you are the keeper of the gates by preventing what foods enter your body, what appears in your eye gates, and what pierces your hearing gate. The gatekeeper must be careful what enters the body and the soul, or you become physically sick or spiritually wounded by depression, lust, and deception.

But remember, you are not alone, for the Holy Spirit, the alongside one, is the spiritual gatekeeper who has entered your gate to open doors, empower you, bring conviction, guide you, and remind you of God's great love and purpose for your life. Remember that the spirit realm is anchored to the earthly realm, so the Holy Spirit is essential, but the Spirit needs us to accomplish things in the earthly realm.

And the devil and demons need a body to connect to the physical realm to accomplish what they want to achieve by creating their dark atmosphere. Thus, there is a war between the saints of God and demonic forces, but Yahweh supports us with His power and hosts of angels.

## HOUSE OF GOD, GATES OF HEAVEN

*And he was afraid and said, "How awesome is this place! This is none other than the house of God, and this is the gate of heaven"* (Genesis 28:17). It is the first time the "house of God" is used in the Bible and paired with the gate of heaven. As a point of access, the gate of heaven is the place where heaven enters the earthly realm, where God's presence, power, righteousness, and love come to establish His kingdom among us. So, it is the desire of those living in the earthly realm for God's **kingdom come and will be done, on earth as it is in heaven** (Matthew 6:10).

Obeying his father, Jacob left toward Haran but stopped for the night at a certain place in Canaan called Luz, where his grandfather Abraham built an altar and called on the name of the Lord (Genesis 12:8). Jacob picked up one of the stones from that place to use as a pillow, which that stone was probably from a ziggurat or other abandoned altars by the Canaanites. Because it was a fallen altar, Jacob didn't realize that spiritual activity existed in that place, and only by the dream did he know that he was on holy ground, a place of Abraham's altar. Jacob was not standing on common ground but sacred space, a place of interaction between heaven and earth, and Jacob slept at a gateway without knowing.

Where a spiritual portal exists, God attaches a special significance to that place, so they are aware of its existence with an awesome sense of fear and respect. Elizabeth Browning said, "Earth is crammed with heaven, and every bush is aflame with God But only those who see, take off their shoes."[139]

*Then Jacob rose early in the morning, took the stone he had put at his head, set it up as a pillar, and poured oil on top of it. And he called the name of that place Bethel, but the name of that city had been Luz previously* (Genesis 28:18, 19). As Jacob poured oil on the rock that was his pillow, he called that place Bethel, which means house of God, designating this as a gate that led to God's dwelling place since he had witnessed God's holy angels ascending and descending to the very throne of God.

Where people have gathered on the face of the earth, God placed gates determining its pre-appointed times. According to His wisdom, He set up the boundaries of their dwellings to entice people to seek the Lord and His anointing and enlightenment, to misstep Him like a blind man hoping to find Him, although He is never far from us.

> *And He has made from one blood every nation of men to dwell on all the face of the earth, and has determined their pre-appointed times and the boundaries of their dwellings, so that they should seek the Lord, in the hope that they might grope for Him and find Him, though He is not far from each one of us; for in Him we live and move and have our being (Acts 17:26-28).*

## OPENING THE GATES OF HEAVEN

*Jesus answered and said to him, "Because I said to you, 'I saw you under the fig tree,' do you believe? You will see greater things than these."; And He said to him, "Most assuredly, I say to you, hereafter you shall see heaven open, and the angels of God ascending and descending upon the Son of Man"* (John 1:5, 51). Though the young Nathaniel was overwhelmed by Jesus' prophetic gift, staring into his eyes, Jesus tells him something greater will come when heaven is open, "for you will see angels ascending and descending on God's son."

The open heavens are a theme throughout scriptures that declare God's heart to reveal the heavenly realm to those who are hungry and seek after Him. From that sacred realm in heaven, wherefrom heaven's view, God and the angels look down from heaven wondering who will seek God, but what they see is humans looking upward, longing to experience Yahweh. *The Lord looks down from heaven upon the children of men, to see if there are any who understand, who seek God* (Psalm 14:2).

The Hebrew *baq·q·šū* means to seek, to strive, to pursue, to search out, to seek with prayer, inquiry, and to please God.[140] And the Hebrew *panim* means face, presence, and attention.[141]

When someone seeks God, heaven's gate will open. *When You said, "Seek My face," my heart said to You, "I shall seek Your face, LORD"* (Psalm 27:8).

David, the prophetic poet, sensed by the Spirit God saying, "Seek My face!" As soon as those words dropped from heaven into his spirit, David's heart seriously considered that command and then spoke and said, "I will seek the Lord's face." Seeking the *Lord* means seeking His *presence*, meaning to desire access to God. To be before His *face* is to be in His *presence*.

Those called as brothers and sisters of the crucified One *have confidence to enter the holy place by the blood of Jesus, by a new and living way which He inaugurated for us through the veil, that is, through His flesh* (Hebrews 10:19, 20). Those who have intimate relationships with God will open gates into the heavenly realm.

After John was told to write what he prophetically saw in a book, he wrote those words in Revelation 2, 3. But, in chapter four, we read John's experience with the throne in heaven. *After these things, I looked, and behold, a door standing open in heaven. And the first voice which I heard was like a trumpet speaking with me, saying, "Come up here, and I will show you things which must take place after this." Immediately I was in the Spirit; and behold, a throne set in heaven, and One sat on the throne* (Revelation 4:1, 2).

Daniel 7:9-14 is an apocalyptic throne room scene. In the biblical and apocryphal narrative, the great throne room is common for the prophets in those apocalyptic stories. Isaiah has his inaugural vision of the Lord, "high and exalted, seated on his throne," surrounded by angelic creatures (Isaiah 6:1-5). Ezekiel's first vision describes the glory of God as a glowing, otherworldly man seated on a throne of lapis lazuli accompanied by strange "living creatures" (Ezekiel 1:25-28). In Enoch 1, he had several throne room scenes similar to Daniel: "And I looked and saw a lofty throne: its appearance was as crystal, and the wheels thereof as the shining sun, and there was the vision of cherubim. And from underneath the throne came streams of flaming fire so that I could not look thereon. And the Great Glory sat there on, and His raiment shone more brightly than the sun and was whiter than any snow" (Enoch 1:18; 20).[142]

> *Now I saw heaven opened, and behold, a white horse. And He who sat on him was called Faithful and True, and in righteousness, He judges and makes war (Revelation 19:11).*

Angels perform a critical role in the heavenly realm, protecting the saints of God, unveiling life on the other side of the veil between heaven and earth, and being Yahweh's messengers and warriors. *Then the voice which I heard from heaven spoke to me again and said, "Go, take the little book which is open in the hand of the angel who stands on the sea and on the earth." So, I went to the angel and said to him, "Give me the little book." And he said to me, "Take and eat it; and it will make your stomach bitter, but it will be as sweet as honey in your mouth"* (Revelation 10:8, 9).

In Revelation 21, John was carried away in the Spirit to a great and high mountain and was shown the great city, maybe like Paul's transport to the third heaven. John saw *the holy Jerusalem descending out of heaven from God, having the glory of God. Her light was like a most precious stone, like a jasper stone, clear as crystal. Also, she had a great and high wall with twelve gates, and twelve angels at the gates, and names written on them, which are the names of the twelve tribes of the children of Israel* (Revelation 21:10-12). In John's spiritual journey, he encounters heaven's gate, and within were gates and angels: twelve high gates and twelve angels that protect the heavenly realm.

The greatest unveiling of the open heavens ensued at Jesus' baptism. Present at His baptism were manifestations of God and the Spirit, joining the three in one. *When He had been baptized, Jesus came up immediately from the water, and behold, the heavens were opened to Him, and He saw the Spirit of God descending like a dove and alighting upon Him. And suddenly, a voice came from heaven, saying, "This is My beloved Son, in whom I am well pleased"* (Matthew 3:16, 17 ).

The poet and the prophet both are crying out with passionate desire that the heavens come down, deliverance for some, and salvation for others, and they know that help comes from the heavenly realm. *Bow down Your heavens, O Lord, and come down; Touch the mountains, and they shall smoke. Flash forth lightning and scatter them; Shoot out Your arrows and destroy them. Stretch out Your hand from above; Rescue me and deliver me out of great waters* (Psalm 144:5-7). *Rain down, you heavens, from above, and let the skies pour down righteousness; Let the earth open, let them bring forth salvation, And let righteousness spring up together. I, the Lord, have created it* (Isaiah 45:8).

The captive Jews in Babylon were probably without prophets or visions from God, which meant they had not received any divine guidance, feeling alone and hopeless. But then, God chose a prophet in their captivity and revealed himself by an extraordinary vision, as he had done to Isaiah in chapter six, Jeremiah in chapter one, and Abraham, as mentioned in Acts 7:2. Ezekiel was the chosen prophet who would speak God's word, and at his inauguration, the heavens were opened in a dramatic display.

While sitting by the River Chebar, the heavenly demonstration begins with a mighty whirlwind from the north, a cloud of raging fire, a brightness radiating with color, and the majestic climax with the four living creatures and the supernatural wheels. *Now it came to pass in the thirtieth year, in the fourth month, on the fifth day of the month, as I was among the captives by the River Chebar, that the heavens were opened, and I saw visions of God* (Ezekiel 1:1).

## INVADING THE GATES OF HEAVEN
## WITH RADICAL PRAYER

Isaiah cried out to Yahweh to tear open the heavens and show Himself to the world that the world might see Him as Isaiah saw Him! *Oh, that You would rend the heavens! That You would come down! That the mountains might shake at Your presence* (Isaiah 64:1). Unwrapping these words, you can feel the intensity of desire in Isaiah's heart. Isaiah's raging desire is seen in his word "Oh," which the Hebrew *lu* means if only, please, oh.[143] And the Hebrew *qâra* means to tear away, to rend, to splint asunder, to make wide.[144] With the intensity of prayer, Isaiah pleaded, "If only You would split the heavens wide open and shake the mountains with God's presence."

In his oft-used words, Augustine expressed his anxious profound desire to uncover a place in God. "For thou has made us for thyself, and our hearts are restless until they find their rest in thee." The longing heart seeks to find a place in God wherein His presence brings favor to our radical praying for cultural change. Feeling the weight of a degrading culture and a needy world should lead us to the place of deep-seated drastic prayer. In those moments, God will come down and rock the world.

One of the most effective prayers in the Bible is what happened in the upper room after Jesus' resurrection. *After they prayed, the place where they were meeting was shaken. And they were all filled with the Holy Spirit and spoke the word of God boldly* (Acts 4:31).

**Hezekiah's prayer is one of the noblest but most drastic prayers for deliverance because he was at the razor's edge.** *O Lord of hosts, God of Israel, enthroned above the cherubim, you are the God, you alone, of all the kingdoms of the earth; you have made heaven and earth. Incline your ear, O Lord, and hear; open your eyes, O Lord, and see; and hear all the words of Sennacherib, which he has sent to mock the living God* (Isaiah 37:16, 17).

So, Isaiah heard Hezekiah's prayer and received a prophetic response from the Lord to the king. *Thus says the Lord, the God of Israel: Because you have prayed to me concerning Sennacherib king of Assyria, this is the word that the Lord has spoken concerning him* (Isaiah 37:21). So, the angel of the Lord descended upon Israel's enemies and trounced 185,000 in the camp of the Assyrians (Isaiah 37:36).

In 2 Chronicles 7, the shekinah glory came down because of Solomon's prayer. God answers prayer. *Now when Solomon had finished praying, fire came down from heaven and consumed the burnt offering and the sacrifices, and the glory of the LORD filled the house* (2 Chronicles 7:1). *Then the Lord heard Solomon's prayer saying, "I have heard your prayer, and have chosen this place for Myself as a house of sacrifice"* (2 Chronicles 7:12).

It was one man's prayer, but now God offers the people a challenge and if they respond, look what will happen if people pray. *If My people who are called by My name will humble themselves, pray and seek My face, and turn from their wicked ways, I will hear from heaven and forgive their sin and* <u>*heal their land*</u> (2 Chronicles 7:14, emphasis added).

Prayer opens God's eyes. He pays attention to the places and people praying with fervor. *Now my eyes will be open, and My ears attentive to prayer made in this place* (2 Chronicles 7:15). So, notice how God comes down in the midst of those who pray regularly and passionately.

## GATES OF PRAYER, THE VEHICLE OF REVIVAL

The great spiritual revivals of history also testify to the central place of prayer in advancing God's purposes and spreading the gospel worldwide. For example, Evan Roberts, the central character of the 1904 Welsh Revival, is said to have prayed every day for thirteen years leading up to the event. The past president of the Evangelical Theological Society, Sam Storms, writes:

"If asked of me why the fire of God fell on Wales, the answer is simple: Fire falls where it is likely to catch and spread. As one has said, 'Wales provided the necessary tinder.' Thousands of believers are unknown to each other, in small towns and villages and great cities, crying to God, day after day, for the fire of God to fall. It was not merely a 'little talk with Jesus,' but daily, agonizing intercession.... One thing is clear: the revival was not the product of someone's personality or another person's preaching or anyone's planning, but God's gracious response to the prayers of his people!"[45]

One could also point to William J. Seymour, a Pentecostal preacher, who is said to have prayed seven hours a day for months leading up to the Azusa Street Revival in Los Angeles (1906-1915).

John Hyde, better known as "Praying Hyde," grew up in an atmosphere of prayer and eventually went to India as a missionary. In deepest India, he sought the Lord, and the strength of meeting his Master face to face prepared him for missionary service. Hyde often spent thirty days and nights in prayer and often was on his knees in deep intercession for thirty-six hours at a time. His work in the villages was so successful that he led four to ten people to Christ each day for years.[146] Prayer changes the atmosphere and shifts things, causing revolution for God's purposes.

I know from experience, having been there, the nation of Nigeria is in full-blown revival. When I went to Africa and saw how the Africans prayed, I told the Lord I needed their passion. I wanted that passion. I want that raw fire to become my normal life.

In the Moravian community of Herrnhut in Saxony, in 1727, commenced an around-the-clock "prayer watch" that continued nonstop for over a hundred years. By 1791, 65 years after the commencement of that prayer vigil, the small Moravian community had sent three hundred missionaries to the ends of the earth. The prayer vigil by Zinzendorf and the Moravian community sensitized them to attempt the unheard-of mission to reach others for Christ.

The Moravians' hearts began to burn with the things that were on the heart of God. Their hearts began to burn for the unreached peoples of the world. Over fifteen years, this small group of three hundred Moravians sent out seventy missionaries who went and lived among unreached people groups, learned their language and culture, then told them about Jesus Christ. One of the churches that the Moravians started sent out two hundred missionaries. One of the Moravian missionary teams voluntarily sold themselves into slavery to identify with enslaved people and share the gospel with them. They were so filled with the spirit of missions, which is the spirit of Christ's self-sacrificing love. The Moravian Brethren, led by Zinzendorf, were responsible for some of the most inspiring and sacrificial stories of missions' history. The Moravians are credited with starting the modern missionary movement.[147]

Your life without God will be natural and predictable; it won't be supernatural. Dr. Peter Wagner said, "The tragedy of America is that we can grow our churches without God. We don't know what to do when God shows up."

## THE KOREAN, AMERICAN, AND GREAT REVIVALS

Dr. David Yonggi Cho is one the greatest examples of the power of prayer. He is the pastor of Oido Full Gospel Church in Seoul, Korea. With its 750,000 members, it is the world's largest church. Every month, as many as 700 new converts are saved from Buddhism, secularism, and nominal Christian backgrounds. How could a church grow this large? Is it possible for other countries to have this kind of revival? Dr. Cho is convinced that renewal is possible anywhere people dedicate themselves to prayer.

Here are his words: "I believe in revival and renewal. It has been historically true that prayer has been the key to every revival in the history of Christianity. Before the church was born on the Day of Pentecost, Luke wrote, 'And [the disciples] were continually in the temple, praising and blessing God' (Luke 24:53). In the Book of Acts, Luke further amplifies what the disciples were doing: 'These all continued with one accord in prayer and supplication' (Acts 1:14). The church was born when the Holy Spirit descended during a time of concentrated prayer. Before the missionary era of the church began, the Holy Spirit revealed to the leaders gathered in Antioch that they should send Barnabas and Saul. Yet, the Holy Spirit only spoke after they had fasted and prayed."[148]

In 1991, after a season of intense prayer and fasting, a prophetic vision began to unfold before my eyes. God began to speak to me about a sweeping revival that would finally come to the United States, a nation that seemed to have been bypassed as God's Spirit flowed throughout other parts. At the Holy Spirit's prompting, I pulled out a map of America and allowed the Spirit to guide my hand to the area where this revival would break out. My finger rested on Pensacola, a Florida panhandle city hardly associated with spiritual fervor. The city was known to the homosexual community as the "gay Riviera."

On that night in 1991, I believed I had heard the voice of the Lord loud and clear: "I am going to send revival to the seaside city of Pensacola, and it will spread like a fire until all of America has been consumed by it." Word spread across the country about the coming revival. In no time, it reached the ears of John Kilpatrick, pastor of Brownsville Assembly of God in Pensacola. And here is his story.[149]

Years earlier, Pastor Kilpatrick had spent an extended time in prayer about the direction of the church's Sunday night services. The Lord prompted him to turn to Matthew 21:13, which reads, "My house shall be called a house of prayer" (NKJV). In 1988, Pastor Kilpatrick shifted the focus of his life to prayer. That began a special and intimate journey with God, as the Lord taught John Kilpatrick deeper and deeper lessons about the nature of prayer. He began to incorporate fasting into his prayer routine, further deepening the well of wisdom God was forming in his spirit. xi-xii

Once he heard of Cho's prophecy, he and the leadership of Brownsville Assembly set aside Sunday nights exclusively for prayer for revival. For three years, they prayed. They prayed for the lost ones, political leaders, church leaders, denominational leaders, and school officials. Brownsville's road to revival was under construction. No one saw it coming. No one predicted the day and the hour. No one even suspected that the Father would come on the most obvious day of all—Father's Day. But nothing laid the foundation for revival as prayer did.[150]

Physically and emotionally drained, he called on Stephen Hill, a colleague in the Assemblies of God and a longtime friend, to preach at the evening service on Father's Day, June 18. The night before, Kilpatrick met with Steve and told him how grieved he was that many people had left the church because of his revival preaching.

At the same moment, Kilpatrick felt the sensation of wind blowing in the sanctuary. One person after another fell to the floor as Hill prayed for them. Others wept, and some shook violently. Hill prayed a simple prayer for Kilpatrick as he stood on the stage. "More, Lord," he said—and the pastor fell to the floor, where he lay for almost four hours. Kilpatrick would be virtually useless to anyone but God Himself for the next forty-eight hours. As the pastor lay on the floor, he felt a heavenly glory resting on him like a heavy blanket. God's presence was tangible at last.[151]

## GATES OF THE EARTH

*The promised land* is a term designating a region of the world that God promised as a heritage to His people, Israel. On_that day, Yahweh made a covenant with Abram saying, *"To your offspring, I will give this land, from the river of Egypt to the great river, the Euphrates river, the land of the Kenites, the Kenizzites, the Kadmonites, the Hittites, the Perizzites, the Rephaim"* (Genesis 15:18-20, LEB, emphasis added).

The promised land was an endowment from earth's Creator to a specific people group, the children of Israel, in which they established their nation. Israel acquired the land but only through God's guidance and His miraculous intervention in history. *For they did not gain possession of the land by their own sword, nor did their own arm save them; But it was Your right hand, your arm, and the light of Your countenance, because You favored them* (Psalm 44:3, emphasis added).

When Israel was ready to take the land, hundreds of years after Abraham, it was inhabited by pagan nations: Canaanites, Amorites, Hittites, Perizzites, Hivites, and Jebusites. When it was time for the Israelites to inherit the promised land, God chose and developed Moses to bring His people out of slavery in Egypt and used Joshua to lead a military conquest of Canaan. And so, it is with us, we must take back the land that demonic forces sought to make it their unholy space, but by the power of God, the earth becomes ours for God's glory. Psalm 48 is a worship song, declaring the greatness of God, rejoicing over the city of God, and honoring the wonder of Mount Zion, the place of worship and nobility. God reserved the land for His unique purposes. *Great is the Lord, and greatly to be praised in the city of our God, in His holy mountain. Beautiful in elevation, the joy of the whole earth, is Mount Zion on the sides of the north, the city of the great King* (Psalm 48:1, 2, emphasis added).

In the typical prophetic allegory, God says that "when I hear the voice of the heavens and earth, I will answer the urgency of revival and renewal for the land is dry and cries out to the heavens to answer," which only the Lord can do. *"It shall come to pass in that day that I will answer,"* says the Lord; *"I will answer the heavens, and they shall answer the earth. The earth shall answer with grain, with new wine, and with oil; They shall answer Jezreel. Then I will sow her for Myself in the earth, And I will have mercy on her who had not obtained mercy; Then I will say to those who were not My people, 'You are My people!' And they shall say, 'You are my God!'"* (Hosea 2:21-24, emphasis added).

Heaven pleads with Jehovah, the earth pleads with heaven, and the soil's product pleads with the earth. To all these prayers, the answer is promised. So, Jehovah answers the heavens with the gifts of dew and rain, answering the cravings of the earth, the corn, wine, and oil. It is a beautiful picture of the harmony between the physical and the spiritual spheres.

The corn, vines, and olive trees represent earth's request and heaven's answer of moisture that they may grow, increase, and bring forth fruit. And the prophetic implications are the fruits and graces of God nourished by the Spirit and the source of the word that perpetuates encouragement and enlightenment that God's people will grow in spirit and truth.

God calls Israel "Jezreel," closing this prophecy. The name "Jezreel" combines the memory of the former punishment, being scattered among the nations, and the future mercy. But God turned His chastisement into mercy to those who believed in Him. Now He changes the word's meaning into, "God shall sow."[152] *And they shall hear Jezreel. Then I will sow her for Myself in the earth, And I will have mercy on her who had not obtained mercy; Then I will say to those who were not My people, 'You are My people!' And they shall say, 'You are my God'* (Hosea 2:22, 23). The apostle Paul considers this great prediction to be truly fulfilled when, by accepting the Divine hope of Israel, both Jews and Gentiles shall be called the children of the living God (Romans 9:25-26).

The term *promised land* can be applied to any space where God appears on earth to glorify His name, as it was for Jerusalem, the city of God, was holy ground. *The earth is the Lord's, and all its fullness, The world and those who dwell therein. For He has founded it upon the seas and established it upon the waters* (Psalm 24:1-2, emphasis added).

The majesty of Jehovah, Lord of the universe, is a reason for the psalmist to insist on morality and sincerity in those who become His worshippers. Paul uses the same truth, referring to the earth that belongs to God (1 Corinthians 10:26). Referencing the poet's words, Paul goes down a different path, saying that we can eat the fruit of the earth without raising questions of conscience because it might be food offered to idols.

*And the fulness thereof* — all these gates of the earth belong to the Lord, for they are of great value in the eyes of the Lord because He is the Maker of all things, the seas and the land, the inhabitants on earth, the lightning, and hail snow clouds, and the winds, mountains, hills, animals; all are points of access from the realm of the spirit. And prophets are the voices of the earth where reform and renewal are necessary through radical ways.

*Lift up your heads, O gates! And lift them up, you ancient doors! And the King of glory shall come in. Who is this King of glory? The Lord of hosts, He is the King of glory* (vs. 9, 10, NASB). Notice the combination of gates and doors. Raising the gates is a sign that the resistance has ended, and wherever there is a gate of glory revealed, rejoice, for Christ has risen and now is the King of glory. The procession has reached the ancient gates, where enemies could never penetrate, and the prophetic poet shouts out loud to lift the esteemed gates higher because the King is making an entrance.

The watchers at the gate, hearing the song, look over the battlements and ask, "Who is this King of glory?" which is a question full of meaning and worthy of eternity's meditations. But the response from the choir echoes of joy, making clear the secret identity: Lord of God's angelic armies and King of glory.

## STORM GATES

Tidal gates have been operating for centuries to block saltwater from penetrating landscapes, while storm gates are relatively new. Storm gates block just severe storm surges while normally remaining open to allow saltwater to move freely back and forth with the tides.[153]

When someone mentions storming the gates of heaven, that references intense prayer, but the storm gates here are the dangerous storms generated by hurricane wind forces. If you study maps, you will discover that most hurricanes start in the western part of Africa and make their way over to the United States.

Voodoo is completely normal in Benin, which is considered the voodoo capital of the world, with a public holiday celebrating voodoo and the national Voodoo Museum. People across West Africa, especially Togo, Ghana, and Nigeria, hold similar beliefs, but in Benin, it is recognized as an official religion, followed by some 40% of the population.

The origins of many storms can be traced more than 3,700 miles from the east of Florida. Low-pressure systems form above the Cape Verde archipelago off the coast of West Africa. As storms move away from the islands and across the Atlantic, they gather strength, first becoming tropical storms, then growing in intensity as they feed off the warm tropical waters until they become a hurricane. These trends were duplicated by the massive hurricane that devastated St. Thomas in the Caribbean.[154]

So besides voodoo activity in Benin, a Nigerian pastor and long-time resident of Cape Verde said the pattern of life of the people in that country is idol worship, not only leaning on voodoo but having much to do with mermaids, which they burn sacrifices to appease the marine spirit, especially among the women.[155]

Those most vulnerable to hurricanes and tropical storms will often pray, desiring that storm to move away from land. I've experienced when the Lord revealed particular storms, and I prayed against them. I remember praying for churches that no one be harmed. Several years ago, I saw a spirit of leviathan striking Pensacola. I had to go back and look at the prophetic word and saw that it happened during the Supreme court nomination for Kavanaugh. When I saw he was nominated, I saw this storm coming, but I didn't correlate the two together until that moment. One of the storms was headed towards where Bishop Hamon lived in Florida. I remember people from Bishop's church calling and chatting with me. One of the main leaders called and asked me about the prophecy because they prayed the storm went in another direction. The storm hit land in their area, but nothing harmed the church. I remember Bill's daughter, Jane Hamon, praying against any damage when a storm hit through that prophetic word. I wanted the storm not to come, but there are times when He saves you from the storm and other times when God opens gates to preserve you amid the storm.

CHAPTER SEVEN

# GATES, TREES, AND THE KINGDOM, PART ONE

Trees provide a framework for the biblical narrative beginning with the obvious story of the trees in Eden's garden. The place God created for Adam as a home was not a palace but a garden. *And out of the ground, the LORD God made every tree grow that is pleasant to the sight and good for food. The tree of life was also in the midst of the garden, and the tree of the knowledge of good and evil* (Genesis 2:9). To the Oriental, the large well-grown tree was a special object of veneration because it was pleasant to the sight, and man lived on the fruit of the trees, for it was delicious and nutritious for the body.

What stood at the center of the garden? Trees—the tree of life with its life-giving fruit and the tree of the knowledge of good and evil, from which humans were not to eat, and we are aware of the garden disaster.

Trees can tell the story of the Bible because many main characters and theological events are associated with trees. A tree stripped of roots and branches became the cross on which Jesus hung for our salvation. *And we are witnesses of all things which He did both in the land* *of the Jews and in Jerusalem, whom they killed by <u>hanging on a tree</u>* (Acts 10:39, emphasis added). *Now when they had fulfilled all that was written concerning Him, they took Him down <u>from the tree</u> and laid Him in a tomb* (Acts 13:29, emphasis added).

*"[Joseph] is a fruitful tree, a fruitful tree by a spring, with branches climbing over a wall* (Genesis 49:22, GW). Jacob had doubtless been made acquainted with the history of his beloved son Joseph from the time of his disappearance until he met him on the borders of Egypt. It had been the meditation and the wonder of his last seventeen years. Joseph is like a fruitful tree planted near a fountain of living water, and of which the branches, or suckers, springing from it overtop the wall built around the spring for its protection. The vast number of his descendants showed this fruitfulness of Joseph.

In Isaiah 53:2, the prophet Isaiah wrote one of the most profound messianic prophecies because its list of details was unquestionably fulfilled in Jesus Christ. *For He grew up before Him like a tender shoot, and like a root out of dry ground; He has no stately form or majesty That we would look at Him, nor an appearance that we would take pleasure in Him* (Isaiah 53:2). Or, to paraphrase it, "Look for the man who resembles a little tree growing out of the barren ground."

Even the trees sing for joy. *Let the heavens rejoice, let the earth be glad; let them say among the nations, "The Lord reigns!" Let the sea resound, and all that is in it; let the fields be jubilant, and everything in them! Let the trees of the forest sing, let them sing for joy before the Lord* (Psalm 96:11, 12). Then shall all the trees rejoice, the forests, oaks, cedars, and pines wave with majesty. If they were conscious of their magnificence and beauty and saw how much wisdom and goodness God has lavished on them in their branches, leaves, flowers, and fruit. If they could know how much they are made to accomplish in rendering the world beautiful and contributing to the happiness of man. If they understood what a bare, bleak, cold, desert world this would be but for the power and mercy of God.

And then there is the prophetic significance with trees. *By the river on its bank, on one side and the other will grow all kinds of trees for food. Their leaves will not wither, and their fruit will not fail. They will bear every month because their water flows from the sanctuary, and their fruit will be for food and their leaves for healing* (Ezekiel 47:12). With every parable, there is a prophetic interpretation, and in the scriptures, one prophetic word in the Old Testament often leads to another in the New Testament. Rivers by the bank, trees for fruit, and leaves for healing, we find the prophetic word in the book of Revelation. *And he showed me a pure river of water of life, clear as crystal, proceeding from the throne of God and of the Lamb. In the middle of its street, and on either side of the river, was the tree of life, which bore twelve fruits, each tree yielding its fruit every month* (Revelation 22:21-22).

Here are the similarities in Ezekiel's prophetic language, but now we arrive at its meaning in Revelation 22:23: *The leaves of the tree were for the healing of the nations. And there shall be no more curse, but the throne of God and of the Lamb shall be in it, and His servants shall serve Him.* One of the principles of interpretation is allowing for scripture to interpret scripture.

Fables about trees speaking and acting like human beings spring from whimsical incarnations, which is characteristic of an early stage of civilization; they were current among the Hebrews, Babylonians, and Assyrians. This fanciful story teaches sensible morality. In the Bible, "trees" seem more favorable as actors than other nations' talking birds and beasts.[156] *Once the trees went forth to anoint a king over them, and they said to the olive tree, "Reign over us!"; Then the trees said to the vine, "You come, reign over us!" But the vine said to them, "Shall I leave my new wine, which cheers God and men, and go to wave over the trees?"* (Judges 9:8, 12 -13).

King David referred to himself as a green olive tree in similar poetic symbolism. *But I am like a green olive tree in the house of God; I trust in the mercy of God forever and ever* (Psalm 52:8).

## KINGDOM METAPHORS

A few years ago, Seth Godin, writer and consultant to many, addressed the power of metaphors, pointing out, "The best way to learn a complex idea is to find it living inside something else you already understand." In other words, "this" is like "that."[157]

Millenniums ago, in Matthew 13, Jesus used seven kingdom metaphors to describe the kingdom of God. Jesus, the master communicator, was the maestro of metaphors in His teaching, common in ancient times, to describe abstract words. *The kingdom of heaven is like a mustard seed, which a man took and sowed in his field, which indeed is the least of all the seeds; but when it is grown, it is greater than the herbs and becomes a tree* (Matthew 13:31, 32, emphasis added).

As seven metaphors in the Bible describe God's kingdom, seven metaphors exist using trees to portray restoring the kingdom. When writing about gates and portals, we have already used other metaphors like doors, tents, and the body, but trees are the potent metaphors expressed in the "branches" of government.

Our U.S. government has three branches of government, like the three parts of a tree: roots, trunks, and the crown, or canopy. Each part of a tree plays an important role in the ecosystem and the tree's health. Albert Einstein's love of nature is reflected in his words: "Look deep into nature, and then you will understand everything better. Understanding each part and its importance can help you know how to keep your tree healthy."[158]

The crown is the most visible and one of the main parts of a tree. The crown is the top portion of any tree where all the branches, leaves, and even fruit reside. The first branches emerge from the trunk and influences how a tree functions and its appearance. Some trees have wide crowns with a dense canopy and are excellent shade trees, while others have tall but narrow crowns.

Defining the spiritual kingdom requires revealing the seven arts of the structural anatomy of a spiritual kingdom. To disclose and apply the key elements of a spiritual kingdom, we employ symbolic elements of a tree to biblically unlock kingdom truths like seeds, roots, trunk branches, bark, leaves, and fruit.

Though trees have beautiful symmetry and wonder of God's kingdom, there is another realm that disgraces the beauty of trees. The Celtic Druids worshiped not in temples but in groves of trees. There is a thing called the Druid Garden, which is found all over the eastern part of the States, especially in the Appalachian Mountains. These sacred trees and plants–branching patterns, wave patterns, spirals, and much more–permaculture learns from these patterns in the trees to help solve environmental problems.[158b] Tree sigils are sigils (signs) created from natural patterns, such as those found in trees. They use nature as a guide to design symbols for a specific purpose. Thus, they look to these sacred trees for inspiration when they need it, inspiration from the phantom world of deception.

"In Wilkesboro, North Carolina, there is a history of a certain tree that was the center of life for this community. The Tory Oak Tree—A stately oak in Wilkesboro, N.C., stood for three hundred years. It symbolized the patriots' yearning for freedom and the bitterness of their conflict with the British crown. In 1779, two tories (Americans loyal to Britain) plundered the home of George Wilfong in neighboring Lincoln County. The tories used Wilfong's clothesline to lead off his horses. Before reaching the British lines, they were captured and brought to the courthouse here. Colonel Benjamin Cleveland found them 'guilty' and hung them from the limbs of the Tory Oak—using Wilfong's clothesline. Later, three other tories retaliated by kidnapping Colonel Cleveland. However, Cleveland's brother, Robert, led the charge to rescue Benjamin, and the three kidnappers also hung from the Tory Oak."[159] Under the belly of this story are other stories not revealed but known, the story of blacks who were hung on that tree.

In 1980, the tree had the distinction of North Carolina's "champion" black oak, with a circumference of fourteen feet, a crown height of fifteen feet, and an overall limb spread of forty feet. It withstood the strain of three operations to remove rotten portions but was replaced with concrete mortar. However, the rotting continued, and heavy winds demolished two-thirds of the tree in June 1989.[160]

## TEARING DOWN STRONGHOLDS

As we build God's kingdom, it necessitates tearing down the kingdom of darkness. If we're tearing down a demonic stronghold, it existed somewhere, and we need to identify the seven anatomies of a kingdom, whether demonic or of God. It will determine whether we're going to tear it down, and if so, how we restructure it.

In the spirit realm, there is an aphorism that says whoever possesses the gate controls the territory. It doesn't matter where people live in the world or sense it. We live in critical times when God's people must build altars and possess the gates influencing communities and people, politics and businesses, technologies, and diverse forms of communication.

A different atmosphere is created with buoyant awareness and dynamic energy, making one spiritually attentive to perceive the spirit's presence and control of a city gate. It is a spiritual truth that the atmosphere in any environment determines the presence of God or Satan, angels or demons. There can be freedom in certain areas but not in others. So, for instance, where I live, there's a certain spiritual freedom, a climate in this area with miracles and wonder. Still, there are other spaces where demonic altars were established, polluting the area with cloaks and daggers, filling the atmosphere with whispers of delusions.

There is a tremendous spiritual heritage in this area. Still, conversely, ungodly altars were established in Wilkes County with generations of racism, which can be traced and seen, and we must remove those dangerous places. Maybe in your area, you have strongholds of prostitution, drug addiction, and even a spirit of poverty. These altars of poverty must be eliminated because they are generational. By recognizing these seven different keys to restoring and rebuilding God's kingdom, we can dismantle those spirits of destitution and replace those places by building an altar of prosperity.

## PART ONE: THE KING

Number one is the king, or whatever ruling person controls their space, big or small, because they have authoritarian rule over places and people. Whatever major force is ruling over a community, state, or nation and in whatever field of control, they must be identified. *The LORD is our judge and our ruler; the LORD is our king and will keep us safe* (Isaiah 33:22, CEV). There is a reference here to Israel's three forms of government: Rulers, Judges, and Kings. But Israel was a theocracy, and the prophet's words ascend human rule to the true divine Reality. Albert Barnes, the profound theologian, painted a powerful picture of Isaiah's declaration. Yahweh will be nothing but a source of happiness, truth, and prosperity to us. His presence will be only a blessing and a means of success and joy for us. The repetition of the name Yahweh three times is common in the Scriptures.[161]

Only one can say, King of kings and Lord of lords, and He shall reign forever and ever. *For to us a child is born, to us a son is given; and the government shall be upon his shoulder, and his name shall be called Wonderful Counselor, Mighty God, Everlasting Father, Prince of Peace. Of the increase of his government and of peace there will be no end, on the throne of David and over his kingdom, to establish it and to uphold it with justice and with righteousness from this time forth and forevermore* (Isaiah 9:6, 7). The gospel of Matthew was written to prove that Jesus Christ is Israel's long-awaited, promised Messiah, the King of all the earth, and to reveal God's kingdom.

The testimonies of Paul and John celebrate Christ as King and sovereign Lord. *Therefore, God also has highly exalted Him and given Him the name which is above every name that at the name of Jesus every knee should bow, of those in heaven, and of those on earth, and of those under the earth* (Philippians 2:9, 10). *They will make war on the Lamb, and the Lamb will conquer them, for he is Lord of lords and King of kings, and those with him are called and chosen and faithful* (Revelation 17:14).

Though they call it the Bible Belt, it does not mean that the King of glory is ruling over that area, but a religious spirit rules along with other spirits. Those with authority have the power to control the spheres of false shepherds. *"Awake, O sword, against my shepherd, against the man who stands next to me," declares the LORD of hosts. "Strike the shepherd, and the sheep will be scattered; I will turn my hand against the little ones"* (Zechariah 13:7, ESV). The envy and hatred of Satan combined with the blind fury of the chief priests, Herod's contempt, and Pilate's guilty cowardice, they freely accomplished Christ's death on a tree, which God had before decreed for the salvation of the world, and His disciples scattered. But His hand of grace and mercy, power, and protection was placed on the young ones who had scattered but became apostles who changed the world.

In ancient times, a shepherd symbolized protection, power, and authority. A divine symbol of kingship was the shepherd's crook, even in Egypt.[162] Indeed, the idea of a shepherd as the leader was not exclusive to the Bible. However, we know that God, the ultimate shepherd of His people, takes this concept to a level not current in other cultures.

Any shepherd breaking the rule of authority and protection should be judged. *What sorrow awaits this worthless shepherd who abandons the flock! The sword will cut his arm and pierce his right eye. His arm will become useless, and his right eye completely blind* (Zechariah 11:17, NLT).

Whoever rules in a city with drug kings and mob bosses must be eliminated like the worthless abusive shepherds. The approach of the police department is to go after the kingpin and take them out, but even that is a never-ending battle. Ministries like Teen Challenge have done phenomenal jobs in drug rehabilitation, but there has been a surge in drug abuse and death. The police departments and drug rehab centers have done their job; still, the missing element is tearing down altars of corruption plus the contrast of building altars to Jehovah and reforming God's kingdom within the degraded culture that has been avoided. It must begin with spiritual discernment of the root cause rather than the effects. Then you can focus on growth and maturation.

Vibrant growth can mature into a crown that produces the fruit of wickedness or the fruit of righteousness. The levels of kingdom maturation involve cultural change, prophetic insight, and courage to shift the ineffective and foolish attempts at changing the inner cities. Undoubtedly, the church needs to do better, but it won't change until it understands this process. It will require people of godly authority who have courage, gifting, and wisdom, building from the bottom up and shifting the atmosphere with an invasion of the supernatural realm, which is the starting point.

## NUMBER TWO: THRONES

Paul uses the didactic of things in heaven and things on earth to infer Christ's ultimate power and authority as one who sits on the throne. God's throne is one of authority and honor, righteousness, and justice.

The apostle Paul wrestled for words to convey the dignity and glory of Christ as the sovereign ruler. As one who sits on the throne of heaven, Jesus is higher, far above any worldly government, worldly wisdom, and all creation (principality). *Far above all principality, and power, and might, and dominion, and every name that is named, not only in this world but also in that which is to come* (Philippians 2:10).

In the prophet Isaiah's inauguration, he began his ministry with news of the death of King Uzziah and the manifestation of God Almighty. *I saw the Lord sitting on a throne, high and lifted up, and the train of His robe filled the temple* (Isaiah 1:1).

High and lifted up—He was not merely "above" the ranks of the heavenly beings, as the head; he was not one of their ranks, placed by office a little above them, but he was infinitely exalted over them, as of different rank and dignity. The power and dominion of one on the throne reflect the King's lordship at the highest level far above the heavenly and earthly realm. There is no competition on His throne, and insurgence is impossible.

When Joseph's dream was fulfilled, he ascended to the highest governmental position in Egypt except for the one sitting on heaven's throne. *You shall be over my house, and according to your command, all my people shall do homage; only in the throne, I will be greater than you* (Genesis 41:40).

*And of all my sons, for the LORD hath given me many sons—but He hath chosen Solomon, my son, to sit upon the throne of the kingdom of the LORD over Israel* (1 Chronicles 28:5, JPS Tanach). The throne of the kingdom of the Lord—this expression is unique in the Old Testament (compare 1 Chronicles 29:23, 1 Chronicles 17:14). It strongly reinforces the idea that the Israelite monarchy was a representative with delegated authority, not David nor Solomon, but Yahweh Elohim is the true King of heaven and earth.

Micaiah said, "*Therefore, hear the word of the Lord. I saw the Lord sitting on His throne and all the host of heaven standing by Him on His right and on His left*" (1 Kings 22:19). In his vision, Micaiah was shown the heavenly council chamber with Jehovah sitting on His throne as ruler of the universe. And standing by Jehovah is all the host of heaven, the celestial powers, cherubim, angels, archangels, who surround the Lord of glory.

*I beheld till thrones were placed, and one that was ancient of days did sit: His raiment was as white snow, And the hair of his head like pure wool; His throne was fiery flames, and the wheels thereof burning fire* (Daniel 7:9, JPS Tanakh, emphasis added). It would be easy to pass by accepting the King James Version of casting down thrones, but to reach a biblical view requires a bit of research. The Hebrew text analysis reads, "I watched until thrones were put in place."[163] Maurer and Lengerke suppose that the allusion is to the thrones on which the celestial beings sat in the solemn judgment that was to be pronounced—the throne of God, and the thrones or seats of the attending inhabitants of heaven, coming with Him to the solemn judgment.[164]

In Daniel's vision is a setting up or a placing of thrones to administer judgment on the beast. The use of the plural is per the language elsewhere employed to denote that God, the great Judge, would be surrounded by others associated with administering justice, either angels or redeemed spirits. Prophetically speaking, it would involve the overthrow of the Gentile nations in the Old Testament.

As a takeaway, there are thrones in heaven and earth who perform righteous judgment. But others have created ungodly thrones to occupy with perversions and deceptions against God, the King who sits on His throne.

Every king has a throne accompanied with authority and power to rule over a nation of people. Thrones empowered by the king fill the space of unrighteousness and injustice. But where there are empty spaces, it becomes filled with demonic forces establishing their kingdom and authority. Space will be filled with something. Where there is light, you can have peace that the King is on His throne, but where there is darkness, be aware because the enemy has situated his sphere for ruling over people.

Sometimes the darkness is allowed to rule simply because of the ignorance of believers instead of choosing to rule, and that's why the Bible says He *raised us up together and made us sit together in the heavenly places in Christ Jesus* (Ephesians 2:6). We are so tightly joined together in Christ that we were raised with Him from the dead to sit in the heavenly realm with Him, sharing His honor, glory, power, and authority. *Listen carefully: I have given you authority [that you now possess] to tread on serpents and scorpions, and [the ability to exercise authority] over all the power of the enemy (Satan); and nothing will [in any way] harm you.* (Luke 10:19, AMP).There is no reason you should not take your place with Christ on His throne. *To him who overcomes I will grant to sit with Me on My throne, as I also overcame and sat down with My Father on His throne* (Revelation 3:21).

God cannot be confined to one location. The essence of God is in everything and everywhere and ineffable. As taught by Saint Gregory Palamas, you can't locate His essence, but you may locate His energies. While God is unknowable in His essence, He can be known and experienced in His energies, and such experience changes do not change God's essence; only by experience are you changed, being raised with Christ.

*He raised us up together with Him [when we believed], and seated us with Him in the heavenly places, [because we are] in Christ Jesus* (Ephesians 2:6). So, we understand that sitting in heavenly places in Christ means not just one place but multiple different places of rulership for those who sit with Him.

Before His resurrection, Jesus joined His disciples for a final word, saying, "*All authority has been given to Me in heaven and on earth. Go therefore and make disciples of all the nations, baptizing them in the name of the Father and of the Son and of the Holy Spirit, teaching them to observe all things that I have commanded you; and lo, I am with you always, even to the end of the age*" (Matthew 28:18-20). All authority was given to Christ, in heaven, and on earth, and then He sends them to the world, being empowered with authority in His name.

So, in Acts 26:17-19, a word of authority is given: *I am sending you to open their eyes, so that they may turn from darkness to light and from the power of Satan to God, that they may receive forgiveness of sins and a place among those who are sanctified by faith in me.*

Christ made an open display of His authority and power that releases us to a place of victory that must be established on the earth. *Having disarmed principalities and powers, He made a public spectacle of them, triumphing over them in it* (Colossians 2:15).

The Greek *apekdysamenos* means to strip for one's advantage or despoil (plunder) and disarm a rival.[165] The Greek *archas* means ruler, principality, demons, or first to commence something.[166] And the Greek word *exousias* means the power of authority (influence) and right (privilege), the power of rule or government, the sign of regal authority, a crown, or authority over humanity.[167] The Greek *deigmatizó* means a spectacle, disgraced, exposed, held as an example by publicly displaying them.[168] The Greek *thriambeusas* means to lead one as their prisoner in a procession, to celebrate a triumph, publicly exalting the victor who leads a victory-procession.

Combining these five interpretations, it reads like this. As one who sits on the throne, Christ has effectively stripped, plundered, and disarmed all rival rulers, including demonic powers and principalities who desired to crush God's kingdom from the beginning. Still, Messiah ended ruling governments or authorities that were the antithesis of God's rule. And because of Christ's victory, He leads Satan and his demonic forces in chains in a public victory procession celebrating the glorious victory.

> *But the LORD sits as King forever; He has established His throne for judgment, And He will judge the world in righteousness; He will execute judgment for the peoples fairly (Psalm (9:7, 8).*

*Therefore, the LORD longs to be gracious to you, and therefore He waits on high to have compassion on you. For the LORD is a God of justice; How blessed are all those who long for Him (Isaiah 30:18).*

Our responsibility is to enforce Christ's victory starting on the cross, ending with His resurrection, then sitting on the throne while we reign with Him. We must be cautious and alert to discern those areas of resistance to God's style of authority, mercy, and justice, for it is the foundation of a heavenly throne.

## CHAPTER EIGHT

# GATES, TREES, AND THE KINGDOM, PART TWO

*"As Moses stretched forth his rod on God's behalf over Egypt, so the church by its prayers stretches forth Christ's authority over the nations and their rulers"* (Derek Prince).

We live in challenging times with the rise of ungodly activity, and many doubt their faith in God. The rising storm of satanic activity leads many into the dark places of despair and deception. But there is a king whose power brings down demonic strongholds; if we pray.

*Lift up your heads, you gates, And be lifted up, you ancient doors, That the King of glory may come in* (Psalm 24:7). So, we pray that the Lord of glory would descend into the gates of our cities and nations. No battle can be lost because the King of glory is mighty in battle and surrounded by the angelic armies, ready to respond at the command of the Lord of hosts.

*"He rules now in the midst of his enemies and rules by the rod of His strength (Psalm 110:2). The rod is*

*the mark of the ruler's authority so the rod of Christ's authority, exercised in His name, is sent forth through our prayers. In every direction that the rod is extended, the forces of evil are compelled to yield, and Christ, in turn, is exalted, and His kingdom advanced" (Derek Prince).*

## NUMBER THREE: FOUNDATIONS OF MERCY, LOVINGKINDNESS, AND RIGHTEOUS JUSTICE

God's strong hand and mighty arm are divine instruments to execute His plans. *You have a strong arm; Your hand is mighty; Your right hand is exalted. Righteousness and justice are the foundation of Your throne; Mercy and truth go before You* (Psalms 89:13,14). Righteousness and justice are the pillars and foundations supporting God's throne, and wherever God moves, there will be mercy and truth. Wherever God appears in our world, it will be attended with kindness and faithfulness.

*Clouds and thick darkness are all around him; righteousness and justice are the foundation of his throne* (Psalm 97:2). Clouds and darkness—imagery borrowed from the theophany at Sinai, God's holy mountain. Though Jehovah envelops Himself in mystery and comes with dominant intervening might, it is comforting for His people to know that His kingdom is founded upon righteousness.

In Hebrew, *tzedakah* connotes charitable contributions, but the term originates in another realm. In the Bible, tzedakah means "righteous behavior" paired with "justice." Although the term tzedakah is applied to giving to needy individuals only in post-biblical Judaism, the Bible is replete with warnings to show concern for the poor. Biblical laws like those calling on farmers to set aside some of their crops during harvest for the landless become in rabbinic Judaism the basis for an extensive social welfare system built on individual initiative and shared responsibility. These and other laws were the foundations for Jewish life and worship.[169]

It is derived from the root *tzisedek,* which means fulfilling duties towards others, particularly the responsibilities imposed on a person based on moral virtues, such as remedying those injured.Justice precedes righteousness, and thus, it appears from the order of God's wording that His courtroom justice precedes His remedy for our injustice. In the words of the sages: "Justice is the declaration of God's will and our means of serving and approaching Him."[170]

And God's remedy for our injustice establishes His righteousness, thereby enabling Him to extend His mercy. In other words, God's love is an outpouring of Him remedying our injuries by taking upon Himself the payment for our debt to sin. It is written, *"For the law was given through Moses, but grace and truth came through Jesus Christ"* (John 1:17).

Pirkei Avot is a compilation of Rabbinic Jewish tradition's ethical teachings and maxims, part of didactic Jewish ethical literature. Much of these writings are part of the Orthodox *Sayings of the Desert Fathers*.[171] So, Pirkei Avot 1:2 teaches that the world stands on three pillars: Torah, work in the service of G-d, and acts of human kindness, where the Mishna teaches that we are not alone in the world but must live and coexist with others. Thus, by studying Torah and gleaning its eternal lessons, we have an opportunity to become closer to G-d.[172]

The Hebrew *chesed* means lovingkindness, mercy, grace, and goodness. It denotes the unbounded lovingkindness with which God created the worlds and permeated all creation. Most translations include compassion and grace. Illustrating the diversions of interpretations in Isaiah 89:1, 2 requires these three translations to view *chesed* fully: *I will sing of the mercies of the LORD forever. Mercy shall be built up forever* (NKJV, emphasis added). *I will sing of the lovingkindness of the LORD forever. Goodness and lovingkindness will be built up forever* (AMP, emphasis added). *I will sing of the graciousness of the LORD forever. Graciousness will be built up forever* (NASB, emphasis added). Mercy, lovingkindness, and graciousness are three interpretations of the Hebrew *chesed. There is no confusion but a diversity of thought based upon accurate interpretations.*

One of the common mentions in the Old Testament is "mercy" (*racham*)," mentioned 262 times. For example, Deuteronomy 4:31 declares, *The Lord your God is a God of mercy (rachum)*. Lamentations 3:32 says that God's **mercies *(rachamav) never come to an end.***

In the Hebrew language, the other word for "mercy" *(racham)* shares the same three-letter root as the word for "womb" *(rechem)*. Based on the close linguistic connection between these terms, **God's "mercy" toward humanity denotes the same kind of divine protection that a baby has in its mother's womb.**

In Psalm 22, the psalmist recounts a lifelong devotion to the Lord, saying, *"I was cast upon you from the __womb__ (rechem); you are my God from my mother's belly"* (Psalm 22:10, emphasis added).[173]

## FOUNDATIONS FROM THE SCRIPTURES

> *But God's firm foundation stands, bearing this seal: "The Lord knows those who are his," and, "Let everyone who names the name of the Lord depart from iniquity" (2 Timothy 2:19, ESV).*

*For no one can lay a foundation other than that which is laid, which is Jesus Christ* (1 Corinthians 3:11, emphasis added). The apostle was a wise master-builder, but it will not support the church's structure without a firm foundation which is Christ. The doctrine of Christ is not the foundation, but Christ Himself is the foundation, who He is and what He has done. That is why Paul points to Christ as the foundation of what He has accomplished.

*And the king commanded them to quarry large stones, costly stones, and hewn stones, to lay the foundation of the temple* (1 Kings 5:17). Using this imagery of laying the temple's foundation, the prophet Isaiah moves into a mode of prophetic communication, countering the absurdity of ungodly rulers making a covenant with death. *Because you have said, "We have made a covenant with death, And with Sheol we are in agreement. When the overflowing scourge passes through, It will not come to us, For we have made lies our refuge, And under falsehood we have hidden ourselves"* (Isaiah 28:15).

But God counters the extraordinary stupidity of Israel's rulers in

Jerusalem by laying a sure foundation in Zion, expecting the people to be patient. *Therefore, thus says the Lord GOD, "Behold, I am the one who has laid as a foundation in Zion, a stone, a tested stone, a precious cornerstone, of a sure foundation: 'Whoever believes will not be in haste'"* (Isaiah 28:16). In reading this, you can almost feel the prophet about to declare the judgment of God upon the nation. But God speaks, not the prophet. The general sentiment is that though there is an approaching calamity and the temple is about to be destroyed because of their sin, God's purpose was that this earthly empire should not be destroyed. In Barnes notes, it says, a foundation, a cornerstone was to be laid that would be unshaken and unmoved by all the assaults of the foes of God, and all who were truly resting on that should be safe. Therefore, the essential idea in this passage is the perpetuity of His kingdom and the safety of His true people.[74]

In contrast with the insecure refuge and false ground of confidence on which the nobles relied, the prophet presents the one sure rock, which is Christ. *For no one is able to lay another foundation, besides the one being already laid, which is Jesus Christ* (1 Corinthians 3:11). As members of God's family, we are *built on the foundation of the apostles and prophets, Jesus Christ Himself being the chief cornerstone* (Ephesians 2:20).

From the elevation of a despised beggar to the highest and most dignified rank, possesses a seat of honor, the throne of glory. *He raised up the poor out of the dust, He lifted up the needy from the dunghill, To make them sit with princes, And inherit the throne of glory; For the pillars of the earth are the LORD'S, And He has set the world upon them* (1 Samuel 2:8, JPS Tanakh). The pillars of the earth are the Lord's and He set the world upon them. The earth is the Lord's and the fulness thereof. Its foundations on which it is laid and its pillars by which it is supported belong to the power and providence of God; otherwise, the earth hangs on nothing.

*When my enemies retreat, they stumble and perish before You. For You have upheld my just cause; You sit on Your throne judging righteously* (Psalm 9:4, Berean Study Bible). David does not subscribe to his abilities but God's favor. When the enemies come against us, God sits on His heavenly throne, administering justice, awarding defeat to the unrighteous who attack His people, giving victory, glory, and honor to the faithful ones who stood strong against the aggressors. There is no God like Jehovah!

*It is an abomination for kings to commit wickedness, For a throne is established by righteousness* (Proverbs 16:12). It is a vigorous challenge for all who live in a place of leadership, especially kings and presidents. When a ruler performs honorably and wisely, punishes the corrupt, rewards the righteous, acts as God's representative with integrity, and sets his authority based on godliness, he wins the affection of his people and they will willingly obey him. *And a throne shall be established with mercy (chesed); and one shall sit upon it with truth in the tabernacle of David, judging, and earnestly seeking judgments, and hasting righteousness* (Isaiah 16:5, Brenton Septuagint Translation).

## NUMBER FOUR: SCEPTERS

Since ancient times, a staff or scepter indicated secular or religious authority. They were used in Egypt as early as the fifteenth century BC and in Cyprus as early as the twelfth century BC. Among the early Greeks, the scepter was a long staff used by aged men, the elders among them, and it came to be used by others placed in authority, such as judges, military leaders, and priests. Under the Romans, an ivory scepter was a mark of consular rank. Victorious generals, who received the title of imperator, also used it. Under the Roman Empire, the emperors used a scepter of ivory, tipped with a golden eagle.[175]

The Hebrew *shebet* means rod, shepherd's staff, club, scepter mark of authority, tribes of Israel, and shaft of a spear.[176] When *shebet* applies to a newly crowned king, they are handed a scepter, and kingly authority has been given to him. A king without a scepter is a crown prince or a king in waiting where there is no scepter. No scepter, no authority.

A broken scepter symbolizes squandered authority and position: *The LORD has broken the staff of the wicked, the scepter of rulers, that struck the peoples in wrath with unceasing blows, that ruled the nations in anger with unrelenting persecution* (Isaiah 14:5, 6). The "staff" and the "scepter" are similar symbols of power, the former in which a man supports himself, the other which he wields with the King of Babylon's arm to smite those who oppose him. Because of the Babylonian abusive power and anger by persecuting the people, God squashed their staff and scepter eliminating his power.

When the word *scepter* pertains to God, it refers to His absolute rule over His creation. The scepter of God also appears in prophetic passages describing the coming Messiah who will rule the nations and restore righteousness. *A star shall come out of Jacob, and a scepter shall rise out of Israel* (Numbers 24:17), prophetically referring to Jesus, the coming Messiah.

In the book of Esther, King Ahasuerus spared Queen Esther's life when he extended his golden scepter as she approached him in the courtyard. *When the king saw Esther the queen standing in the courtyard, she obtained favor in his sight; and the king extended to Esther the golden scepter which was in his hand. So Esther approached and touched the top of the scepter* (Esther 5:2, NASB).

Only these three words—throne, scepter, and anointed—are mentioned together in Psalms 45:6,7 and Hebrew 1:8, 9. *But of the Son, He says, "Your throne, O God, is forever and ever, And the righteous scepter is the scepter of His kingdom. You have loved righteousness and hated lawlessness; Therefore God, Your God, has anointed You With the oil of gladness more than Your companions* (Hebrews 1:8, 9, emphasis added).

The word "elohim" has a duality of meaning, gods and God, depending on context for its precise significance. If used in a solemn address to a king sitting upon an everlasting throne, it surely implies assigning Divine honors to the king so addressed. In this case, the king's throne refers to God's Son, enthroned on Zion, the Son being addressed as Himself "Elohim." A scepter of righteousness is the scepter of thy kingdom. In this and the following clause is expressed the important idea that the ideal throne of the SON is founded on righteousness, with a peculiar, anointed unction with "the oil of gladness" (Pulpit Commentary).[177]

A scepter is an emblem of royal power, and, accordingly, most look grand and luxurious, often with royal crown jewels. Scriptures mention an assortment of precious metals and gemstones. The following verse describes a scepter made of iron for the victors in the church of Thyatira at the Messiah's return: *And to the one who overcomes and continues in My work until the end, I will give authority over the nations. He will rule them with an iron scepter and shatter them like pottery—just as I have received authority from My Father* (Revelation 2:26, 27, BSB).

There is an allusion here to Psalm 2:9: *You will break them with an iron scepter; You will shatter them like pottery* (BSB). Albert Barnes, the infamous biblical scholar, shines a white light on these words. "It is a slight change, 'he will rule,' instead of 'he will break,' which to rule with a scepter of iron is not to rule with a harsh and oppressive sway but with power that is firm and invincible. It denotes a government of strength, or one that cannot be successfully opposed, one in which the subjects are effectually subdued" (Barnes Notes).[178]

*The Lord will stretch forth Your strong scepter from Zion, saying, "Rule in the midst of Your enemies"* (Psalm 110:2). In this prophetic picture, the divine King sits the gifted earthly ruler by His side to take the scepter from his hand, stretches the symbol of authority out of Zion, God's holy church, to govern in the middle of our enemies, not the edges.

Once God has given you a scepter, a rod of power, you have the authority and responsibility to pronounce judgment, a verdict upon the wicked established in our territory, and crush the wicked enemies lest they do wrong. *The scepter of God is a fearful thing to His enemies. For the scepter of wickedness shall not rest upon the land of the righteous, so that the righteous will not put forth their hands to do wrong* (Psalm 125:3).

## CHAPTER FIVE: COUNCIL OF ELDERS

*But which of them has stood in the <u>council</u> of the LORD to see and hear His word? Who has given heed to His word and obeyed it? (Jeremiah 23:18, BSB, emphasis added).The <u>secret</u> of the LORD is with those who fear Him, And He will show them His covenant (Psalm 25:14, emphasis add-*

*ed). Surely the Lord GOD does nothing Unless He reveals*
*His <u>secret</u> to His servants the prophets (Amos 3:4, emphasis*
*added).*

The Hebrew *sôd* means council, secret, assembly, company, intimacy, as indicated in these verses.[179] William Hamlin, professor of history, and Daniel Peterson, professor of Islamic Studies, add their thoughts on *sod.* Only those who participate in the divine "sod"/council know the "sod"/secret plan, and only those who are given explicit permission may reveal that "sod" to humanity. This concept is illustrated in several biblical passages." [180]

In my book, *Angels: A Biblical Book of Living Light,* I shared that nearly all scholars now agree that, when used in relationship to God, "sod" refers to the heavenly divine council, which prophets may sometimes be invited into the council to learn divine secrets. I opened the section on the divine council with these words: "Mahanaim is the place of two camps, the camp of humans and angels. At Mahanaim, a council is established, secrets shared, and strategies created. Who stands in the counsel of the Lord? It is His prophets and the righteous who are allowed in the council of the Lord."[181]

The Hebrew *Mahanaim* means two camps; two hosts, "referring to the small visible company of faithful followers and the vastly superior invisible host of mighty angels" (Dr. Henry M. Morris, *The Defender's Study Bible*).[182] The two camps were Bethel, where the angels appeared, and Jacob's return from Padam-aram, where an angel appeared again. So Jacob went on his way, and the angels of God met him. When Jacob saw them, he said, "This *is* God's camp." And he called the name of that place Mahanaim (Genesis 32:1, 2 ).

Who stands in the counsel of the Lord? It is His prophets and the righteous who are allowed in the council of the Lord.

> *And all the angels were standing around the throne and*
> *around the elders and the four living creatures, and they*
> *fell on their faces before the throne and worshiped God*
> *(Revelation 3:11). Around the throne were twenty-four*

*thrones, and on the thrones, I saw twenty-four elders sitting, clothed in white robes; and they had crowns of gold on their heads (Revelation 4:4).*

There is much speculation about the twenty-four elders in the book of Revelation. As you can see, they are seated on thrones, dressed in white robes, wearing crowns. Whoever these elders are, one of the things you notice is that they are constantly entering into worship. These verses give plenty of clues to understanding that the twenty-four elders are humans.

The twenty-four elders had access to the throne, and those in the church who overcame sat on thrones. These elders were all dressed in white and wore crowns on their heads. To be dressed in white, especially a white robe, is symbolic of being clothed in the righteousness of Christ. The only ones who will ever be clothed in His righteousness are those who have been redeemed. *"Yet you have a few people in Sardis who have not soiled their clothes. They will walk with me, dressed in white, for they are worthy. The one who is victorious will, like them, be* <u>*dressed in white*</u>*. I will never blot out the name of that person from the book of life but will acknowledge that name before my Father and his angels"* (Revelation 3:4, 5, emphasis added). Because the twenty-four elders are wearing crowns, it symbolizes the crown of life. *Blessed is the one who perseveres under trial because, having stood the test, that person will receive the* <u>*crown of life*</u> *that the Lord has promised to those who love him* (James 1:12, emphasis added).

In *Angels: A Biblical School of Living Light*, I wrote that this is where creative miracles emerge. The angels and four living creatures are in the divine council, and the elders appear, and you never know what they say, but the glory realm is always there. The glory realm is ushered into a meeting on earth by the angels bringing the glorious, miraculous realm from the throne.

The observations created by Jamieson, Fausett, and Brown confirm Clarke's words in his commentary: "Here, the angel acts merely as a ministering spirit (Hebrews 1:4), just as the twenty-four elders have vials full of odors, or incense, which are the prayers of saints

(Revelation 5:8), and which they present before the Lamb. It seems reasonable to suppose that the incense offered in ancient worship was designed to symbolize the prayers of saints. When the prayers of the saints ascended, he would also burn the incense, that it might go up at the same moment. The angel does not provide the incense; it is given to him by Christ, whose meritorious obedience and death are the incense, rendering the saints' prayers well-pleasing to God."[183]

## NUMBER SIX: PRIESTHOOD

Prior to Sinai, we've seen a few priests, Melchizedek and Jethro, but for the most part, sacrifices were offered by a patriarch on behalf of his family. However, as the nation of Israel was formed in the wilderness at the foot of Mount Sinai, God set up a specific pattern for atonement from sin so that the people encamped around Him might be cleansed from their sins and remain a holy people through the sacrifices offered by the priesthood.

*For every high priest taken from among men is appointed on behalf of people in things pertaining to God, in order to offer both gifts and sacrifices for sins* (Hebrew 5:1, NASB). In Hebrew, a priest is *kōhen*, from which we get the common Jewish surname "Cohen." The etymology of the word is obscure.[184] The priests were charged with ministering to the Lord, first and foremost. But their second focus was on the people of Israel by daily offering sacrifices, burning incense in the Holy Place, and tending the lamps on the lampstand. Weekly they renewed the bread of the presence and ate the old loaves.

> *We have such a High Priest, who is seated at the right hand of the throne of the Majesty in the heavens, a Minister of the sanctuary and of the true tabernacle which the Lord erected, and not man (Hebrews 8:1, 2).*

> *He made us into a kingdom, priests to His God and Father—to Him be the glory and the dominion forever and ever (Revelation 1:6). You have made them to be a kingdom*

*and priests to serve our God, and they will reign upon the earth (Revelation 5:10).*

*"Now if you will indeed obey My voice and keep My covenant, you will be My treasured possession out of all the nations—for the whole earth is Mine. And unto Me you shall be a kingdom of priests and a holy nation." These are the words that you are to speak to the Israelites (Exodus 19:5, 6).*

*But you are a chosen generation, a royal priesthood, a holy nation, His own special people, that you may proclaim the praises of Him who called you out of darkness into His marvelous light (1 Peter 2:9).*

In these words, there is a dual interpretation, the priesthood of the Jews and the Gentiles. In 1 Peter 2:9, the audience is Jewish, considered aliens and strangers in a Gentile culture, but Peter encourages them to maintain their faith in Christ. A chosen generation, a royal priesthood, a holy nation is with words Peter invoked Old Testament peculiarities that the Jewish believers would understand and embrace since only the Levites were part of the old covenant priesthood.

God introduces the idea of a royal priesthood, describing Israel as a kingdom of priests and a holy nation in Exodus 19:6. But, later, in John's letter to the seven churches, He declares that we are a kingdom of priests. *He did make us kings and priests to His God and Father, and to Him is the glory and the power to the ages of the ages!* (Revelation 1:6, NLT).

The company of the four living creatures and the twenty-four elders echoes the song of the Lamb, and they are part of His kingdom. *And have made us kings and priests to our God; And we shall reign on the earth* (Revelation 5:10), similar to the royal priesthood concept that Peter references.

As a company of priests, we offer the sacrifice of worship and doing good to our God. *Through Him then, let's continually offer up a sacrifice of praise to God, that is, the fruit of lips praising His name. But do not forget to do good and to share, for with such sacrifices God is well pleased* (Hebrews 13:15, 16).

But there are gifted ones in God's house who are chosen and gifted as priests who care for the body of Christ and leaders who build kingdom structures in their city. The function of a spiritual priest/leader is to be a mediator and maintainer of the balance between the sacred and the profane in the church and society. They are being the voice of the social structures and establishing the foundations of God's kingdom in their communities and nations.

As prophets and priests, they are called to a special responsibility to oversee the nations, tearing down, building, and planting. *See, I have this day set thee over the nations and over the kingdoms, to root out, and to pull down, and to destroy, and to throw down, to build, and to plant* (Jeremiah 1:10). They represent God's word that must be declared with force and love as needed. Moses is the representative prophet, priest, and kingly leader as a servant of God. We need a generation of those like Moses.

## NUMBER SEVEN: RULED BY OTHERS

The life of Gideon was characterized by his noblest act, refusal of kingship. *Then the men of Israel said unto Gideon, Rule thou over us, both thou, and thy son, and thy son's son also: for thou hast delivered us from the hand of Midian. But Gideon said to them, "I will not rule over you, nor shall my son rule over you; the LORD shall rule over you"* (Judges 8:22).

The Divine King seats the earthly king by His side, taking his scepter from his hand, stretches it in token of the wide empire he is to administer from Zion. *The LORD shall send the rod of thy strength out of Zion: rule thou in the midst of thine enemies* (Psalm 110:2). *Righteousness is the heart of what it means to rule as a leader. Behold, a king shall reign in righteousness, and princes shall rule in judgment* (Isaiah 32:1).

Earthly relations, such as father, magistrate, governor, and prince, are partial types and manifestations of the divine headship. And Christ's humanity is but the revelation and manifestation of His Father and, in the end, will put all things He accomplished at God's feet. *Then [cometh] the end, when he shall have delivered up the kingdom to God, even the Father; when he shall have put down all rule and all authority and power* (1 Corinthians 15:24).

The elders (or presbyters) to whom Timothy was to receive some honor in the congregations of so great a city like Ephesus. In addition to their many duties connected with organization and administration, they distinguished themselves by their preaching and teaching. *Let the elders that rule well be counted worthy of double honor, especially they who labor in the word and doctrine* (1 Timothy 5:17).

There can be no doubt that the man child in Revelation is Christ. The combination of features is too distinct to admit doubt. He is the one who will feed His flock like a shepherd (Isaiah 40:12), and not only to have His people, but all nations as His inheritance (Psalm 2:7-9), and whose rule over them is to be supreme and irresistible. *And she brought forth a man child, who was to rule all nations with a rod of iron: and her child was caught up unto God, and [to] his throne* (Revelation 12:5).

You are either ruled by God or by a demonic entity. So, it becomes our responsibility to set the territory free to live in a region where God breathes in that place where freedom rules. Freedom is in that place because God set the captives free of ungodly rule.

The elders and leaders of the city must be aware of the tragic issues that are hurting our community. Can your leaders answer these questions about their area, and what will they do? What is the suicide rate? What is the incarcerated rate? What are the murder and robbery rates? What is the homeless rate in your area, and single mothers also?

Where God rules and the leaders achieve, the godly altars of intercession open the portals to angelic encounters. Godly thrones have been established and kings are ruling. Where communities are devasted by crime and addictions, the leaders must bravely rule by exercising God's supernatural power. Transformation is the direct result of godly, spiritual leaders acting on God's word, giving prophetic leaders direction. It requires reestablishing a godly altar where satanic altars have ruled the city.

In ancient times, the city gates represented the eldership of the realm and its justice systems. In the city gate, through which people constantly flowed, agreements were verbally sealed in the presence of witnesses, a necessity in an era before the written contract. Everything happened at the gates.

The city's gate was also a podium for the Israelite prophets of old, the spirited social reformers of their day. *Hate evil and love good,* declaimed Amos, *and establish justice in the gate (Amos 5:15). Even though we live in modern times, our responsibility is to guard, cleanse, and transform the gates. Jesus told Peter that He would build the church and the gates of hell would not prevail against it, implying every level of government and* the strength of the immovable church planted on the rock.

The prophets must discern areas needing radical change and the collapse of demonic strongholds. *Then the LORD put forth His hand and touched my mouth, and the LORD said to me: Behold, I have put My words in your mouth. See, I have this day set you over the nations and over the kingdoms, to root out and to pull down, To destroy and to throw down, To build and to plant* (Jeremiah 1:9-10).

The Spirit of the Lord will travel with Jeremiah in a fresh prophetic anointing to articulate God's word with boldness. The hand is the instrument of making and doing; the touching of Jeremiah's mouth by the hand of God is consequently a token that God frames in his mouth what he is to speak. God has consecrated him to be His prophet and endowed him to discharge his duties.

He may now entrust Jeremiah with His commission to the peoples and kingdoms and set him over them as His prophet who proclaims to them His word. With the words of the Lord, he is to destroy and build up peoples and kingdoms. The work at first seems one simply of destruction—to root out and ruin and to destroy and rend asunder.

But beyond that, there is the hope of healing restoration work. He is to "build up" the fallen ruins of Israel, to "plant" in the land made desolate. The whole sequel of the book is a comment on these words.

It passes through terror and darkness to the new covenant's glory and blessing (Jeremiah 31:31). We should be meditating day and night on these words because of the times of sorrow defining this season in our world.

Sometimes it takes radical action to cleanse people and a nation when demonic altars and ungodly gates exist to control the atmosphere and earthly territory. *Instead, this is what you are to do to them: tear down their altars, smash their sacred pillars, cut down their Asherah poles, and burn their idols in the fire. For you are a people holy to the LORD your God. LORD your God has chosen you to be a people for His prized possession out of all peoples on the face of the earth* (Deuteronomy 7:5, BSB).

*Be delighted, heavens from above, and clouds shall sprinkle righteousness! The earth shall be opened, salvation will multiply, and righteousness will sprout as one. I AM LORD JEHOVAH, who have created these things* (Isaiah 45:8, Aramaic Bible in Plain English). We end this on a glorious note when heaven's gates are opened, clouds of rain sprinkle the land with holy righteousness, and salvation sprouts like a fast-growing plant. Now is the day to put your full trust in Jehovah Elohim.

> *Serve the LORD with gladness; Come before His presence with singing. Know that the LORD, He is God; It is He who has made us, and not we ourselves; We are His people and the sheep of His pasture. Enter into His gates with thanksgiving, And into His courts with praise. Be thankful to Him and bless His name. For the LORD is good; His mercy is everlasting, And His truth endures to all generations (Psalm 100:2-5).*

CHAPTER NINE

# ALTARS OF COVENANT

The scene would look quite ominous to those attending church— five bloody animal carcasses on the ground, three split in half, and the halves separated a short distance. But in ancient times, it would not have been so menacing. The arrangement of divided animal carcasses would have been instantly recognized as an arrangement of a type of blood covenant.

In Genesis 15, an intense conversation commenced between God and Abram concerning the birth of a child to Sarah. Though Abram had a son through Hagar, God made a covenant with him to receive a son from Sarah, a son of promise. As a token of the covenant, God said, "*Bring Me a three-year-old heifer, a three-year-old female goat, a three-year-old ram, a turtledove, and a young pigeon.*" *Then he brought all these to Him and cut them in two, down the middle, and placed each piece opposite the other; but he did not cut the birds in two* (v. 9, 10).

However, there was an important difference in God's blood oath with Abraham. When the evening came, Abraham fell into a deep sleep, and thick and intimidating darkness came over him (v. 12), and there appeared a smoking firepot and flaming torch passing between the pieces. The smoking oven and burning torch symbolized God. In many biblical situations, God represents Himself through the image of fire, like Moses' experience with God in the burning bush and the pillar of fire.

Thus, God alone passed through the pieces of dead animals, and the covenant was sealed by God alone (v. 17). Nothing depended on Abraham. Everything depended on God, who promised to be faithful to His covenant. God fashioned a promise to Abraham *since there was no one greater for him to swear by; he swore by himself* (Hebrews 6:13). Abraham and his descendants could trust, count on, and believe everything God promised. On that day, Yahweh made a covenant with Abram, saying, *"To your descendants, I have given this land, from the river of Egypt to the great river, the River Euphrates"* (Genesis 15:18).

Apart from blood ties, covenants were how people of the ancient world formed wider relationships with each other. The accounts of the relationship between David and Jonathan are the only unequivocal mention of a compact between two individuals in the Old Testament. *Then Jonathan made a covenant with David because he loved him as himself* (1 Samuel 18:3).

Often accompanied with the covenants were signs, witnesses, memorials, shared meals, sacrifices, and solemn, binding oaths, sealing the relationship with promises of blessing for keeping the covenant and curses for breaking the covenant. The Theological Dictionary of the New Testament indicates that in ancient times, there were written documents on which the words of the covenant with its terms in the form of promises and stipulations were spelled out, witnessed to, signed, and sealed.[185]

## THE INAUGURATION OF THE COVENANT NARRATIVE

There is no consensus on the number of biblical covenants mentioned in the Bible, but the five precise covenants forming the soul of the scriptures are Noah, Abraham, Israel, David, and the New Covenant. The narrative continues till the great climax with Jesus, the Messiah.

The Noahic Covenant, found in Genesis 9, is God's promise to Noah and his descendants after the flood that destroyed the world.

The Noahic Covenant is distinguished with an unconditional covenant and includes Noah, all his descendants, and every living creature on the earth. *And as for Me, behold, I establish My covenant with you and with your descendants after you, and with every living creature* (v. 9, 10). Then God seals the covenant with a token, the rainbow. *I set My rainbow in the cloud, and it shall be for the sign of the covenant between Me and the earth* (v. 13).

We approach God's promises differently by reviewing the Abrahamic Covenant as an unconditional covenant initiated upon Yahweh's words. *I will make you a great nation; I will bless you and make your name great; And you shall be a blessing. I will bless those who bless you, And I will curse him who curses you; And in you all the families of the earth shall be blessed* (Genesis 12:2, 3). Jehovah's solitary action indicates that the covenant is effectively His promise by binding Himself to the covenant. On the same day, the Lord made a covenant with Abram, saying, *"To your descendants I have given this land, from the river of Egypt to the great river, the River Euphrates"* (Genesis 15:18). God reiterates the Abrahamic Covenant to Isaac and his son Jacob, whose name God changes to *Israel*. The great nation was ultimately established in the land where Abraham had dwelled.

The Mosaic Covenant is a conditional covenant made between God and the nation of Israel at Mount Sinai. It is sometimes called the Sinai Covenant but is more often referred to as the Mosaic Covenant since Moses was God's chosen leader of Israel. The covenant pattern is very similar to other ancient covenants because it is between a sovereign king (God) and his people (the children of Israel).

It is centered around God's divine law given to Moses on Mount Sinai, differing significantly from the Abrahamic Covenant and later biblical covenants. The covenant is conditional on being directly related to Israel's obedience to the Mosaic Law. If Israel is obedient, God will bless them, but God will punish them if they disobey. In Exodus 20, Yahweh positions the key elements of the covenant He will reject and judge. *You shall have no other gods before Me. You shall not make for yourself a carved image, or any likeness of anything that is in heaven above, or that is in the earth beneath, or that is in the water under the earth; you shall not bow down to them nor serve them* (v. 3-5).

The Davidic Covenant is a sequel to the past covenants, promising a Davidic king as the symbol through whom God would secure the promises of land, descendants, and blessing. The details of the Davidic Covenant are referred to David via Nathan, the prophet speaking as God's representative. It centers on key promises made to David. First, God reaffirms the promise of the land that He made in the first two covenants with Israel, the Abrahamic and Mosaic Covenants. This promise is seen in 2 Samuel 7:10: *I will provide a place for my people Israel and will plant them so that they can have a home of their own and no longer be disturbed. Wicked people will not oppress them anymore.* God then promised that David's son would succeed him as king of Israel and that Solomon would build the temple. *I will raise up your offspring to succeed you, your own flesh and blood, and I will establish his kingdom. He is the one who will build a house for my Name* (2 Samuel 7:12-13).

But then the promise continues and expands with a house, throne, and kingdom. *He shall build a house for My name, and I will establish the throne of his kingdom forever* (2 Samuel 7:13). The promise that David's "house," "kingdom," and "throne" will be established forever is significant because it shows that the Messiah will come from the lineage of David and that He will establish a kingdom from which Christ will reign.

The old covenant God established with His people required strict obedience to the Mosaic Law. But Moses predicted that Israel would fail in keeping the old covenant (Deuteronomy 29:22–28); he then sees a time of restoration when they return to Yahweh Elohim to obey His voice, according to all that God commanded, with all their heart and with all their soul, which Moses said, *"The Lord your God will circumcise your hearts and the hearts of your descendants, so that you may love him with all your heart and with all your soul, and live"* (Deuteronomy 30:6 ).

The prophet Jeremiah also predicted the new covenant. *Behold, the days are coming, says the Lord, when I will make a new covenant with the house of Israel and with the house of Judah not according to the covenant that I made with their fathers. But this is the covenant that I will make with the house of Israel after those days, says the Lord: I will put My law in their minds, and write it on their hearts, and I will be their God, and they shall be My people* (Jeremiah 31:31, 33 ). Jesus came to fulfill the law of Moses (Matthew 5:17) and establish the new covenant between God and His people. The old covenant was written in stone, but the new covenant is written on our hearts.

## ALTARS AND COVENANTS

The altar of a covenant is a place and a promise, geography, and people. It includes places like heaven and earth, light and darkness, geography where you see the bright light of God's presence among us, and the darkness of satanic locations. It is also a place where covenants are cut and vows made. Altars and covenants are solemn and sacred moments to be considered and embraced with commitment. The altar of the covenant is where we establish identity and return to remember our identity.

We have described altars as places, many different places that were hallowed and weighty but sometimes evil and unholy. But the word covenant is not commonly used in modern cultures. We talk about contracts, litigating, and agreements, but a covenant is rarely used, and most lack biblical meaning. But it is used almost three hundred times in the Hebrew Old Testament and thirty-three times in the Greek New Testament.

The majority of Old Testament uses of *beriyth* are translated as covenant, treaty, compact, agreement between two parties, and first used in God's covenant with Noah in Genesis 6:18: *but I will establish My covenant with you, and you shall enter the ark—you and your sons and your wife, and your sons' wives with you.*[186]

Genesis 12:7 is the first mention of a theophany in the patriarchal narrative, and Yahweh appears in a continuation mode with the divine promises to Abram. *And YHWH appears to Abram and says, "To your seed I give this land"; there he builds an altar to YHWH, who has appeared to him* (Genesis 12:7, LSV). The altar is erected on the spot and is consecrated by the appearance of the Lord. By this sincere act of devotion, Abram made an open pronouncement of his religion, established the worship of the one true God, and declared his faith in the promise. The altar was a sign of the covenant made between Yahweh and Abram.

## THE ALTAR OF YAHWEH

One of the challenges for Moses was the mixed multitude.*A mixed multitude went up with them also, and flocks and herds—a great deal of livestock* (Exodus 12:38). Some were Egyptians through intermarriages, and others joined to avoid the plagues. No doubt others were induced by Yahweh's signs and wonders in Egypt and sought their good among the Israelites.

What appeared to be a place of refuge for this great mixture of people afterward became problematic to Moses and its leaders. This swarm of foreigners became an issue because most were accustomed to making altars to worship other gods. The practice of altars continued until Moses led Israel out of bondage into the wilderness on their way to the promised land. Once they reached Mount Sinai and inaugurated the covenant, a new rule was added concerning what kind of altars could be built.

> *An altar of earth you shall make for Me, and you shall sacrifice on it your burnt offerings and your peace offerings, your sheep and your oxen. In every place where I record My name I will come to you, and I will bless you. And if you make Me an altar of stone, you shall not build it of hewn stone; for if you use your tool on it, you have profaned it (Exodus 20:24-25).*

> *You shall make no covenant with them or with their gods (Exodus 23:22).*

Some practiced their worship of God by building altars to please Yahweh. Still, among the mixed multitudes, the Egyptians and other idolatrous nations commonly sacrificed to idols or devils in the fields or any places.

*For this reason, the Israelites will bring to the LORD the sacrifices they have been offering in the open fields. They are to bring them to the priest at the entrance to the Tent of Meeting and offer them as sacrifices of peace to the LORD* (Leviticus 17:5). Because of the abuse of building altars, Moses ended the freedom to build altars requiring they bring their sacrifices to the tent of meeting. Once the tabernacle was built, altars in the field ended. Despite the laws on altars, building altars continued like Gideon, Saul, David, and Ezekiel. Nor did it terminate building idols to false gods.

What was once altars in the fields now became a sanctuary, the Ark of the Covenant, a wooden box covered with gold and topped with a lid known as the Seat of Atonement, the earthly throne of Yahweh. This holy chest, copied from what Moses saw in heaven, was placed in the Holy of Holies in the desert tabernacle and later in the Jerusalem temple.

*And let them construct a sanctuary for Me, that I may dwell among them. According to all that I am going to show you as the pattern of the tabernacle and the pattern of all its furniture, so you shall construct it; And there I will meet with you, and I will speak with you from above the mercy seat, from between the two cherubim which are on the ark of the Testimony, about everything which I will give you in commandment to the children of Israel; And see to it that you make them according to the pattern which was shown you on the mountain* (Exodus 25:8, 9, 22, 40 ). From that moment on, it was called the Ark of the Covenant.

The ancient altars of the patriarchs became the sanctuary of God, then the tabernacle, with the Ark of the Covenant, which is the altar of Yahweh. But the writer of Hebrew prophetically declares that we now live in a new time, a time of replacing the shadows with a better covenant, a different sanctuary, a glorious high priest, and a righteous priesthood. *We have such a High Priest, who is seated at the right hand of the throne of the Majesty in the heavens, a Minister of the sanctuary and of the true tabernacle which the Lord erected, and not man. For every high priest is appointed to offer both gifts and sacrifices. Therefore, it is necessary that this One also have something to offer. For if He were on earth, He would not be a priest, since there are priests who offer the gifts according to the law, who serve the copy and shadow of the heavenly things, as Moses was divinely instructed when he was about to make the tabernacle. For He said, "See that you make all things according to the pattern shown you on the mountain." But now He has obtained a more excellent ministry, inasmuch as He is also Mediator of a better covenant, which was established on better promises* (Hebrews 8:1-6).

## HANDLING DEMONIC ALTARS

Moses was apparently concerned about Israel's future life in the promised land because they would be surrounded by the Canaanites who worshiped other gods, so he made this commandment: *You shall utterly destroy all the places where the nations which you shall dispossess served their gods, on the high mountains and on the hills and under every green tree. And you shall destroy their altars, break their sacred pillars, and burn their wooden images with fire; you shall cut down the carved images of their gods and destroy their names from that place. You shall not worship the Lord your God with such things* (Deuteronomy 12:2-4).

Instead of tearing down the false altars in Canaan, they began using those pagan altars to sacrifice to the Lord, using something profane to try to honor God and in a profane method! God told them, *"You must not worship the Lord your God in their way, because in worshiping their gods, they do all kinds of detestable things the Lord hates. They even burn their sons and daughters in the fire as sacrifices to their gods"* (Deuteronomy 12:31). Eventually, a history resulted in Israel's kings building idols to their gods.

Ahaz, king of Judah, did all those things God said not to do, including making idols and altars and sacrificing his sons to Molech. *Ahaz shut the doors of the Lord's temple and set up altars at every street corner in Jerusalem. In every town in Judah, he built high places to burn sacrifices to other gods...* (2 Chronicles 28:24-25). *King Hezekiah was a faithful king and brought about reforms, but then his son Manasseh rebuilt the pagan altars his father had torn down! He built altars in the temple of the Lord to all the starry hosts. Manasseh sacrificed his sons in the fire, practiced sorcery, divination, and witchcraft, and consulted mediums and spiritists. Then, he took the carved image he had made and put it in God's temple* (2 Chronicles 33:4-7). This is how far the kings of Judah and Israel had fallen, and the people followed them blindly, willingly. No wonder God allowed them to be carried off into exile and experience destruction, first Israel and then Judah!

Gideon was facing an enigma—though God was with Israel, he wondered where the wonders and miracles were. *The angel of the Lord appeared to Gideon and told him, "The Lord is with you," and Gideon asks, "If the Lord is with us, why has all this happened to us? Where are all his wonders that our fathers told us about?"* (Judges 6:13). Gideon should have asked, "Are we with the Lord?" After another encounter with God, Gideon breaks down his father's false altar he built to Baal, and Gideon constructs a proper altar where sacrifice could be offered to the Lord.

Whatever spirits are invoked at their altars will determine what is acceptable to the Lord and the atmosphere created in that place. *I beseech you therefore, brethren, by the mercies of God, that you present your bodies a living sacrifice, holy, acceptable to God, which is your reasonable service* (Romans 12:1). Righteousness begins with a sacrifice at a holy altar in your lives, an altar of our heart. Let your heart be an altar to God, and may your prayer rise to God like the sweet smell of incense, and when you lift your hands in prayer, may it be like the evening sacrifice (see Psalm 141:2 ).

In guarding the altar of your heart, be aware of any demonic altars like a coven of witches, New Age groups, or altars that existed in your family or an area for generations. *You shall make no covenant with them or with their gods* (Exodus 23:32).

In Ephesians 4:27, Paul says *do not give the devil an opportunity*. The Greek *topos* means occasion, opportunity, any portion or space marked off, location, or room.[187] So, be cautious giving the devil a space, room to gain access, through the door of your heart. Those marked-off locations of altars of deception require you to be strong in the word of God when dealing with deception at any level. It could be through false teachings, lies, pride, false religion, ungodly dreams, or illusions of reality that God does not exist.

You face two dangers: deceptions and the danger of going to places to confront false idols, like going to those religious sites in Katmandu, thinking you can deliver them without being sent by God and empowered to do it. Pride can spawn a risk leading you into treacherous places unprepared by boasting in the authority you do not have. The key to overcoming the deceptive work of Satan is knowing how to use the weapons of your warfare by casting down arguments and every high thing that exalts itself against the knowledge of God, bringing every thought into captivity to the obedience of Christ (2 Corinthians 10:5).

In John Paul Jackson's book, *Needless Casualties of War*, he offers wisdom for all who seek to engage in spiritual warfare. If you haven't read it, you should, especially when engaging in the realm of the spirit. You do not want to go somewhere and engage in something that will cause harm to your family, that opens the door of deception and unnecessary attacks that you don't need in your life. In his book, John Paul said that if you have gifts of intercessory prayer and discernment of spirits, be careful to focus on God and not on Satan and his kingdom. And he went on to say that discovering the results of this newfound jurisdiction over demonic spirits on earth caused His seventy followers to rejoice greatly. But Jesus cautioned them about becoming prideful or overconfident about their authority.[188]

In Numbers 23, a curious dialogue begins between Balaam, Balak, and God. Its fascinating story of Balak and Balaam's failed attempts to curse the Jewish people illustrates that prophets can't control God's decisions. Numbers 22-23 record how, after being thoroughly humiliated by his talking donkey, Balaam, the non-Jewish sorcerer/prophet commissioned by Balak King of Moab to curse the Jews, found himself incapable of cursing them. Instead, he bestowed four tremendous blessings on the Jews, making Balaam a bigger donkey than the talking donkey.

*Out of the same mouth come blessing and cursing. My*
*brothers, this should not be! Can both fresh water and salt*
*water flow from the same spring? (James 3:10, 11).*

We must understand that there are certain immutable laws God
has established in the spirit realm. Satan doesn't get to make up his
own rules and definitely not humans. The enemy has to move within
the boundaries of the created laws, even if they try, like Balaam and
Satan.

As seen throughout the scriptures, you never know what will
happen when heaven's gates open. In the supernatural realm, such
physical laws are broken, such as Saint Francis of Assisi, who was recorded as having been "suspended above the earth, often to a height
of three, and often to a height of 4-6 feet. St. Alphonsus Liguori, when
preaching, was lifted before the eyes of the whole congregation several feet from the ground. Liguori is also said to have had the power
of bilocation. In the Orthodox tradition, St. John the Wonderwork-
er (1896-1966) was said to be levitating while in prayer, which an individual witnessed while checking in on him while the saint was in
prayer."[189]

Manifestations are not demonic but depend on the source behind the manifestation that determines whether it's from God or evil.
The same is the way with altars, for the source determines whether to
live in open heaven or an open hell.

Abraham has arrived at the moral elevation of self-denial and
submission to the will of God. The angel of the Lord now confirms
all his special promises to him with an oath, on their deepest terms.
The multitude of his seed has a double parallel in the stars of heav-
en and the ocean's sands. In Genesis 22:15-18, the angel called Abraham for the second time, making that holy ground: *And the angel of*
*the LORD called unto Abraham out of heaven the second time, And said, By*
*myself have I sworn, saith the LORD, for because you have done this thing,*
*and have not withheld your son, your only son: That in blessing I will bless*
*you, and in multiplying I will multiply your seed as the stars of the heaven,*
*and as the sand which is upon the sea shore; and your seed shall possess*

*the gate of his enemies. And in thy seed shall all the nations of the earth be blessed because thou hast obeyed my voice.*

When the scent of the prophet's sacrifice reached heaven, the Lord secured a great victory for Israel, and then Mispah became sacred ground. *While Samuel was sacrificing the burnt offering, the Philistines drew near to engage Israel in battle. But that day, the LORD thundered with loud thunder against the Philistines and threw them into such a panic that they were routed before the Israelites; Then Samuel took a stone and set it up between Mizpah and Shen. He named it Ebenezer, saying, "Thus far has the LORD helped us"* (1 Samuel 7:10, 12 , NIV).

I believe in geographical locations where heaven and the face of God touch the earth. Thin places are locations where the distance between heaven and earth sort of collapses, and the windows of perception are washed; you can catch glimpses of God, as happened to King Nebuchadnezzar. King Nebuchadnezzar ordered the three young Israelites burned in an exceptionally hot furnace. Still, they did not perish in flames and were accompanied by one who had the appearance of a god. *King Nebuchadnezzar was astonished and rose up quickly. He said to his counselors, "Was it not three men that we threw bound into the fire?" They answered the king, "True, O king." He replied, "But I see four men unbound, walking in the middle of the fire, and they are not hurt; and the fourth has the appearance of a god"* (Daniel 3:24-25). God was walking with them in the fire; not only Shadrach, Meshach, and Abednego, but all those present around the furnace were standing on holy ground–a thin place.

I believe you can attend a thin revered place, and the same atmosphere and anointing remain. You can visit a house, and their prayers are still vibrating through the walls of the buildings from years past. I went to Wesley's prayer room, and my friends and I were so messed up in the presence of God, which was smaller than a closet, laying down in God's presence.

Revivals are like the thin places where God visits humans, coming down dramatically and kissing the earth like God did in Columbia, Argentina, and Brazil. Describing Argentina as a flashpoint of revival, C. Peter Wagner wrote, "Like a burning, dry undertone, the Spirit of God has ignited an extraordinary spiritual bonfire in Argentina. From the southern tip of Tierra del Fuego to breath-taking Iguazu Falls in the northeast, the flames of revival blazed through Argentina and beyond, making the country one of the flashpoints of church growth today." The Argentinian revival ministries of Claudio Friedson, Hector Giminez, Carlos Annacondia, and Omar Cabrera won hundreds of thousands to the Lord. They all have powerful ministries in evangelism with signs, wonders, healing, and miracles. Unprecedented unity, fervent prayer, and New Testament ministries of signs and wonders gave Argentina's revival worldwide flame, where people like John Arnott visited seeking a fresh touch from God, which led Randy Clark and Arnott to launch another significant revival, all of them being thin places where God appeared in His glory.[190]

## BUILD AN ALTAR, MAKE A HOUSE

The poet-prophet David craved for God and a place of habitation, the courts of the Lord. *How lovely are Your dwelling places, O Lord of hosts! My soul longed and even yearned for the courts of the Lord; My heart and my flesh sing for joy to the living God* (Psalm 74:1, 2, NASB). The Hebrew *mishkan* means dwelling places, resting place, tabernacle, tent, and where to dwell.

The birds are always at the Western Wall, for they found a home nestled into cracks above the folded intentions with prayers preparing to fly to heaven.

> *The bird also has found a house, And the swallow a nest for herself, where she may lay her young, Even Your altars, O Lord of hosts, My King and my God. How blessed are those who dwell in Your house! They are ever praising You. Selah. How blessed is the man whose strength is in You, in whose heart are the highways to Zion! Passing through the valley of Baca they make it a spring; The early rain also covers it with blessings. They go from strength*

*to strength, every one of them appears before God in Zion (Psalm 84:3-7, NASB).*

In ancient Greece and the East, the birds that nested in temples were accounted sacred, and the swallow sought the temple enclosure at Jerusalem as a secure and safe nesting habitation. Often the pathway to God's presence is through many valleys. In this verse, David mentions the valley of Baca, which the Literal translation called the Valley of Weeping, which was probably the Valley of Rephaim. However, one of his great victories over the Philistines was a dry place, but the rain covered its pools. *And He will cause the rain to come down for you— The former rain, And the latter rain in the first month* (Joel 2:23). The rain gives us strength to strength as we finally appear before God in Zion.

One of the most important things we must do is build an altar of compassion and righteousness with people passionate about encountering God's presence in the heavenly place and learning how to move from strength to strength. If we make our locations a priority, then the Holy Spirit can enter through the gates and change the face of the earth. If you are hungry to change the world, you can start by building an altar in your family, community, and nations, according to your calling.

A well is about more than water. It's the symbol of a thriving community, and there are things in this world we do not want to thrive. Genesis 26:12–33 tells a contentious story of wells during a time of famine, when God commands Isaac to remain in the land of his father, Abraham, and dig for water. The land is blessed because of God's promise to Abraham, and therefore Isaac is blessed in his tenacious task. Abraham dug and defended wells that thrived —but his enemies loathed it. Years later, Isaac accepted the challenge to restore and refurbish the wells. When he did, he too faced opposition from the Philistines by driving him away from his wells. So, Isaac directed his community toward the difficult task of re-digging Abraham's wells. Once again, the Lord fulfilled His promise to past generations, and Abraham's act of faith bore fruit in future generations.

As it is with Isaac's well, so it is with altars: you have to tend to the altar, keeping it burning and making sure that nothing is coming to trigger the spirits from hell to bring anything against holy altars, like causing sickness to families, chaos to communities, or creating torment that distracts people from building altars.

Gates were not only found in the cities but also churches. As a people and a church, we can open and close gates. In Isaiah 22:22, we are reminded about the power of keys to open and close doors: *And I will place on his shoulder the key of the house of David. He shall open, and none shall shut, and he shall shut, and none shall open.* In ancient times, he who holds the keys to the royal household has powerful authority to open or close it. In God's kingdom, He is the keeper of the door, opening doors you cannot close and closing doors you cannot open.

But Christ had conferred unlimited authority on the apostles when He said, "*I will give you the keys of the kingdom of heaven, and whatever you bind on earth will be bound in heaven, and whatever you loose on earth will be loosed in heaven*" (Matthew 16:19).

## REBUILDING AN ALTAR SO FIRE CAN FALL

The account of Elijah's skirmish with the prophets of Baal recorded in 1 Kings 18 is one of the historic events of a cosmic conflict between prophets and the false gods that many Israelite kings embraced. After Israel had gone more than three years without rain as a judgment for their idolatry, the prophet Elijah confronts the evil king Ahab, challenging him to a spiritual showdown. The king summoned Israel to gather at Mount Carmel, along with the 450 prophets of the false god Baal and the four hundred prophets of the false goddess Asherah (v. 19). After the children of Israel and the prophets of Baal gathered at Mount Carmel, Elijah challenges them to a decision saying, *If the Lord is God, follow Him; but if Baal, follow him* (v. 22). Forcing them to a decision, he challenges the prophets of Baal to prepare a bull as an offering for their god—Elijah would do the same—with this catch: they could light no fire on their altar. The God who answered with fire from the sky would be considered the true God (v. 23–25).

The people agreed that this was a good strategy, so the prophets of Baal went first. The pagan prophets shouted and danced around their altar from morning till noon with no answer from Baal, and the prophet mocked them, telling them to cry out louder (v. 26, 27). Despite what seemed like unending hours of effort, nothing happened. The historian's comment intimates at the vacancy of Baal worship: "*There was no response, no one answered, no one paid attention*" (v. 29).

*Elijah then called the people to him as he repaired the altar of the Lord. Once the sacrifice was ready, Elijah prayed, "Lord, the God of Abraham, Isaac and Israel, let it be known today that you are God in Israel and that I am your servant and have done all these things at your command. Answer me, Lord, answer me, so these people will know that you, Lord, are God, and that you are turning their hearts back again"* (v. 36, 37).

Then God did what Baal could never do: the fire of the LORD fell from heaven and consumed the burnt offering and the wood and the stones and the dust, *and also licked up the water in the trench* (v. 38). *The people of Israel bowed down and declared the Lord as God* (v. 39). No one who witnessed that event doubted that Yahweh was the only God, and that Baal was a powerless imitator. God's provision of rain soon followed the repentance of the Israelites.

## BREAKING DOWN ALTARS

As servants of the Most High God, we must enforce His judgment upon workers of iniquity in our region, area, or nation. Begin by demolishing old altars or repenting for idolatry and worshiping other gods . When creating an altar to the Lord, ensure that you are not building upon an existing altar constructed by the kingdom of darkness.

In deciding to tear down a demonic altar, there has to be repentance, as it was with the children of Israel. When the fire of God reveals His power, the people will repent for lack of faith, and the rains of restoration will come. *Now when they had come and gathered the church together, they reported all that God had done with them and that He had opened the door of faith to the Gentiles* (Acts 14:27).

Before you can build an altar, some altars must be removed. In the battle of the prophets, the Baal prophets expected to win by creating fire in their altars, but their side lost. Whoever you choose determines who wins in the end. *And if it seems evil to you to serve the LORD, choose for yourselves this day whom you will serve, whether the gods which your fathers served that were on the other side of the river, or the gods of the Amorites, in whose land you dwell. But as for me and my house, we will serve the LORD* (Joshua 24:15).

As Gideon would do, now is the time to repent and break down all evil altars in your community or nation. *On that night, the LORD said to Gideon, "Take your father's young bull and a second bull seven years old, tear down your father's altar to Baal, and cut down the Asherah pole beside it"* (Judges 6:25, BSB). As Gideon destroyed the altar in his family, so should we do if they exist. It is a war against all evil altars. Demonic forces are setting up ungodly altars in families, cities, and nations as a war against the progression of God's people and His kingdom; they must be exposed and exterminated. And those in communion with God should not have communion with the works of darkness. *And have no fellowship with the unfruitful works of darkness, but rather expose them* (Ephesians 5:11).

*When God made man in his image, the moral law was written in his heart, by the finger of God, without outward means. But since the covenant made with man was broken, the Lord used the ministry of men, both in writing the law in the Scriptures and in writing it in the heart* (Exodus 34:4). Those under a curse caused by breaking the moral law must renounce and squelch every existing agreement between Satan and those building evil altars and breaking the covenant established by God. *Keeping mercy for thousands, forgiving iniquity and transgression and sin, by no means clearing the guilty, visiting the iniquity of the fathers upon the children and the children's children to the third and the fourth generation* (Exodus 34:7).

Here is the second revelation of the name of the God of Israel to Moses. The first revelation was of Yahweh as the self-existent One, who purposed to deliver His people with a mighty hand (Exodus 3:14); this was the same Yahweh who is a loving Savior who now forgives their sins. In the commandment, there is divine love associated with divine justice.

In Ezekiel 18:4, a reiteration exists between the words in Exodus and Ezekiel: *Behold, all souls are mine; as the soul of the father, so also the soul of the son is mine: the soul that sinned, it shall die.* But then the prophetic word in verses five through nine becomes clear that *if a man be just, and do that which is lawful and right,* and then mentions a litany of things you don't do or righteous things you do, then he surely lives. But in Ezekiel 18:10-13, it is the opposite, for if they have done all these abominations, they shall die, and his blood shall be on him.

Spiritual oppression can appear outside our safe place through curses and witchcraft and from within ourselves because we harbor hatred, bitterness, malice, and unforgiveness in our hearts (Matthew 18:21-35). Such spiritual oppression can also stem from involvement in the occult, false teaching, sexual immorality, or keeping idols or magic books in the home (Deuteronomy 7:24-26). Christians can be oppressed, hindered, and harassed, like the temple in Jerusalem, which, in the time of Jeremiah and Ezekiel, had idol worship and evil practices occurring while God's glory still dwelt in the Ark of the Covenant inside the Holy of Holies. Therefore, Christians often had to cleanse the temple and break all association with such practices. *Therefore, repent and return, so that your sins may be wiped away, in order that times of refreshing may come from the presence of the Lord* (Acts 3:19).

The good news is that forgiveness and deliverance are possible through the power of the Holy Spirit, repentance, and righteousness, as indicated in God's word. *Not by might nor by power, but by my Spirit* (Zechariah 4:6). *Therefore, repent and return so that your sins may be wiped away, in order that times of refreshing may come from the presence of the Lord* (Acts 3:19, NASB). *A man is not established by wickedness, But the root of the righteous cannot be moved* (Proverbs 12:3).

There are only two paths to the way of life: righteous living and repentance. So, if you enter an evil covenant, especially something established by your ancestors, radical repentance is required if you are to be freed from its bondage. Curses and evil covenants are responsible for our culture's many tribulations and trials. After the victory over the Baal prophets, Elijah was in a depression, so while at the cave, when God appeared, he outlined his concerns. *I have been very zealous for the Lord God of hosts; for the children of Israel have forsaken Your covenant, torn down Your altars, and killed Your prophets with the sword* (1 Kings 19:10), but Israel did repent and returned to Yahweh, and the rain came.

Jehovah-Jireh is one of the different names of God found in the Old Testament. Jehovah-Jireh, *YHWH-Yireh* means "The LORD Will Provide." *And Abraham named that place The LORD Will Provide, as it is said to this day, "On the mountain of the LORD it will be provided"* (Genesis 22:14).

Abraham's name was honored and celebrated when God provided the ram to be sacrificed in place of Isaac. The account of Abraham on Mount Moriah thus becomes more than a dramatic illustration of faith and obedience. It is a presentation of the Lord's amazing grace, constant prevention, and extensive wisdom. Jehovah-Jireh is not "The LORD *Did* Provide," but "The LORD *Will* Provide." In other words, the name does not simply memorialize a past event; it anticipates a future action for those who embrace God's covenant of blessing.

Mary J. Evans, a former lecturer at the London School of Theology, wrote these words concerning blessings and cursings: "New Testament teaching echoes the Old Testament view of blessing and cursing as relational. The ultimate and only important blessing is that of belonging to God being part of his family. The only real curse is separating from God outside the community of blessing. Both blessings and curses can be described in material terms in temporal contexts, but their material dimension is secondary. Although bad things can happen to those who belong to the kingdom, those who are part of God's people cannot be under the curse; rather, they are blessed!"[191]

## CHAPTER TEN

# TERRITORIAL SPIRITS

Since the early days of our world, people have been formed into groups with others in authority over them. Those territories began to grow from Babylon to Rome, and now look how our world grew. The entire world is divided into continents, while continents are further sub-divided into countries. Then countries are divided into regions or states. These nations and regions are divided into local government areas or boroughs. Finally, local government areas are divided into cities, towns, and townships. From the continent right down to the village, all these territories, people rule through political authorities that rule over them and manage their affairs.

This final chapter deals with territorial spirits and parallel spiritual governmental authorities that rule over them. According to scriptures, these are called principalities, powers, rulers of darkness, and spiritual hosts of wickedness in the heavenly places (Ephesians 6:12). The Greek text reads, "*We don't wrestle with flesh and blood but against rulers, against the authorities, against the cosmic powers of this darkness, and the spiritual forces of evil in the heavenly realms.*"[192] It means that continents, countries, regions, states, cities, towns, and villages all have spirit overlords, unseen rulers that exercise consequential influence over them. These spirit rulers resist God and oppose Christ, the

Son whom He has appointed heir of all things. And never doubt that they are against the plans and purposes of God for humanity, creating mayhem in key places.

Two powerful stories demonstrate the truth concerning territorial spirits that war against humans: the prince of Persia in the book of Daniel and the man with an unclean spirit. The first reference of war in the heavens materializes in Daniel 10 when an angel appears and touches Daniel. Daniel the prophet received a disturbing vision concerning a great war (v.1). So intense was the vision that he went into three weeks of mourning, fasting, and prayer. Responding to Daniel's prayer, God sent a heavenly messenger to explain the vision. During those three weeks, the angelic messenger was delayed, which the angel described to Daniel.

The narrative implies that wicked territorial spirits under the command of Satan were assigned to nations to oppose God's will and people. This prince of Persia was responsible for attempts at manipulating the king's decision to release many of the Jews held in captivity. His evil plotted maneuverings were overpowered by the support of God's chief angel, Michael, by assisting the heavenly messenger. Events play out on earth as a corresponding movement happens in the spiritual realm.

Then the second account is the story of a Gadarene, who was possessed by an evil spirit. The Gadarenes (Gergesenes) country is one of the few areas Jesus visited where Gentiles composed most of the population. Once landing in that area, Jesus confronted a man whose possessed state gave him a level of superhuman strength like Samson, but the demons tormented him, and he was uncontrollable (Mark 5:3-5).

The demonically possessed man who came to Jesus cried out his name was Legion. This name refers to a Roman military regiment that varied in soldier strength from 4,000 to 6,000. [193] Even as the purpose of the Roman legions was to enforce the emperor's will, the goal of the multiple evil spirits was to carry out the devil's will of bringing pain, destruction, and chaos to humans!

In great mercy, the Lord freed the Gadarene by casting the demons out of him and allowing them to enter a nearby herd of pigs. The swine then immediately killed themselves by rushing off a cliff. When the nearby townspeople heard of the great miracle (and not wanting to suffer further economic loss), they begged Christ to leave the Gadarenes and never come back!

Spiritual warfare is a reality, and a titanic, cosmic battle is going on in the supernatural, invisible realm all around us. We can't see it, but Yahweh's angels battle with demonic forces in a conflict to determine who will persuade and control nations and individuals. But we are called to engage in the spiritual battle on the earthly level. *Therefore, take up the whole armor of God, that you may be able to withstand in the evil day, and having done all, to stand* (Ephesians 6:13).

For generations, Christians have focused on "Satan" as the main opponent when they have engaged in spiritual warfare, but there are other enemies. C. Peter Wagner developed an approach to spiritual warfare that involves three levels. The first is *ground-level spiritual warfare*, which refers to casting demons out of believers. The second is *occult-level spiritual warfare*, which refers to "dealing with powers of darkness that are more coordinated and organized than one or more demons who might be afflicting a certain person at a certain time."[194] The third is *strategic-level spiritual warfare*, which involves confrontation with high-ranking territorial spirits which Satan has assigned to coordinate the activities of the kingdom of darkness over a certain area to keep the people's minds blinded to the "gospel of the glory of Christ," as in 2 Corinthians 4:3, 4.[195]

There is an entire hierarchy of demons, many with specific geographic territories.

Once a territorial spirit's power is broken, ministry in that area can be far more effective. Even though Christ, by His death and resurrection, has snatched back the dominion and authority from Satan and given them back to man, these evil forces refuse to give up and continue to fight against humans. Hence, anyone anywhere on earth is fair game, as far as Satan is concerned.

## THE MYSTERIOUS NUMBER SEVEN

At the latest, the diverse Sumerian words containing the number took firm root in their culture by the twenty-second century BCE. But the question is, why did they select the number 7 as a mystical or sacred number? In religious or mythological cosmology, the **seven heavens** refer to seven levels or divisions of the heavens. The ancient Mesopotamians regarded the sky as a series of domes (usually three, but sometimes seven) covering the flat earth as they knew it. Understanding that the heavens can influence things on earth when presented with heavenly, magical properties to the number seven itself, as in stories of seven demons, spirits, or thrones.

The number seven frequently appears in Babylonian magical rituals. And the second Book of Enoch, also written in the first century CE, describes Enoch's mystical ascent through a hierarchy of ten heavens.

When he reaches the seventh heaven, Enoch sees the fiery armies of archangels and a wide variety of angelic beings (chapter 20). Enoch is so frightened the angelic guides must pick him up and strengthen him. They show him the throne of the Lord at a great distance (it is in the tenth heaven). He moves to the very edge of the seventh heaven to see the seraphim. The angel guides depart and are replaced by Gabriel, the archangel (chapter 21). With Gabriel, he sees the eighth heaven, which contains the Zodiac. Michael then brings Enoch into the presence of the Lord in the tenth heaven (chapter 22).

> *"And those two men lifted me up thence on to the <u>seventh heaven</u>, and I saw there a very great light, and fiery troops of great archangels, celestial forces, and dominions, orders and governments, Cherubim and seraphim, thrones and many-eyed ones, nine regiments, the Ioanit stations of light" (2 Enoch 20:1, emphasis added).*[196]

Numbers in biblical times were often symbolic of a deeper meaning. The number seven is especially prominent in scriptures, appearing over 700 times. From the seven days of creation to the many "sevens" in Revelation, the number seven was used in various ways, including the dark side of the number seven. The first use of the number *seven* in the Bible relates to the creation week in Genesis 1. God spends six days creating the heavens and the earth and then rests on the seventh day. It was a template for the seven-day week observed worldwide to this day. The seventh day was "set apart" for Israel, and the Sabbath was a holy day of rest.

Throughout the scriptures, manifold references exist of the number 7 with biblical meaning attached. But the number 7 is used more than fifty times in the book of Revelation in a variety of contexts: there are seven letters to seven churches in Asia and seven spirits before God's throne (Revelation 1:4), seven golden lampstands (Revelation 1:12), seven stars in Christ's right hand (Revelation 1:16), seven seals of God's judgment (Revelation 5:1), seven angels with seven trumpets (Revelation 8:2), etc. In all likelihood, the number 7 again represents completeness or totality: the seven churches represent the completeness of the body of Christ, the seven seals on the scroll, and the book of Revelation, with all its 7s, is the capstone of God's word to man.

## THE SEVEN SPIRITS OF GOD

*John to the seven churches that are in Asia: Grace to you and peace from Him who is, and who was, and who is to come, and from the seven spirits who are before His throne (Revelation 1:4, NASB).*

*To the angel of the church in Sardis, write: He who has the seven spirits of God and the seven stars (Revelation 3:1, NASB).*

*Out from the throne came flashes of lightning and sounds and peals of thunder. And there were seven lamps of fire burning before the throne, which are the seven spirits of God (Revelation 4:5, ESV).*

> *And between the throne and the four living creatures and among the elders I saw a Lamb standing, as though it had been slain, with seven horns and with seven eyes, which are the seven spirits of God sent out into all the Earth (Revelation 5:6, NASB).*

It is impossible to say with complete certainty what or who the Bible refers to when it describes the "seven spirits of God" in these verses. From the references that mention the seven spirits, we know they are "held" by Christ and likened to seven lamps burning in front of God's throne. They also said, "sent out into all the earth" and equated it with the "seven eyes" of the Lamb of God.

These descriptions are mysterious and compact with symbolic meaning, as is much of the book of Revelation. However, there is no indication that these seven spirits of God do not exist. That is, they are more than simple metaphors. John refers to them as a literal entity, similar to the angels or the cherubim. One view is that the seven spirits are indeed angels of some kind.[197]

Enoch mentions seven angels who have specific assignments which seem to fit with the seven angels of God. "And these are the names of the holy angels who watch. Uriel, one of the holy angels, is over the world and Tartarus. Raphael, one of the holy angels, is over the spirits of men. Raguel is one of the holy angels who takes vengeance on the world of the luminaries. Michael, one of the holy angels, to wit, he that is set over the best part of mankind and over chaos. Saraqael, one of the holy angels, who is set over the spirits, who sin in the spirit. Gabriel, one of the holy angels, who is over Paradise and the serpents and the Cherubim. Remiel, one of the holy angels, whom God set over those who rise" (Enoch 19:1-8).[198]

Another view takes a verse from Isaiah 11:2 and uses it to enumerate and name the seven spirits of God. *Rested on him hath the Spirit of Jehovah, the spirit of wisdom and understanding, The spirit of counsel and might, The spirit of knowledge and fear of Jehovah* (Isaiah 11:1, 2, Young's Literal Translation).

## THE SEVEN STARS

The stars invoked humanity's greatest creative and intricate legends and myths. Both the Egyptians and the Babylonians assigned stars to their myriad of deities. The practice of star worship also thrived under the Assyrians and especially the Chaldeans. In Joseph's dream, the twelve tribes of Israel are represented as stars.

After the seventh seal is opened, John sees these seven angels who stand before God, also known as the seven stars. *The mystery of the seven stars which you saw in My right hand, and the seven golden lampstands: <u>The seven stars are the angels of the seven churches,</u> and the seven lampstands which you saw are the seven churches* (Revelation 1:20, emphasis added).

In Joseph's dreams, the twelve tribes of Israel are symbolized as stars. *Then he dreamed still another dream and told it to his brothers, and said, "Look, I have dreamed another dream. And this time, the sun, the moon, and the eleven stars bowed down to me"* **(Genesis 37:9).**

God warns the people not to worship the stars and *beware not to lift up your eyes to heaven and see the sun and the moon and the **stars**, all the host of heaven, and be drawn away and worship them and serve them, those which the LORD your God has allotted to all the peoples under the whole heaven* **(Deuteronomy 4:19).**

The stargazers were legitimate observers of the skies, but, finally, the greater part of the astronomers launched into astrology and undertook to predict events from the changing phenomena of the heavens, which became a spiritual problem. These **astrologers read the stars but were powerless.** *Let now the astrologers, those who prophesy by the **stars**, Those who predict by the new moons, stand up and save you from what will come upon you* **(Isaiah 47:13).**

The ancients often assigned particular stars to false idols. *You also carried along Sikkuth your king and Kiyyun, your images, the <u>star</u> of your gods which you made for yourselves* **(Amos 5:26, emphasis added).**

## THE SEVEN MOUNTAINS

Here is the mind which has wisdom. *The seven heads are seven mountains on which the woman sits. There are also seven kings. Five have fallen, one is, and the other has not yet come. And when he comes, he must continue a short time* (Revelation 17:9, 10). In verse five, the woman is referred to as a city, Babylon the great, the mother of harlots.

Rome is called the city of seven hills, and many Bible teachers believe the mountains refer to the seven hills that Rome sits on. But the false religious system is worldwide, and in the original Greek language, the next verse says these seven heads are seven kings. In the scriptures, mountains often represent the power of kingdoms and individual kings (Jeremiah 51:25; Daniel 2:35; Zechariah 4:7).

The woman sitting on the seven mountains can be described in two different ways; it either means the place where the woman is sitting, or she controls the seven mountains (kings). Since the woman represents the worldwide false religion, it's best to say she controls the seven kings and the beast she sits on. False religions have been a manipulating factor in governments since Nimrod established Babel, and even today, false religions are influencing factors in many nations around the world.

*And they are seven kings; five have fallen, one is, the other has not yet come; and when he comes, he must remain a little while* (Revelation 17:10). The seven kings are political systems, not religious ones—the mountains represent the seven kings of the seven world empires on earth that came out of the political and religious Babel that God used for His purposes in dealing with Israel. The five that have fallen are Egypt, Assyria, Babylon, Persia, Greece, and Rome, which had not fallen during John's visions. All of this is manipulated by satanic influence.[199]

## SEVEN ALTARS

The Moabites were terrified of the Jews, especially after they defeated the Emori, the Moabites' guardians. Although natural enemies,

Moab and Midian banded together and appointed a Midianite, Balak son of Zippor, as king over them. Balak recognized that the power of the Jews was supernatural, so he sought a way of undermining them supernaturally.

Together with the elders of Midian, he hatched a plan to hire Balaam, a well-known and powerful sorcerer and prophet, to curse the Jews at a diviner's fee. In the past, if he placed a curse on someone, it happened, but Balaam knew about the true God, not of some vague, demonic spirit. Because of his love for money, Balaam essentially tried to manipulate God into granting him a special exception. Still, Balaam's two visits with Balak's representatives flopped. First, God told him not to go with the first group, and the next time God told him to go, knowing full well that God was on Israel's side.

But that was not the worst, because the encounter with the donkey and the angel sent him back to Balak. God had sent the angel and made the donkey speak to bring about this humiliation, shattering Balaam's ego.

Having been humiliated by his donkey and pushed around by God, Balaam arrived in Moab's capital city and was greeted by Balak. So, the next day, Balak took Balaam up to the mountain of the high places of Baal, that from there, he might observe the extent of the entire Jewish camp.

First, Balaam said to Balak to construct seven altars and have seven bulls and seven rams ready to sacrifice on those seven altars (Numbers 23:1). *Then Balaam and Balak offered a bull and a ram on each altar, and Balaam the prophet told Balak the king of Moab to stay by his burnt offerings, while Balaam went to meet with God on a barren height. And God met Balaam, and he said to Him, "I have prepared the seven altars, and I have offered on each altar a bull and a ram." Then the Lord put a word in Balaam's mouth, and said, "Return to Balak, and thus you shall speak"* (v. 4, 5). After being at the third different location overlooking the camp of Israel and going through the same rituals, the Spirit of God comes upon Balaam delivering a third positive prophecy concerning Israel. The seven altars' sacrifices to their gods were an utter flop because there is only one God, and Yahweh is His name.

As long as you rest in the divine alignment with the Lord, your life is purified and protected. Despite what false prophets attempt at curses, building a sacrificial altar to their gods, or any encroachment of satanic forces, we have set our minds on the heavens, not on earth, and our life is hidden with Christ in God (Colossians 3:2, 3).

**Ecliptic, Solstice, Equinox**

Now we explore the place of untangling the Babylonian star system and everything related to understanding how the created heavens work. Then we will shift to the misuse of God's creative work.

The *ecliptic* is an imaginary line in the sky that marks the sun's path. The moon and planets also travel along the path of the ecliptic. It's the projection of the earth's orbit onto the celestial sphere, and it marks the plane of the solar system. Tracing the paths of the planets in front of the background stars, you'll see that the ecliptic passes through the constellations of the Zodiac.

The ancients could predict when eclipses would occur by paying attention to the movement of bodies along the ecliptic. This invisible line across the sky is the starting point for the celestial coordinate system used by astronomers to pinpoint the location of every star, nebula, and galaxy.

Astronomy has been important to people for thousands of years. The ancient construction of Stonehenge in England may have been supernaturally designed, among other purposes, to attribute honor to the solstices and equinoxes. These are the times and locations during earth's journey around the sun that we humans have long used to mark our seasons.

There are only two times of the year when the earth's axis is tilted neither towards nor away from the sun, resulting in a nearly equal amount of daylight and darkness at all latitudes. And these events are referred to as the equinoxes.

The sun's migration appears to halt on two days of the year and then switches directions. Those two days are the solstice days based on the Latin derivative *solstitum,* which means "sun stopped or stationary." The summer solstice happens in late June—23.5° north of the equator—called the Tropic of Cancer, and the winter solstice happens in late December—23.5° south of the equator—called the Tropic of Capricorn.²⁰⁰

## THE ZODIAC AND GOD'S CREATIVE ACT

The **Sumerians in Mesopotamia**—a historical region of Western Asia—were the first to start noticing the movements of the planets and stars. Around 3000 BCE, they recorded and identified the prominent constellations and patterns. Within Mesopotamia, the **Babylonians** (also known as the *Chaldeans*) became the first great astronomers. Continuing with the Sumerians' research, the Babylonians created the first **zodiac wheel.**

At around the end of the 5th century BCE, Babylonian astronomers divided the ecliptic into 12 equal "signs" that correspond to the 12 months of the year at 30 days each. Each sign contained 30° of celestial longitude, creating the first known **celestial coordinate system.** The name of an animal often identifies each segment. The Greeks later provided the term for the Zodiac when they described it as the *zodiakos kyklos,* aka "animal circle."

After the occupation of Alexander the Great in 332 BCE, Egypt came under Hellenistic rule. In the city of Alexandria—founded by Alexander during the 3rd and 2nd centuries BCE—scholars created **Horoscopic astrology** by merging Babylonian astrology with the Egyptian tradition of the **Decanic Zodiac.**²⁰¹

Later, when the Egyptian and Mesopotamian astrological traditions were synthesized around the 1st century BCE, the 36 decans were merged with the 12 signs of the Zodiac.²⁰² A decan is the subdivision of a sign. Each sign is allocated a triplicity, consisting of three of the four classical elements—air, water, earth, or fire—and subdivided into three equal parts of 10 degrees each; these parts are decans or decanates. Decans are a way of breaking down the qualities of each sign by separating each one into thirds of ten degrees each. Every sign will have three decans, and each decan has a planetary ruler who becomes the co-ruler of that particular sign.²⁰³

## ASTROLOGY, A CORRUPTIVE
## DECEPTION, AND BOOMING BUSINESS

Astrology is not to be confused with science; there's no evidence prov-ing zodiac signs correlate with personality. It's simply a method of predicting earthly and human events based on the placement of the sun, the moon, and the planets within the astrological constellations.

It has been rejected by the scientific community as having no ex-planatory power for describing the universe and has not demonstrat-ed its effectiveness in controlled studies, has no scientific validity, and is thus regarded as pseudoscience. There is no proposed mechanism of action by which the positions and motions of stars and planets could affect people and events on earth in the way astrologers say they do that does not contradict well understood basic aspects of bi-ology and physics.[204]about:blank - cite_note-Vishveshwara-6

And so, everything became a system of corruptive deceit that could be easily manipulated by darkness, no matter what the sign was. And so, when the cultic astrologist prophesizes or decrees over a particular sign, and without knowing can affect you by creating false hope, taking you down a river of exploitation.

Besides the perversion of truth, it leads to profits in the astrology industry, which is what it is, a booming business. As insider Barbara Smith previously reported, revenue for astrology apps grew to near-ly $40 million in 2019—a 64% increase . According to Sensor Tower and IBISWorld, "mystical services" grew by 1.4% from 2016 to 2019. The industry as a whole is worth $2.2 billion.[205] Such business partly brought down the Babylonian empire.

*And these two things come to you, in a moment, in one day: childless-ness and widowhood, they have come on you according to their perfection, In the multitude of your sorceries, In the exceeding might of your charms* (Isaiah 47:9, LSV). They were secure in their wickedness, but their knowledge led them astray (v. 10). So, catastrophe fell upon them like a giant heavenly boulder crushing their nation. *But disaster will come upon you; you will not know how to charm it away. A calamity will befall you that you will be unable to ward off. Devastation will happen to you suddenly and unexpectedly* (v.11).

With cunning irony and hints of prophetic mockery, Isaiah push-
es their leaders and people forward on their pathway to Babylonian
destruction, not slowly but quickly it will come. *Persist, then, [Baby-
lon] in your enchantments and your many sorceries with which you have
labored from your youth; Perhaps you will be able to profit [from them],
Perhaps you may prevail and cause trembling* (v. 12). The prophet gave
them a contrived encouragement to Babylon, Israel's adversaries. "If
Babylon uses all the resources of her magical art, perhaps she may
succeed—who knows? Perhaps she may strike terror into the hearts
of her assailants. An enormous disruption will come upon you, not
discerning how to charm it away. It reflects Yahweh's pathos towards
astrology, stargazing, or your monthly prognostication."

In Stephen's last address to the Sanhedrin, he compares the fall of
Babylon to the hard hearts of the Jewish leaders. *Then God turned and
gave them up to worship the host of heaven, as it is written in the book of the
Prophets: Did you offer Me slaughtered animals and sacrifices during forty
years in the wilderness, O house of Israel? You also took up the tabernacle
of Moloch, And the star of your god Remphan, Images which you made to
worship; And I will carry you away beyond Babylon* (Acts 7:42, 43).

*You are stiff-necked and uncircumcised in heart and ears! You always
resist the Holy Spirit; as your fathers did, so do you. Which of the prophets did your fathers not persecute? And they killed those who foretold the
coming of the Just One, of whom you now have become the betrayers and
murderers* (v. 51, 52).

It is not typical in today's language of someone who would use
harsh language against those resisting biblical truth, persecuting
people who speak the truth and those who engage in prophetic divination.

## SPIRIT GUIDES, HOLY AND UNHOLY

The Holy Spirit has many functions. Not only does He distribute
spiritual gifts according to His will, but He also comforts us, teaches
us, and remains as a seal of promise upon our hearts until the day of
Jesus' return. But the Holy Spirit also takes on the role of a guide and

counselor. *When the Spirit of truth comes, he will guide you into all the truth, for he will not speak on his own authority, but whatever he hears he will speak, and he will declare to you the things that are to come* (John 16:13, ESV).

When we receive the Spirit of God, we are in position to know all things. But when we speak, we are guided by the Spirit, *which things we also speak, not in words taught by human wisdom, but in those taught by the Spirit, combining spiritual thoughts with spiritual words* (1 Corinthians 2:13, NASB).

When we know the will of God but do not follow it, we are resisting the Spirit's work in our lives, which could open doors to the other spirit guides. Despite the claims of New Agers, spirit guides are anything but benevolent. They are not the spirits of dear, departed loved ones, nor are they ascended masters who have crossed over some mystical plane, but the Bible does refer to familiar spirits and those who associate with them. *You must not turn to mediums or spiritists; do not seek them out, or you will be defiled by them. I am the LORD your God* (Leviticus 19:31).

While one is sleeping, an enemy sows tares and then leaves after creating the disaster. *But while men slept, his enemy came and sowed tares among the wheat and went his way* (Matthew 13:25). These are not human enemies but Satan's minions planting bad seeds of false doctrine and devastating lies that will ruin them as the seeds grow in their souls.

> *Have respect to the covenant; For the dark places of the earth are full of the haunts of cruelty (Psalm 74:20).*

These dark places are places of wickedness and wrath. ***And we know that we are of God and the whole world lieth in wickedness*** (1 John 5:19). And in Revelation 12:12, they prophetically speak of a time of demonic anger: ***Woe to the inhabitants of the earth and of the sea! for the devil has come down unto you, having great wrath.***

*And have no fellowship with the unfruitful works of darkness but rather expose them* (Ephesians 5:11). Fully a third of the recorded miracles of Saint Columba involve evil spirits. On one occasion, Columba was fasting alone on Iona. In a vision, he saw a wave of black creatures holding iron darts, attacking and striking down the monks of his monastery.... Protected by the armor of God, Columba spent the entire day in violent combat, taking on the demonic forces singlehandedly, a true warrior of the Spirit. When the exhausted saint returned to the monastery, he informed his fellows that they had been spared from the plague due to his spiritual warfare on their behalf *(Water from an Ancient Well).*[206]

## SATANIC MEDIATORS AND INTERCESSORS

In the scriptures and especially the apocalyptic writings, we meet a cast of fallen characters—Satan, demons, and other nefarious beings, like the beast and false prophet—that indicate supernatural realities, earthly administrators of evil with structures of power. Satan is the force behind those nefarious beings, prince of the power of the air, and his unseen forces influence or even control what happens in the mundane earthly realm. If these demonic powers are the boot that seeks to press down upon the human face, then God is the ultimate power that crushes all satanic powers in their diverse forms, creating an army empowered by the Spirit.

Satan is the mediator of those incorporated into the community of wickedness and deception, including witches, sorcerers, voodoo priests, occult masters, and wizards. These are members of the satanic war machine. They cut covenants with different spirits to cause havoc in people's lives and renew their covenants every year through rituals and festivals.

A magician, also known as an enchanter/enchantress, magic user, sorcerer/sorceress, spell-caster, warlock, witch, or wizard, is someone who uses or practices magic derived from the supernatural. When Manasseh became king, he did evil in the sight of the Lord, according to the abominations of the nations. *He sacrificed his children in the fire in the Valley of Ben Hinnom, practiced divination and witchcraft, sought omens, and consulted mediums and spiritists. He did much evil in the eyes of the LORD, arousing his anger* (2 Chronicles 33:5, 6).

Fetish Priest— In West Africa, a fetish priest is a person who serves as a mediator between the spirits and the living. Fetish priests usually live and worship their gods in enclosed shrines. The fetish shrine is a simple mud hut with an enclosure or fence. The priest or priestess performs rituals to consult and seek favor from his gods in the shrine. The priest is usually chosen through divination. Though, at times, they help people in their spiritual matters and physical in people's life. But all the people fear them most often because fetish priests claim they can kill people spiritually.[207]

Witches—Early witches were people practicing witchcraft, using magic spells, calling upon spirits for help, or bringing about change. Most witches were thought to be pagans doing the devil's work. One of the earliest records of a witch is in 1 Samuel 28, when King Saul sought the Witch of Endor to summon the dead prophet Samuel's spirit to help him defeat the Philistine army. The witch roused Samuel, who then prophesied the death of Saul and his sons. The next day, according to the Bible, Saul's sons died in battle and Saul committed suicide. Other Old Testament verses condemn witches, such as Exodus 22:18, which says, *thou shalt not suffer a witch to live*. Other biblical passages caution against divination, chanting, or using witches to contact the dead.

In a famous case in 1324 in Ireland, Lady Alice Kyteller was charged with performing magical rites, attempting to divine the future, and poisoning her first three husbands by having sexual intercourse with demons similar to the watchers in Genesis 6.

Charismatic Witchcraft—In Steven Lambert's book, *Charismatic Control: Witchcraft in Neo-Pentecostal Churches,* he exposes the multitudes of sincere and trusting believers caught unawares in the virtually invisible web of religious captivation in certain Charismatic/Neo-Pentecostal churches. Unconscious victims of spiritual abuse, psychological enslavement, and various forms of exploitation are perpetrated under excessive coercive authoritarianism. Such control exploits their followers for personal gain and builds their own

kingdom privately. The truth of the matter is that ecclesiastical enslavement and exploitation are widespread in some sectors of Chris-
tendom, but the perpetrators, many of whom are prominent and re-
spected church leaders, often go to great lengths to disguise it and
have thus far been successful in concealing it. It includes a cross-sec-
tion of average Americans—individuals and families—of every race,
education level, station, and walk of life, rather than radical, fringe
religious sects and cults as many would suppose.[208]

Dr. Robin Harfouche sees Charismatic Witchcraft as the interces-
sor praying that the pastor would take the church differently. It's a
young woman praying that a certain man would have feelings for her.
It's the individual who gives parking lot prophecies or lays hands on
another with the intent of forcing a desire on them through spiritual
means. For this reason, many ministers have shied away from teaching the saints the true word of God concerning spiritual gifts. They
don't want to deal with charismatic witchcraft in the church.[209]

In his article, "The Seeking of Control," Derek Prince defines
witchcraft from a dictionary as "the art or exercise of magical powers, the effect of the influence of magical powers, or an alluring or
seductive charm or influence."[210] Seeking control of people is one of
the great arts of witchcraft, and unfortunately, it can be discovered in
many churches and must be exposed and confronted.

Magic and Sorcerers—In its widest sense, magic attempts to influence persons and events by recourse to superhuman powers: it is
"the science of the occult." The word derives from the Magi, a priest-
ly caste in Media whose functions have largely been associated with
"magic." They claimed to mediate between gods and men; conducted
sacrifices; supervised the disposal of the dead; interpreted dreams,
omens, and celestial phenomena; and foretold the future. "Magic"
came into the Greek world from Persia and thence into Rome, which
the word "sorcery" has possessed to an even greater degree. Magic is
considered mostly white magic and sorcery black magic because of
the evil consequences of their actions.

The word φαρμακεία (pharmakeia) translated as "sorcery" or
"witchcraft" in most English versions, literally means "the use of

medicine, drugs or spells." **Sorcery** was the practice of malevolent magic derived from casting lots to divining the future in the ancient Mediterranean world. Magic is considered mostly white magic and sorcery black magic because of the evil consequences of their actions.

But sorceries will be cut off by the hand of God. *And I will cut off sorceries from your hand, and you shall have no more tellers of fortunes* (Micah 5:2).

> *And when Babylon falls, all evil will be terminated deceived by its sorceries. Then a strong angel picked up a stone like a great millstone and threw it into the sea, saying, "So will Babylon, the great city, be thrown down with violence, and will never be found again. For your merchants were the great ones of the earth, and all nations were deceived by your sorcery" (Revelation 18:21, 23 ).*

Voodoo Doctors—The history of slavery in the Caribbean brought religious practices from enslaved West Africans into contact with Roman Catholicism in French and Spanish colonies and result-ed in distinct New World religions like Haitian *Vodou* and Louisiana Voodoo. Voodoo drifted into spiritual practices involving charmed objects, loosely inspired the so-called "voodoo doll," with the prac-tice of stabbing an effigy with pins to punish people, which is attested in the practice of VOODOO or *Hoodoo.* In *Vodou,* the "zombie" is a living but soulless individual whose free will has been taken by a powerful sorcerer or *bocor.* Voodooism is also considered a religious cult involv-ing witchcraft and communication by trance with ancestors and ani-mistic deities, common in Haiti and other Caribbean islands.[211]

Wizards—In *A Wizard of Earth Sea*, every act of magic distorts the equilibrium of the world, which has far-reaching consequences that can affect the entire world and everything in it. As a result, competent wizards do not use their magic frivolously. The extent of a wizard's knowledge is limited to which spells a wizard knows and can cast. Magic may also be limited by its danger; if a powerful spell can cause grave harm if miscast, wizards are likely to be wary of using it.[212]

## POWERS OF THE DARK NIGHT
## OF TERRITORIAL SPIRITS

This will seem strange and unbelievable for most Christians, but it is a real thing for others, and they need help.

Something about the devil's hour instills a sense of dread into your soul. You know you're safe in your bed, and there is nothing in your room that wasn't there before. But, waking up suddenly at 3 AM fills your body with fear. The phrase "Witching Hour" was first recorded sometime around 1835. However, the origins seem to be from a period in 1535 when the Catholic Church forbade activities during the 3-4 AM window due to rising concerns about witchcraft in Europe. The powers of the dark night are when demonic activity, exorcisms, and rituals have all become intertwined with the Witching Hour.

Household pursuers are demonic powers that move upon your family members and attack them. The signs of satanic interruptions in the family are revealed in multiple ways that seem hereditary. These are some of the attacks that happen in families, especially when these things in each generation: patterns of early death, inherited diseases, multiple divorces, no marriage, a spirit of polygamy, poverty, failure at the edge of a breakthrough, issues with firstborn babies, and a parent who abandons their family. Pray and fast to break curses and covenants which enforce these evil patterns. Look at your life. What seeds are you sowing for your children? By the life you are living right now, you create a pattern for future generations.

The spirits of death and hell seek to operate at night, causing unreasonable death by the perpetrators whom satanic forces have influenced. Over the years, with deep sorrow, we have observed young kids influenced by demons who have killed children at school. Some forces intend to destroy goodness and good things, but it is our responsibility to stand in the place of resisting what demonic forces seek to do.

*You shall not eat any flesh with the blood in it. You shall not interpret omens or tell fortunes* (Leviticus 19:26). Satanic feeding or evil consumption is a very common problem. It is one of the weapons that the devil

uses to carry out his satanic agenda of killing, stealing, and destroying good things in people's lives (John 10:10). Some people have found
themselves eating flesh or drinking blood in their dreams while they
slept at one time or another. But God will give you peace and rest
when you look to Him and pray. *When you lie down, you will not be
afraid; Yes, you will lie down, and your sleep will be sweet* (Proverbs 3:24).

Dream manipulation seems real, and most of us have experienced nightmares that woke us up with fear and anxiety that lasted
for a while. Nightmares are dreams that produce a strong negative
emotional response, such as fear or horror. Nightmare sufferers usually awake in a state of extreme distress, even to the point of a severe
physical response—racing pulse, sweating, nausea—and often cannot go back to sleep for some time. If you can be demon-possessed,
then demons can impact your dreams. According to an article at the
Boston University, it is an interesting clinical fact that even today,
most cases of involuntary spirit possession across the world occur
overnight. The person wakes up possessed.[213]

Satan has secret agents that he uses to fulfill his demonic plans.
These agents have been taught by Satan, who himself was able to
transform into an angel of light. *For such are false apostles, deceitful
workers, transforming themselves into apostles of Christ. And no wonder!
For Satan himself transforms himself into an angel of light. Therefore, it is
no great thing if his ministers also transform themselves into ministers of
righteousness, whose end will be according to their works* (1 Corinthians
11:13-15).

Be careful of wandering spirits as it will be in this wicked generation. In Matthew 12:43-45, Jesus warned them of wandering spirits: *When an unclean spirit goes out of a man, he goes through dry places,
seeking rest, and finds none. Then he says, "I will return to my house from
which I came." And when he comes, he finds it empty, swept, and put in order. Then he goes and takes with him seven other spirits more wicked than
himself, and they enter and dwell there, and the last state of that man is
worse than the first. So shall it also be with this wicked generation.*

Unfortunately, even in the church, some husbands and wives
have had ungodly sexual affairs with demonic implications, as the

Apostle Paul says, *or do you not know that he who is joined to a harlot is one body with her? For "the two," He says, "shall become one flesh"* (1 Corinthians 6:16, emphasis added).

Isaiah had to speak out to some of his disciples who were tempted to engage with familiar spirits. In their troubles and embarrassments, instead of looking to Yahweh, they turned to converse with a spirit of divination. In the case of Saul, he applied to the woman of Endor, who professed to have a familiar spirit, in 1 Samuel 28:7-25.

> *Beware of those who chose to consult with familiar spirits, and when they say unto you, "Seek unto those having familiar spirits, and unto wizards, who chatter and mutter, Doth not a people seek unto its God? For the living unto the dead" (Isaiah 8:19, Young's Literal Translation). Any movement in that direction is a dangerous step because it will influence your future with God. If a person turns to mediums and necromancers, whoring after them, I will set my face against that person and will cut him off from among his people (Leviticus 20:6).*

## MARINE POWERS AND WATER SPIRITS

Poseidon is a god in Greek mythology and one of the Twelve Olympians. He is one of the three most powerful Greek gods (along with Zeus and Hades) and rules over the ocean and all bodies of water. He was especially important to Greek sailors and fishermen.

Aigaios is one of the old sea gods, the god of the ocean storms who helped protect Princess Andromeda from Poseidon. After the gods won, Aigaios fled back into the depths of the sea. Then among the Greek gods, Aeolus commands winds, *Keto*, a female sea god, manifests as a whale, like a whale that swallowed Jonah, *Oceanids*, sea nymphs, *Thalassa*; the mother spirit that rules fish.

These are the Greek gods, but Leviathan and other mentions of sea monsters in the Bible are real. The Leviathan is a large aquatic creature of some kind. The Bible refers to it as a fearsome beast having monstrous ferocity and great power. The Hebrew word for "Leviathan" has the root meaning of "coiled" or "twisted," speaks of "Leviathan the fast-moving serpent, Leviathan the squirming serpent . . . the sea monster."[214] Whatever this monster of the sea is (or was), its strength and wild nature were well known for it was the strongest of the sea, unkillable and uncatchable. Well, until Leviathan meets God!

## DESTROYING MARINE/WATER SPIRITS

Though the description of these water spirits seems massive and unbeatable, no doubt rules the waters, God the creator, and the Spirit who hovers over the waters. *In the beginning, God created the heavens and the earth. The earth was without form and void, and darkness was on the face of the deep. And the Spirit of God was <u>hovering over the face of the waters</u>* (Genesis 1:1, 2, emphasis added). And the Spirit still hovers over the chaos created by the marine powers.

> *The earth is the LORD's, and all its fullness, The world and those who dwell therein. For He has founded it upon the seas and established it upon the waters (Psalm 24:1, 2).*

> *The voice of the LORD is over the waters, the God of glory thunders, the LORD, over many waters.... The LORD sits enthroned over the flood; the LORD sits enthroned as king forever (Psalm 29: 3, 10).*

> *You who laid the foundations of the earth, so that it should not be moved forever. You covered it with the deep as with a garment; The waters stood above the mountains (Psalm 104:5, 6).*

And Job 41:1 questions the ability to crush Leviathan: *Can you pull in Leviathan with a hook or tie down his tongue with a rope?* But in Psalm 74:14, you get the answer to that question: *You crushed the heads of Leviathan; You gave him as food for the creatures of the wilderness.*

In that day, the LORD, with His severe sword, great and strong, *Will punish Leviathan the gliding serpent, Leviathan the coiling serpent; he will slay the monster of the sea* (Isaiah 27:1).

Jesus also understood the manifestation of the water spirits and their willingness to confront Jesus. When Jesus was walking on the water, first he had to help Peter get back in the boat. Jesus was tired and went to sleep, and while asleep, the water spirits created a furious storm trying to overturn the boat. Normally, Jesus would not be concerned because nature would not challenge the Son of God. But in this case, the water spirits did challenge Jesus, and he recognized the storm as an evil manifestation of water spirits.

It was the same spirit Jesus sent into the herd of swine, and suddenly the swine ran violently down the steep slope into the sea and perished there. The swine would never dive into the water, but the water spirits drove them into the water and killed them with the demons.

Yahweh broke the heads of Leviathan. *You divided the sea by Your strength; You broke the heads of the sea serpents in the waters* (Psalm 74:13).

Break the proud waters over my soul. *Yes, the raging waters of their fury would have overwhelmed our very lives* (Psalm 124:5, LVT).

Let the deep waters be dried up and destroy all marine spirits. *He makes the deep boil like a pot; He makes the sea like a pot of ointment* (Job 41:31).

Cast out all mind control spirits of the marine kingdom. *Who says to the deep, 'Be dry! And I will dry up your rivers'* (Isaiah 44:27).

Expose the works of the marine spirits and let them stumble and fall. *The arrogant one will stumble and fall With no one to raise him up* (Jeremiah 50:32).

Leviathan will not oppress me. *Do not let the proud oppress me* (Psalm 119:122).

## JESUS OVERCAME ALL OUR ENEMIES

The temptations of Jesus in the wilderness of Judea happened right after John baptized Jesus in the Jordan River. Once Jesus was supernaturally identified as the Messiah, you would think that He would start facing masses of people. No one could find Him because the Spirit had led Jesus into the wilderness to be tempted. Mark's opening statement addresses Jesus' victorious conflicts with Satan and the wild beasts. *And He was there in the wilderness forty days, tempted by Satan, and was with the wild beasts; and the angels ministered to Him* (Mark 1:13).

While the wild beasts would be a threat to anyone in the desert places, Jesus illustrates the essence of the restored creation where the lion lays down with the lamb, which is also reflected in David. *Every beast of the forest is mine, and the cattle upon a thousand hills. I know all the fowls of the mountains: and the wild beasts of the field are mine* (Psalm 50:10).

These words that John wrote reflect Jesus' three temptations in the wilderness. *For all that is in the world—the lust of the flesh, the lust of the eyes, and the pride of life—is not of the Father but is of the world* (1 John 2:16). **The first temptation that Jesus faced was the "lust of the flesh"—in this case, the desire for food. Nest is the lust of the eyes is a second temptation Jesus faced when Satan took him on a high mountain and showed Him the world's kingdoms, with unfettered access to kingdoms, cities, wealth, and all the world's riches. Finally, the temptation we often face is the pride of life, like how Satan tempted Jesus to prove His status as the Son of God.**

> *When He had disarmed the rulers and authorities, He made a public display of them, having triumphed over them through Him (Colossians 2:15).*

So, Christ passed through the heavens and became the High Priest over the altar of our hearts. *For we do not have a High Priest who cannot sympathize with our weaknesses but was in all points tempted as we are, yet without sin* (Hebrews 4:15).

CHARLIE SHAMP is the Co-Founder and President of Destiny Encounters Intl. He is a sought after international key note speaker. He has been commissioned by Heaven as a Prophet to bring healing and revival in the nations. He has ministered both nationally and internationally with radical demonstrations of faith seeing lives transformed through the power of the Holy Spirit. He resides in Moravian Falls, North Carolina with his wife, Brynn, and their three children.

*For more information, connect with the ministry at:*

**DESTINYENCOUNTERS**.COM

# ENDNOTES

1.  https://www.goodreads.com/en/book/show/42642026-finding-narnia (Accessed January 18, 2022).
2.  https://hebrewwordlessons.com/2020/08/23/panim-paneh-seek-my-face/ (Accessed January 18, 2022).
3.  Ibid (Accessed January 18, 2022).
4.  https://www.moravian.org/2018/07/a-brief-history-of-the-moravian-church/(Accessed January 24, 2022).
5.  https://biblehub.com/greek/3857.htm (Accessed January 19, 2022).
6.  Ibid
7.  https://blogs.ancientfaith.com/wholecounsel/2020/09/22/death-by-holiness/ (Accessed January 20, 2022).
8.  https://enduringword.com/bible-commentary/1-corinthians-5/ (Accessed January 24, 2022).
9.  https://www.oca.org/orthodoxy/the-orthodox-faith/worship/the-sacraments/holy-eucharist (Accessed January 20, 2022).
10. https://www.ancient-hebrew.org/names/Nimrod.htm (Accessed January 21, 2022).
11. Michael Heiser, Unseen Realm (Belinham, WA, Lexham Press, 2015) 113
12. https://www.thegatheringplacehome.com/abraham-issac-and-jacob-t5049.html (Accessed January 24, 2022).
13. Barnes Notes, https://www.studylight.org/commentary/hebrews/12-18.html (Accessed January 22, 2022).
14. https://www.biblestudytools.com/lexicons/greek/kjv/chrematizo.html (Accessed January 22, 2022).
15. Pulpit Commentary, https://biblehub.com/commentaries/hebrews/12-26.htm (Accessed January 22, 2022).
16. https://www.preceptaustin.org/hebrews_1227-29
17. https://www.biblestudytools.com/isa_iah/22-22.html (Accessed January 23, 2022).
18. https://www.gotquestions.org/Jachin-and-Boaz.html (Accessed January 23, 2022).
19. https://biblehub.com/greek/4740.htm (Accessed January 23, 2022).

20.  https://biblehub.com/greek/4599.htm (Accessed January 23, 2022).

21.  https://www.bibletools.org/index.cfm/fuseaction/topical.show/RTD/cgg/ID/8253/Taking-Gods-Name-Vain.htm (Accessed January 24, 2022).

22.  https://www.bibletools.org/index.cfm/fuseaction/topical.show/RTD/cgg/ID/8259/Name-as-Description-Character.htm (Accessed January 23, 2022).

23.  https://discoveringthejewishjesus.com/yahweh-tsidkenu/ (Accessed January 24, 2022).

24.  https://discoveringthejewishjesus.com/yahweh-shammah/ (Accessed January 24, 2022).

25.  Pulpit Commentary, https://biblehub.com/colossians/1-26.htm (Accessed January 25, 2022).

26.  https://bibleapps.com/greek/458.htm (Accessed January 25, 2022).

27.  Dustin Benge, The Anointed Cherub: The Fall of Satan, https://www.reformandamin.org/articles1/2019/7/22/the-anointed-cherub-the-fall-of-lucifer#_ftn4 (Accessed January 28, 2022).

28.  Johnathan Edwards, Ibid

29.  https://biblehub.com/hebrew/5175.htm (Accessed January 28, 2022).

30.  https://www.studylight.org/lexicons/eng/greek/3789.html (Accessed January 28, 2022).

31.  https://www.britannica.com/topic/Elohim (Accessed January 28, 2022).

32.  Don Milam, The Ancient Language of Eden (Destiny Image Publishers, Shippensburg, Pa 2003) 68-72

33.  S. D. Gordon, Quiet Talks About Jesus (Destiny Image Publishers, Shippensburg, Pa 2003) 21, 22

34.  https://biblehub.com/hebrew/2400.htm (Accessed January 29, 2022).

35.  https://www.chaimbentorah.com/2016/10/word-study-transgressions-%D7%A4%D7%A2%EF%AC%AA/ (Accessed January 29, 2022).

36.  https://biblehub.com/hebrew/5766.htm (Accessed January 29, 2022).

37.  https://www.ancient-hebrew.org/definition/iniquity.htm (Accessed January 29, 2022).

38.  https://en.wikipedia.org/wiki/Son_of_perdition#:~:text=The%20New%20International%20Version%20translates,character%20and%20to%20his%20destiny. (Accessed January 30, 2022).

39.  https://www.jstor.org/stable/26373865 (Accessed January 30, 2022).

40.  https://www.gotquestions.org/antitype-in-the-Bible.html (Accessed January 30, 2022).

41.  Thayer's Greek Lexicon, https://biblehub.com/greek/2722.htm (Accessed January 30, 2022).

42.  Thayer's Greek Lexicon, https://biblehub.com/greek/601.htm (Accessed January 30, 2022).

43. https://www.biola.edu/blogs/good-book-blog/2017/jesus-in-genesis-3-15 (Accessed February 4, 2022).
44. https://biblehub.com/hebrew/342.htm (Accessed February 1, 2022).
45. https://biblehub.com/hebrew/2233.htm (Accessed February 1, 2022).
46. https://www.studylight.org/lexicons/eng/hebrew/7779.html (Accessed February 1, 2022).
47. https://biblehub.com/hebrew/7218.htm (Accessed February 1, 2022).
48. https://biblehub.com/hebrew/6119.htm (Accessed February 1, 2022).
49. A. Even-Shoshan, ed., A New Concordance of the Old Testament (Jerusalem: Kiryat Sefer, 1997) 340–42
50. E. Kautzch, ed., Gesenius' Hebrew Grammar (rev. A. W. Cowley; 2nd English ed.; Oxford: Clarendon Press, 1910) 123
51. Jack Collins, "A Syntactical Note (Genesis 3:15): Is the Woman's Seed Singular or Plural?" Tyndale Bulletin 48 (1997): 144.
52. Max Wilcox ("The Promise of the 'Seed' in the New Testament and the Targums")"
53. Dempster, Dominion and Dynasty, 69 n. 26.
54. Wilcox, "The Promise of the 'Seed' in the New Testament and the Targumim," 2–3.
55. James Hamilton, The Skull Crushing Seed of the Woman: Inner-Biblical Interpretation of Genesis 3:15 https://sbts-wordpress-uploads.s3.amazonaws.com/equip/uploads/2010/07/sbjt_102_sum06-hamilton.pdf (Accessed February 2, 2022).
56. Ibid, Dempster, Dominion and Dynasty, 223.
57. https://jwa.org/encyclopedia/article/jael-wife-of-heber-kenite-midrash-and-aggadah (Accessed February 2, 2022).
58. https://biblehub.com/hebrew/2342.htm (Accessed February 2, 2022).
59. Gills Exposition, https://biblehub.com/commentaries/jeremiah/30-9.htm (Accessed February 2, 2022).
60. https://biblehub.com/hebrew/4899.htm (Accessed February 3, 2022).
61. https://biblehub.com/hebrew/6168.htm (Accessed February 3, 2022).
62. C. E. B. Cranfield, A Critical and Exegetical Commentary on the Epistle to the Romans (Baker Exegetical Commentary on the New Testament; Grand Rapids: Baker, 1998), 804–05
63. D. J. Moo, The Epistle to the Romans (New International Commentary on the New Testament; Grand Rapids: Eerdmans, 1996), 516
64. https://www.wordsense.eu/%CE%B4%CF%81%CE%AC%CE%BA%CF%89%CE%BD/ (Accessed February 4, 2022).
65. https://www.biblestudytools.com/lexicons/greek/nas/satanas.html (Accessed February 4, 2022).

66. https://biblehub.com/greek/4108.htm (Accessed February 4, 2022).

67. https://www.biblestudytools.com/lexicons/greek/nas/oikoumene.html (Accessed February 4, 2022).

68. https://sbts-wordpress-uploads.s3.amazonaws.com/equip/up-loads/2010/07/sbjt_102_sum06-hamilton.pdf (Accessed February 10, 2022).

69. http://www.newhumanityinstitute.org/pdfs/article-odes-of-solomon.pdf (Accessed February 4, 2022).

70. https://www.reformation21.org/blogs/the-mystery-and-glory-of-the-i.php (Accessed February 4, 2022).

71. https://www.studylight.org/lexicons/eng/hebrew/01319.html (Accessed February 5, 2022).

72. Irenaeus of Lyons. Against Heresies, Book III, Chapter 23, 7

73. https://theopolisinstitute.com/leithart_post/protoevangelium/ (Accessed February 6, 2022).

74. https://biblehub.com/hebrew/1869.htm (Accessed February 6, 2022).

75. https://biblehub.com/hebrew/6620.htm (Accessed February 6, 2022).

76. https://biblehub.com/hebrew/8577.htm (Accessed February 6, 2022).

77. https://blogs.timesofisrael.com/adam-and-eve-what-was-the-sin/ (Accessed February 6, 2022).

78. https://www.studylight.org/lexicons/eng/hebrew/5753.html (Accessed February 6, 2022).

79. https://www.ancient-hebrew.org/names/Adam.htm (Accessed February 8, 2022).

80. http://thebiblenet.blogspot.com/2015/11/havel-abel.html (Accessed February 8, 2022).

81. https://www.ancient-hebrew.org/names/Seth.htm (Accessed February 8, 2022).

82. https://www.abarim-publications.com/Meaning/Enosh.html (Accessed February 8, 2022).

83. https://www.abarim-publications.com/Dictionary/q/q-n-he.html (Accessed February 8, 2022).

84. https://www.ancient-hebrew.org/names/Enoch.htm (Accessed February 8, 2022).

85. https://www.ancient-hebrew.org/names/Methuselah.htm (Accessed February 8, 2022).

86. https://www.ancient-hebrew.org/names/Cain-and-Abel.htm

87. https://www.abarim-publications.com/Meaning/Lamech.html

88. https://oxfordre.com/religion/view/10.1093/acre-fore/9780199340378.001.0001/acrefore-9780199340378-e-144 (Accesse February 9, 2022).

89.  https://yrm.org/yahweh-or-jehovah/ (Accessed February 9, 2022).
90.  https://hermeneutics.stackexchange.com/questions/66388/why-is-yhwh-the-name-of-the-god-replaced-by-a-title-the-lord-why-is-the-ar (Accessed February 9, 2022).
91.  https://www.bibletools.org/index.cfm/fuseaction/Lexicon.show/ID/H2490/chalal.htm (Accessed February 8, 2022).
92.  https://www.ccel.org/c/charles/otpseudepig/enoch/ENOCH_1.HTM (Accessed February 9, 2022).
93.  https://www.alittleperspective.com/genesis-426-then-men-began/ (Accessed February 9, 2022).
93b. https://www.google.com/search?q=For+all+sad+words+of+tongue+and+pen%2C+The+saddest+are+these%2C+%27It+might+have+been%27.+John+Greenleaf+Whittier&rlz=1C1CHBF_enUS895US895&oq=For+all+sad+words+of+tongue+and+pen%2C+The+saddest+are+these%2C+%27It+might+have+been%27.++John+Greenleaf+Whittier&aqs=chrome..69i57.2672j0j15&sourceid=chrome&ie=UTF-8
94.  https://www.alittleperspective.com/genesis-426-then-men-began/ (Accessed February 9, 2022).
95.  https://www.studylight.org/encyclopedias/eng/tje/e/evil-spirits.html (Accessed February 11, 2022).
96.  https://www.gotquestions.org/synonymous-parallelism.html (Accessed February 10, 2022).
97.  https://www.thetorah.com/article/god-shelters-the-faithful-the-prayer-of-psalm-91 (Accessed February 12, 2022).
98.  Erich Zenger, Psalms 2, Hermeneia (Minneapolis: Fortress, 2005), 430
99.  xcx https://www.thetorah.com/article/god-shelters-the-faithful-the-prayer-of-psalm-91
100. http://qbible.com/brenton-septuagint/psalms/91.html
101. https://biblehub.com/hebrew/6620.htm (Accessed February 12, 2022).
102. https://biblehub.com/hebrew/8577.htm (Accessed February 12, 2022).
103. https://www.ibiblio.org/expo/deadsea.scrolls.exhibit/Library/enoch.html (Accessed February 12, 2022).
104. https://researchsupportsthetruth.wordpress.com/2013/07/03/new-light-on-the-book-of-enoch/ (Accessed February 6, 2022).
105. https://biblehub.com/hebrew/5303.htm (February 6, 2022).
106. https://biblehub.com/hebrew/5307.htm (February 6, 2022).
107. https://www.ccel.org/c/charles/otpseudepig/enoch/ENOCH_1.HTM (February 12, 2022).
108. Ibid

109. https://www.ccel.org/c/charles/otpseudepig/enoch/ENOCH_1.HTM (Accessed February 12, 2022).
110. https://leefjougeloof.co.za/mount-hermon-gate-of-the-fallen-angels/ (Accessed February 13, 2022).
111. https://everything.explained.today/Samyaza/ (Accessed February 12, 2022).
112. Ibid
113. Ibid
114. Ibid
115. Ibid
116. Cambridge Bible for Schools and Colleges, Accessed November 30, 2020, https://biblehub.com/commentaries/matthew/17-2.htm
117. https://joshbenner.org/2018/05/02/dietrich-bonhoeffer-cheap-grace-vs-costly-grace/ (Accessed February 13, 2022).
118. https://penelope.uchicago.edu/Thayer/E/Roman/Texts/secondary/SMIGRA*/Ara.html (Accessed February 15, 2022).
119. The Oxford History of Greece and the Hellenistic World (Oxford, England: Oxford University Press, 2001).
120. https://books.openedition.org/pulg/501?lang=en (Accessed February 15, 2022).
121. https://biblehub.com/commentaries/acts/17-23.htm (Accessed February 15, 2022).
122. https://books.openedition.org/pulg/501?lang=en (Accessed February 15, 2022).
123. Ibid
124. https://www.biblestudytools.com/dictionary/altar/ (Accessed February 17, 2022).
125. https://www.setapartpeople.com/possessing-gates-of-your-enemy (Accessed February 16, 2022).
126. https://www.internationalstandardbible.com/B/bethel.html (Accessed February 17, 2022).
127. Ibid
128. https://www.studylight.org/lexicons/eng/greek/1210.html (Accessed February 18, 2022).
129. https://www.studylight.org/lexicons/eng/greek/3089.html (Accessed February 18, 2022).
130. http://articles.ochristian.com/article1935.shtml (Accessed February 18, 2022).
131. http://articles.ochristian.com/article1935.shtml (Accessed February 18, 2022).

132. https://www.biblestudytools.com/dictionary/covenant-book-of-the/ (Accessed February 20, 2022).
133. https://www.biblestudytools.com/dictionary/hallow-hallowed/ (Accessed February 20, 2022).
134. https://www.biblestudytools.com/dictionary/sabbath/ Accessed February 21, 2022).
135. https://www.ancient-hebrew.org/ebooks/mtg.pdf (Accessed February 20, 2022).
136. Ibid
137. https://home.agh.edu.pl/~szymon/Tolkien/?fn=2#:~:text=Still%20 round%20the%20corner%20there,and%20sloe%2C%20Let%20them%20 go! (Accessed February 23, 2022)/
138. https://www.history.com/this-day-in-history/kkk-founded (Accessed February 24, 2022).
139. https://crammedwithheaven.org/poets/ (Accessed February 25, 2022).
140. https://www.studylight.org/lexicons/eng/hebrew/1245.html (Accessed February 26, 2022).
141. https://biblehub.com/hebrew/6440.htm (Accessed February 26, 2022).
142. https://www.sacred-texts.com/bib/boe/boe017.htm (Accessed February 26, 2022).
143. https://biblehub.com/hebrew/3863.htm (Accessed February 27, 2022).
144. https://www.studylight.org/lexicons/eng/hebrew/7167.html (Accessed February 27, 2022).
145. https://www.samstorms.org/enjoying-god-blog/post/10-things-you-should-know-about-the-welsh-revival-of-1904-06 (Accessed February 27, 2022).
146. https://christianhof.org/hyde/ (Accessed February 27, 2022).
147. https://www.revivalandreformation.org/resources/all/the-moravian-100-year-prayer-movement (Accessed February 27, 2022).
148. David Yonggi Cho, Prayer That Brings Revival, (Lake Mary, FL, Creation House, 1998) ix
149. Ibid x-xi
150. Ibid xii
151. Ibid xiii-xiv
152. Barnes Notes, https://biblehub.com/commentaries/hosea/2-23.htm (Accessed February 28, 2022).
153. https://www.tandfonline.com/doi/abs/10.1080/08920753.2022.2037387?src=&journalCode=ucmg20 (Accessed February 28, 2022).
154. https://www.bbc.com/future/article/20201014-the-desert-that-gives-birth-to-the-most-powerful-hurricanes (Accessed February 28, 2022).

155. https://dailytrust.com/the-mystic-story-about-cape-verdean-women (Accessed February 28, 2022).
156. Cambridge Bible for School and Colleges, https://biblehub.com/commentaries/judges/9-8.htm (Accessed March 3, 2022).
157. https://slideplayer.com/slide/17617872/ (March 4, 2022).
158. https://www.goodreads.com/quotes/32930-look-deep-into-nature-and-then-you-will-understand-everything (Accesssed March 4, 2022).
158b. http://www.westacre.org.uk/2017/03/24/druid-circles-and-the-patterns-of-nature/
159. https://www.hmdb.org/m.asp?m=183068#:~:text=The%20Tory%20Oak.,Wilfong%20in%20neighboring%20Lincoln%20County (Accessed March 4, 2022).
160. https://www.ncpedia.org/tory-oak#:~:text=The%20Tory%20Oak%2C%20sometimes%20referred,%2Dfilled%2C%20deteriorating%20dark%20stump. (Accessed March 5, 2022).
161. Barnes Notes on the Bible, https://biblehub.com/commentaries/ephesians/1-21.htm (Accessed March 5, 2022).
162. John J. Davis, The Perfect Shepherd; Studies in the 23 Psalm (Grand Rapids, Michigan, Baker House, 1979), 100
163. https://biblehub.com/text/daniel/7-9.htm (Accessed March 7, 2022).
164. Barnes Notes, https://biblehub.com/commentaries/daniel/7-9.htm (Accessed March 7, 2022).
165. https://www.studylight.org/lexicons/eng/greek/554.html (Accessed March 6, 2022).
166. https://www.studylight.org/lexicons/eng/greek/746.html (Accessed March 6, 2022).
167. https://www.biblestudytools.com/lexicons/greek/nas/exousia.html (Accessed March 6, 2022).
168. https://biblehub.com/greek/1165.htm (Accessed March 6, 2022)/
169. https://www.myjewishlearning.com/article/tzedakah-101/ (March 6, 2022).
170. https://www.chabad.org/library/article_cdo/aid/111261/jewish/Tzedek-amp-Chessed-Righteousness-and-Kindness.htm (Accessed March 6, 2022/
171. https://en.wikipedia.org/wiki/Sayings_of_the_Desert_Fathers (Accessed March 6, 2022).
172. https://jhvonline.com/judaisms-three-pillars-and-the-days-of-awe-p29513-112.htm (Accessed March 6, 2022).
173. https://www.patheos.com/articles/the-original-hebrew-meaning-of-mercy (Accessed March 7, 2022).

174. Barnes Notes, https://biblehub.com/commentaries/isaiah/28-16.htm (Accessed March 10, 2022).

175. https://www.cgg.org/index.cfm/library/weekly/id/654/scepter-of-king-dom-god-part-one.htm (Accessed March 8, 2022).

176. Brown, Driver, Briggs https://biblehub.com/hebrew/7626.htm (Accessed March 8, 2022).

177. https://biblehub.com/commentaries/hebrews/1-8.htm (Accessed March 8, 2022).

178. https://biblehub.com/commentaries/revelation/2-27.htm (Accessed March 8, 2022).

179. https://www.studylight.org/lexicons/eng/hebrew/05475.html (Accessed March 9, 2022).

180. https://www.deseretnews.com/article/765621073/Old-Testament-divine-council-called-a-sod.html (Accessed April 20, 2019).

181. Charlie Shamp Angels: A Biblical School of Living Light (Moravian Falls, SC, Destiny Encounters International, 2020) 89

182. https://christiananswers.net/dictionary/mahanaim.html (Accessed March 9, 2022).

183. Jamieson, Faucett and Brown, https://biblehub.com/commentaries/revelation/8-4.htm (Accessed March 8, 2022).

184. J. Barton Payne, kōhen, TWOT #959a.

185. https://www.preceptaustin.org/covenant_definition (Accessed March 11, 2022).

186. https://www.preceptaustin.org/covenant_definition (Accessed March 11, 2022).

187. https://biblehub.com/greek/5117.htm (Accessed March 14, 2022).

188. https://bookmate.com/books/IZp6cZmD/quotes (Accessed March 14, 2022)

189. https://en.wikipedia.org/wiki/Saints_and_levitation#cite_note-2 (Accessed March 14, 2022).

190. Geoff Waugh Flashpoints of Revival, (Renewal Journal Publications, 2020) 144, 145

191. https://digitalcommons.andrews.edu/cgi/viewcontent.cgi?article=1358&context=jams (Accessed March 16, 2022).

192. https://biblehub.com/text/ephesians/6-12.htm (Accessed March 18, 2022).

193. Strong's #G3003

194. C. Peter Wagner, Confronting the Queen of Heaven (Colorado Springs, CO: Wagner Institute for Practical Ministry, 1998), pp. 11-13

195. Engaging the Enemy: How to Fight and Defeat Territorial Spirits, (Ventura, California: Regal Books, 1999) 12

196. http://www.pseudepigrapha.com/pseudepigrapha/enochs2.htm (Accessed March 20, 2022).

197. https://www.compellingtruth.org/seven-spirits-God.html (Accessed March 20, 2022).

198. https://www.ccel.org/c/charles/otpseudepig/enoch/ENOCH_1.HTM (Accessed March 20, 2022).

199. https://agairupdate.com/2016/10/01/the-seven-mountains-and-seven-heads/ (Accessed March 19, 2022).

200. https://www.weather.gov/cle/Seasons (Accessed March 20, 2022).

201. https://mymodernmet.com/history-of-astrology/ (Accessed March 20, 2022).

202. http://theastrologydictionary.com/d/decans/ (Accessed March 21, 2022)

203. https://neeness.com/what-does-decanate-mean/ (Accessed March 21, 2022)

204. Bennett, Jeffrey; Donohue, Megan; Schneider, Nicholas; Voit, Mark, The Cosmic Perspective 4th ed, (San Francisco, CA: Pearson/Addison-Wesley 2007) 82-84

205. https://www.businessinsider.com/astrology-indus-try-boomed-during-pandemic-online-entrepreneurs-2020-12#:~:tex-t=As%20Insider's%20Barbara%20Smith%20previously,whole%20is%20worth%20%242.2%20billion. (Accessed March 21, 2022).

206. http://www.anamcharabooks.com/blog/2017/2/15/resistance-in-this-present-darkness-by-kenneth-mcintosh (Accessed March 21, 2022).

207. https://www.definitions.net/definition/fetish+priest (Accessed March 21, 2022).

208. https://www.amazon.com/Charismatic-Control-Witchcraft-Neo-Pente-costal-Churches/dp/188791501X (Accessed March 21, 2022).

209. https://www.xpmedia.com/article/202/charismatic-witchcraft (Accessed March 21, 2022).

210. https://www.derekprince.com/teaching/06-3 (Accessed March 21, 2022).

211. https://www.dictionary.com/browse/voodoo (Accessed March 21, 2022). 18 Michael Kern, The Limits of Magic, The Victorian Web, archived from 10, 16, 2013

212. Michael Kern, The Limits of Magic, The Victorian Web, archived from 10, 16, 2013

213. https://www.bu.edu/bostonia/spring09/nightmares/index.shtml(Accessed March 22, 2022).

214. https://www.gotquestions.org/leviathan.html (Accessed March 22, 2022).

Printed in Great Britain
by Amazon